LITERARY CRITICISM AND CULTURAL THEORY

Edited by

William E. Cain
Professor of English
Wellesley College

A ROUTLEDGE SERIES

LITERARY CRITICISM AND CULTURAL THEORY

WILLIAM E. CAIN, *General Editor*

NEGOTIATING COPYRIGHT

Authorship and the Discourse of Literary
Property Rights in Nineteenth-Century America

Martin T. Buinicki

Routledge
Taylor & Francis Group

NEW YORK AND LONDON

A portion of Chapter Three appeared previously in my article "Walt Whitman and the Question of Copyright." *American Literary History* 15.2 (2003): 248-75.

A portion of Chapter Four appeared previously in my article "Staking a Claim: Samuel L. Clemens' Pragmatic Views on Copyright." *American Literary Realism* 37.1 (2004): 59-82. Copyright 2004 by Board of Trustees of the University of Illinois.

Quotations from manuscript materials found in the American Antiquarian Society, Worcester, MA, are published by permission of the curator.

Quotations from manuscript materials owned by The Harriet Beecher Stowe Center, Hartford, CT, are published by permission of the curator.

Published in 2006 by
Routledge
Taylor & Francis Group
711 Third Avenue,
New York, NY 10017

Published in Great Britain by
Routledge
Taylor & Francis Group
2 Park Square,
Milton Park, Abingdon,
Oxfordshire OX14 4RN

First issued in paperback 2015

Routledge is an imprint of the Taylor and Francis Group, an informa business

© 2006 by Taylor & Francis Group, LLC

International Standard Book Number-13: 978-0-415-76282-3 (pbk)
International Standard Book Number-13: 978-0-415-97625-1 (Hardcover)

Library of Congress Cataloging-in-Publication Data

Catalog record is available from the Library of Congress

Taylor & Francis Group
is the Academic Division of Informa plc.

Visit the Taylor & Francis Web site at
http://www.taylorandfrancis.com

and the Routledge Web site at
http://www.routledge-ny.com

For Andrea

Contents

List of Figures

Acknowledgments

When glancing through acknowledgment pages, one rarely recognizes the daunting task they represent for a grateful author. I begin here with the knowledge that nothing I say can adequately express my gratitude to the many who helped me see this book through to publication. In doing my research, I benefited from the assistance of a number of patient librarians at the University of Iowa, particularly in the Special Collections and Government Publications Departments. In Worcester, MA, the staff of the American Antiquarian Society was exceedingly helpful, as were the librarians at the Harriet Beecher Stowe Center in Hartford, CT. The assistance of these professionals was invaluable.

I also owe a debt of gratitude to many professors who have encouraged me over the past several years. I am grateful to Ben Varner at the University of Northern Colorado for recommending that I go to graduate school, and to Dan Miller for teaching me what to do once I was there. While at the University of Iowa, I had the good fortune to work with, among others, Dennis Moore, Kathleen Diffley, Miriam Gilbert, David Wittenberg, and Laura Rigal. I am also grateful to Mark Janis for his insights regarding legal matters discussed in the text. Ed Folsom has been that rarest of mentors: he has pushed me to improve my scholarship while at the same time encouraging my love of literature. His advice and support have already helped me in countless ways, and he is a model of the kind of scholar and teacher I hope one day to become.

I am also grateful to my colleagues at Valparaiso University for their encouragement, and I want to pay a special note of thanks to my student assistant, Sarah Werner, who carefully tracked down references to confirm their accuracy. Her patience and attention to detail were invaluable.

Finally, words fail to express the thanks I owe to my parents, Judy and Martin Buinicki, and to my wife, Andrea. They have always believed in me, even when I failed to believe in myself. I could not have completed this book without Andrea's help. She has read it cover to cover (multiple times, I'm afraid), and it would take a volume easily three times as long to express the love, gratitude, and admiration I feel for her.

Introduction

In 1853, a prominent opponent of expanding American copyright laws wrote, "The advocates of free trade and international copyright are, to a great extent, disciples in that school in which it is taught that it is an unjust interference with the rights of property to compel the wealthy to contribute to the education of the poor" (Carey 85). This was one of his more temperate statements. He also wrote that any expansion of copyright laws, including granting authors rights to control translations and adaptations, would perpetuate monopolies in Eastern publishing houses, add to the already unfair compensation authors received for a minimal amount of actual labor, and limit access to knowledge to upper-class New England elites. When a volume of his remarks was released in a second edition in 1868, he added that copyright laws perpetuated the earlier efforts of slaveholders to keep slaves ignorant.

The text, Henry C. Carey's *Letters on International Copyright*, was an important volley in the long-raging battle over copyright, and it attracted numerous responses, including a public rebuttal in the United States House of Representatives in 1872. Copyright opponents were not the only ones who engaged in this type of heated rhetoric, however, and they were not alone in attempting to link their position with America's democratic principles. In 1843, writer Cornelius Mathews proclaimed,

> As a great nation, standing in the very front rank of the guides and examples of mankind, America should desire to possess a literature, whether foreign or native, only under the broadest and clearest sanctions of right and justice. [. . .] She owes it to herself, and to the great cause of which she is an acknowledged representative, to stand forth, and gathering her pure robes about her, repel by instant action aspersions so unworthy of her faith and her fame. (7)

Declarations such as these were common as arguments over copyright law, particularly over the creation of a law that would apply to foreign works, attracted the attention of authors, publishers, editors, readers, congressmen, judges, and clergymen. Such a high degree of public, judicial, and legislative commentary contributed to the creation of a discourse of literary property rights that often served to position the interests of authors as firmly opposed to the interests of readers. By examining how authors carefully framed their public support for copyright law, and by tracing how the logic and terms of the discourse emerge in the literary works of prominent authors, we can see that copyright was more than a legal or business matter. Authors wrote within a discourse of literary property rights that forced them to defend not only their texts but also their democratic principles; as a result, they were put in the uncomfortable position of negotiating copyright not only with publishers, but with readers as well.

The apparent division between authors and readers was in part a function of the constitutional language authorizing the creation of a copyright law in the United States. Article I, Section 8 of the Constitution authorized Congress to pass a copyright law "To promote the Progress of Science and the useful Arts, by securing for limited Times, to Authors and Inventors, the exclusive Right to their respective Writings and Discoveries" (qtd. in Leaffer 6). As legal scholar Marshall L. Leaffer has noted,

> [L]ittle is known about what the Framers had in mind in drafting this particular constitutional clause or about the scope of the various terms of the constitutional language. Consequently, one is left with the language of the Clause itself, which does not even use the term 'copyright.' As revealed in the constitutional language, the dominant idea is to promote the dissemination of knowledge to enhance public welfare. (6)

As Leaffer points out, "copyright" does not seem to be the focus of this clause; instead, any rights granted to "Authors and Inventors" seem only a means to an end: intellectual development supersedes the protection of intellectual property. The "limited Times" reference in the clause, and the emphasis on the public welfare, provide a rather unstable foundation for an author's literary property rights. Because the copyright law subsequently passed by Congress in 1790 offered protection only to certain types of texts for a finite duration of time, the legislative, judicial, and even at times the executive branches of government were called upon again and again throughout the nineteenth century (and, indeed, down to the present day) to expand and redefine the nature of protection granted.

Over the past fifty years, literary critics and historians have paid an increasing amount of attention to the subject of copyright law. What had previously been the purview of library-science and legal scholars entered the literary field with the growth of "book" studies and consideration of the conditions of publishing and selling texts in early America. William Charvat emphasized the importance of copyright in his study of nineteenth-century authorship, noting that the passage of the copyright law in the United States in 1790 made the profession of authorship possible (*Profession* 6). Writing much later, Grantland S. Rice adopted a very similar formula, although his reading suggests that copyright law led not only to the emergence of authorship as a profession, but also to a new method of institutional control and censorship: "It was the separation of the economic from the political domain and the concomitant rewriting of the political legislation of censorship into the economic laws of copyright and literary property which allowed the birth of the professional writer" (79–80). Rice is concerned with the transformation of writing in the United States from a public activity pursued mostly in anonymous political tracts or a small number of privately circulated texts to a government-sanctioned, market-regulated transaction between professional writers and a consuming public. His analysis picks up on the influential work of Mark Rose, who, while focusing primarily on British writers, formulated the notion of "authors as owners," once again imagining copyright law as a method of transformation in which authors are defined primarily in relation to their ownership of literary property.

While the act of taking out a copyright certainly may mark these types of transformations, many recent critics have failed to contextualize this act in a way that adequately accounts for both the changes in copyright law in the nineteenth century and the contested meanings of the law. The notion of "literary property" was far from fixed, and, while some argue that texts were pieces of property no different from tracts of land, this conception of books as property left literary property rights vulnerable to the same kinds of politically charged challenges that other forms of ownership faced, challenges ranging from agrarianism to abolitionism. Central to the critiques of literary property rights were questions of individual rights within a democracy and the limits of monopoly power, as well as assumptions about the affordable and accessible diffusion of knowledge and the role of the author in the process of the creation of the text. Meredith McGill has correctly observed that copyright should be viewed as a "pivot point for a number of interlocking transitions" rather than an easily delineated mechanism of transformation. Those transitions include the transition to a market economy, which enables the shift from a patronage system to a market for books; the ideological shift that reconfigures the relation of the individual to the state, reformulates monarchical legal structures as republican ones, and creates a demand for a national literature; [. . .]; and significant changes in the technology of print systems of distribution which make possible the mass publication and mass marketing of books. ("Matter" 24)

McGill's formulation is a significant advance over earlier views of copyright law. By presenting it as a "pivot point" for a number of institutional shifts, she suggests much more clearly the numerous social, legal, and economic interests that converge in copyright law.

If copyright is a pivot point, however, it is a constantly shifting one, like a point on a drafter's compass that, rather than staying fixed and allowing for the creation of a perfect circle, slides across the page creating overlapping and divergent arcs. McGill focuses on the Supreme Court decision in *Wheaton* v. *Peters,* which is certainly a significant turning point in both copyright law and the debate surrounding it, but it was only one among several moments that affected public and legal perceptions of concepts central to the debates over literary property. This is most clear in the arguments over the very notion of authorship: in the shifts that McGill describes, this was often a site of contention. With the emergence of mass publication and marketing, the central role of the author as the producer of a text was thrown into question: why privilege the writer over the printer or binder? Since the rights granted to authors were limited in their relation to the "public good," the "relation of the individual to the state," at least as far as authors were concerned, was never fully established by the passage of a copyright law or by any single legal decision. In shifting from a "patronage system to a market for books," authors were placed into a relationship with their readers that not only influenced the type of material they wrote, as Rice suggests, but also the ways in which they defended their rights. The shifts never simply marked a single transition such as "author to owner"; rather, they changed the grounds on which an on-going attempt to define such notions as authorship was taking place.

It is necessary, therefore, to examine not simply the legal developments of copyright, but the discourse of literary property rights that emerged from and alongside them. It is within this discourse that concepts such as authorship and literary property were debated, and it is through analysis of these debates that authorship in the nineteenth century can begin to be understood. Approaching authorship in this way acknowledges the impact of judicial and legislative decisions without privileging them, allowing for the changes that may have resulted while recognizing that questions, such as the authors' relationships with their readers, continued to remain unresolved.

"Discourse" is a term that carries with it a diverse array of theoretical assumptions. In this study, "discourse" is conceived much the way Michel Foucault defines it in *Archaeology of Knowledge*. It is not simply a mode of speaking within a given discipline, or simply a set of repeated terms, although it may encompass these elements. Foucault often describes it along the lines of a recognizable series of "complex relations" (22). Discourse can, therefore, span divergent fields of law and literature and encompass statements in novels and in legal journals. Foucault writes, "The frontiers of a book are never clear-cut: beyond the title, the first lines, and the last full stop, beyond its internal configuration and its autonomous form, it is caught up in a system of references to other books, other texts, other sentences: it is a node within a network" (23). The idea of the text as a "node" is useful, particularly if one conceives of the text as being a part of not just one "network," but of many—lines overlapping like the circles from the shifting compass. Foucault has described such a network as a "discursive formation," present "[w]henever one can describe, between a number of statements, [. . .] a system of dispersion, [and] whenever, between objects, types of statement, concepts, or thematic choices, one can define a regularity (an order, correlations, positions and functionings, transformations)" (38). An examination of the various statements, made from different sites of institutional authority and constituting and re-constituting the text and its relationship to authors, readers, publishers, and tradeworkers, reveals the presence of a discourse of literary property rights, which, even while changing throughout the nineteenth century, maintains the regularity of positions that Foucault suggests is essential.

In an attempt to trace this discourse and its impact on writers during the nineteenth century, this study incorporates a wide variety of documents including letters, congressional testimony, judicial decisions, advertisements, and newspaper editorials. At its center, however, this work explores the effect the discourse of literary property rights had on the relationship between writers and readers, and this can be seen most readily through an analysis of the literary works themselves—usually the most direct way authors addressed their readers. Viewing these texts as part of a "network" has meant expanding the reading of some of these to include the copyright pages and the cover art of these texts, elements of what Gerard Genette has labeled the "paratext," those features that enable an audience's access to a book. Such textual analysis is not the end in itself, but it demonstrates the pervasiveness of the discourse of literary property rights and the attempts of four authors to pursue their emerging profession while shaping and reacting to the terms and oppositions of the discourse.

The writers examined in the following four chapters are James Fenimore Cooper, Harriet Beecher Stowe, Walt Whitman, and Samuel Clemens. While nearly all American authors grappled with protecting their literary property rights, and while many wrote on the subject, these four offer unique advantages. Each of these authors allows for an analysis of the discourse of literary property rights during different periods of time, beginning with Cooper's attempts to secure a British copyright in 1820 and ending with the passage of a U.S. bill extending copyright protection to foreign authors in 1891. This historical scope allows for a discussion of the ways in which terms came to be defined, arguments emerged and re-emerged in relation to public events, and laws changed to reflect the status of authorship within the on-going debates. By studying large portions of these particular authors' careers, rather than isolated moments in the lives of numerous authors, we can see how authors were affected by such changes and how they responded to them while continuing to pursue their profession.

These authors were also chosen because of their unique public personas and their acute awareness of how their attempts to protect their literary property rights could affect their readers' reception of those personas. With the notable exception of Cooper, each of these authors continually attempted to formulate a view of their rights and their profession that was in line with the popular conceptions of their identities and beliefs. This was not merely a matter of bowing to readers' wishes, however. The notions of authorship and literary property developed by these authors were both a result of their personal, political and artistic philosophies and a response to the criticism levied against them by copyright opponents. To demonstrate the importance of examining authorship in relation to the discourse of literary property rights, the conclusion suggests how our understanding of the battles over the possession and publication of the poetry of Emily Dickinson has been shaped by the debates over copyright. A greater understanding of these debates calls into question some of our commonly held assumptions regarding the principles at stake in arguments over intellectual property.

James Fenimore Cooper's oft-cited status as one of the United States' first successful "professional authors" makes for an ideal starting point, and in Chapter One, "James Fenimore Cooper's Literary Estate: Individual Property Rights and Monopoly Power," I argue that this status is as much a function of his early awareness of the public nature of copyright debates as it is a result of his "business-like" approach to publishing. Cooper may have recognized his works as "mere articles of trade" (qtd. in "Cooper," Charvat 133), but he also recognized that the public was not yet prepared to view them as such. As a result, his published writings continually represent arguments in defense of individual property rights, arguments that resonate with the emerging rationales employed by advocates for copyright law. Even at times when he appears to distance himself from the debate, the terms of the discourse of literary property rights are echoed in his texts. At the same time, Cooper's prolific publishing and his comments regarding his literary holdings suggest a conscious effort to expand his literary "estate" and reveal a performative aspect in novels such as *The Littlepage Manuscripts* that have hitherto been viewed primarily as polemics and failures.

Only two years after the death of James Fenimore Cooper, Harriet Beecher Stowe achieved international success that exceeded Cooper's, even at the height of his fame. Not surprisingly, this success made her works attractive targets for unscrupulous publishers. Stowe faced significantly different challenges than Cooper had in dealing with these publishers, however. The second chapter, "Harriet Beecher Stowe and Sentimental Possession," examines the public and private negotiations Stowe undertook to pursue her profession and protect her literary property. Her legal status as a married woman limited her right to sign contracts, so she was forced to negotiate with her husband as well as her publishers in pursuing her profession. The phenomenal success of *Uncle Tom's Cabin* thrust her into the debates over copyright, and, as Melissa Homestead has demonstrated, her failed legal challenge to the publication of a German translation of the novel made her vulnerable to charges of hypocrisy. As the owner of "Uncle Tom," Stowe sought to maintain her right to control her possessions without appearing to endorse a logic of ownership that undermined her abolitionist beliefs. Stowe's works reflect these challenges through their representation of sentimental possession, an emotional obligation to purchase objects (like books) of high quality and to protect and preserve them. She does not separate business and personal matters; instead, she renders business personal. This is not a rejection of the literary marketplace, but rather a re-casting of the discourse of literary property rights in sentimental terms.

Stowe was not the only author vulnerable to charges of hypocrisy. Years before the publication of *Leaves of Grass*, Walt Whitman wrote newspaper articles strongly supporting the establishment of an international copyright law. This support continued throughout his career to the very day that Congress passed the bill granting copyright to foreign authors in 1891. Chapter Three, "'Doing as we would be done by': Walt Whitman, Copyright, and

Democratic Exchange," focuses on the apparent contradiction between Whitman's poetic philosophy of universal possession and his career-long support for the protection of authors' rights, including the passage of an international copyright law. Whitman responded to the discursive counter-positioning of democratic ideals and literary property rights by articulating in his poetry and prose a democratic principle of inter-connectedness grounded in open commercial exchanges supported by laws such as copyright. In seeking a personal connection with his readers, Whitman continually sought to embody himself in his texts, not only by metaphorically linking his body and his book—"Camerado, this is no book, / Who touches this touches a man" (*Walt Whitman: Poetry and Prose* 611)—but in later years by authenticating his presence with numerous supplements. His practice went well beyond autographs: on the title page of the 1888 printing of *Leaves of Grass,* he added a statement that each book had been "handled" by the author (qtd. in Myerson 121). For Whitman, copyright was more than a legal necessity of doing business; it was a means of ensuring that each reader touched the "authentic" Whitman.

If Whitman's and Stowe's support for literary property rights suggests a contradiction with their artistic and political beliefs, most critics have viewed Samuel Clemens primarily as an unflinching supporter of the law: a businessman, first and foremost, if often a failed one. The final chapter, "Protecting and Promoting Mark Twain: Samuel Clemens and the Uses of Copyright," demonstrates that widely accepted views of Samuel Clemens as a fervent copyright advocate have overlooked his pragmatic approach to protecting his literary property. For much of his career, Clemens' views on property were far more influenced by the fluid practices of ownership and promotion he witnessed in the mining camps of Nevada than by the arguments of fellow authors like William Dean Howells. His early career was advanced by the widespread unauthorized re-printing of his writings, just as a mining claim gained value with investors following the circulation of a sample of the riches it was supposed to contain. As his career progressed, Clemens continued to protect his work selectively, even though he knew the consequences of failing to copyright meticulously all of his material. As a result, Clemens viewed copyright more as a matter of authorial responsibility than legislative oversight. At the same time, his keen awareness of his audience and its perception of him led him to take great caution in publicly defending his rights, seeking to blunt possible criticism through humor and "behind the scenes" negotiations.

In his own study of authorship in the nineteenth century, Michael Newbury writes, somewhat apologetically, "while it seems inarguable to me that the capacity of writers to imagine the terms of their labor is limited by observable material conditions and available cultural paradigms, I remain sufficiently romantic to believe in authors as individuals capable of mediating and inflecting these conditions in meaningfully individualized ways" (9). Rather than dismissing the notion of authors' agency as romantic, an increasing number of critics are recognizing the importance of focusing on the author, even if older notions of authors as completely autonomous creators have long fallen by the wayside. Roger Chartier notes of this reconceived author-figure,

> As he returns in literary history or literary sociology, the author is both dependent and constrained. He is dependent in that he is not the master of the meaning of his text, and his intentions, which provided the impulse to produce the text, are not necessarily imposed either on those who turn his text into a book (bookseller-publishers or print-workers) or on those who appropriate it by reading it. He is constrained in that he undergoes the multiple determinations that organize the social space of literary production and that, in a more general sense, determine the categories and experiences which are the very matrices of writing. (9–10)

Chartier is careful to recognize the limits of "the author," but, at the same time, he acknowledges that the function of the author cannot be ignored.

Such a view dovetails with Pierre Bourdieu's analysis of the role of the author in what he describes as an "economy of symbolic exchanges" (38). Within this economy, the "speaker" produces a "product" whose value "depends on the relation of power that is concretely established between the speakers' linguistic competences, understood both as their capacity for production and as their capacity for appropriation and appreciation" (67). While Bourdieu is careful not to grant the speaker's "competences" too much weight in determining the outcome of the symbolic exchange, his willingness to consider the "producers" offers another way to consider the author without simply succumbing to a "romantic" view.[1] The term "negotiation" suggests the tenuous position of authors as their status was debated throughout the nineteenth century. "Negotiating copyright" suggests not only a discussion of copyright intent upon reaching an agreement, but also suggests that authors had to step carefully through the obstacle course of arguments about the law. What it does not imply is that authors possessed the ability to define the terms of their profession independently. While authors responded to the legal necessities and the arguments of copyright law in unique ways, their responses were also constrained. They had to negotiate the changes in copyright law and the marketing and publishing professions, as well as the demands and expectations of their readers; the ways they attempted these negotiations helped shape their understanding of their profession.

Theoretical arguments regarding the nature of authorship and the right to own texts took place throughout the nineteenth century; however, they were not merely the purview of scholars. These debates were public and present everywhere from newspapers to Congress. In the midst of these debates, authors were still attempting to pursue their profession, still writing and selling books, all the while working to defend and define this activity. As participants in these debates, authors shaped, at least to some extent, the notions of authorship that emerged. As scholars continue to consider the status of authorship in the United States, it will be useful to recall how the present discourse took shape: not solely through a progression of court decisions or market innovations, but also through a series of negotiations between writers and readers.

Chapter One

James Fenimore Cooper's Literary Estate: Individual Property Rights and Monopoly Power

THE FIRST PROFESSIONAL AUTHOR

James Fenimore Cooper has long been viewed as one of America's first professional authors, not only because of his artistry, but also because of his surprising early success and entrepreneurial approach to his craft. William Charvat, for example, has argued, "Though his self-respect as a writer was unmitigated, he exploited literature in a brisk and business-like fashion" ("Cooper" 133). This attitude, Charvat suggests, as much as his book sales, sets him apart from Irving and other American writers of the period (128). Cooper's comment in a letter to a British publisher in 1826 regarding publication of *The Prairie* and his other novels seems representative of this new sensibility. Cooper writes, "It is necessary to speak of these works as mere articles of trade" (qtd. in Charvat 133). His statement is a perfect expression of the emergence of the new profession of authorship: it illustrates the transition from the novel as individual work of art to "mere article of trade," a commodity to be bought and sold. His language is, presumably, no longer the language of a gentleman hobbyist, pursuing authorship as a pleasant pastime. The author becomes a businessman, the pastime a profession.

Even as Cooper took care to tend to his business interests, he was keenly aware of himself as an American writer writing of American subjects. As Ezra Greenspan notes of *The Spy,* Cooper's first success, "He publicized in its 1821 preface the fact that he had written that novel on what he saw as 'untrodden' native grounds. Its situatedness on such grounds and before an American reading public was a matter that was then very much in Cooper's authorial consciousness and that would remain so as he worked his way through the remainder of his career as a writer of works of fiction and nonfiction alike" ("Pioneering" 109). While Greenspan acknowledges the importance of the reception and popularity of Cooper's early novels, he emphasizes that a large part of Cooper's "pioneering" American authorship was his attention to American concerns and the formulation of authorship as a means of examining and reflecting the history and contemporary concerns of the young nation. From Cooper's time to the present, critics have offered his attention to political and social questions as important evidence of his status as one of the first professional American authors.

What is missing from both of these accounts of Cooper's work and his place in American literary history is an understanding of how Cooper's professional and "business-like" approach to his writing intersects with his awareness of his American audience. If, as Greenspan points out, "subsequent American writers would have a clearer sense of the narrative lay of the land and the conditions of literary professionalism for themselves as authors in America" (119), it was not only because Cooper imagined a literature that could embrace the country's origins and development (118). Perhaps even more importantly, Cooper recognized and reacted to a unique dilemma: if authorship were to succeed in becoming a viable profession in the United States, then Cooper would have to negotiate his economic needs with the demands of his emerging audience as well. The profession of authorship itself would therefore become one of his subjects. His work would argue in favor of the principles of literary property and authorial self-interest that would make the profession both profitable and acceptable to a growing market of readers.

Copyright was an ever-present issue in these negotiations. While Charvat may be correct in arguing that the passage of a federal copyright law in 1790 made the profession of authorship possible (*Profession* 6), it by no means guaranteed its viability. Setting aside the then still questionable social acceptability of writing for profit, would-be authors were forced to confront the popularity of writers from England. American publishers had little need for native works. As Cooper wrote in his 1828 work *Notions of the Americans, Picked up by a Traveling Bachelor,* "Unlike the progress of the two professions in the countries of our Hemisphere, in America the printer came into existence before the Author. Reprints of English works gave the first employment to the Press" (337). While today we can see this as an over-simplification of the history of American publishing and writing, Cooper's comment does point to a persistent obstacle faced by American authors throughout much of the nineteenth century. Because there were no provisions in American copyright law granting rights to foreign authors, American publishers were at liberty to print the most successful English authors without having to pay those authors for the privilege. Although this practice could cause a substantial amount of grief to publishers racing with each other to get their books into the marketplace, it saved them considerable expense and was standard when Cooper began writing in 1820 and remained so throughout much of the century.[1]

Authors also had to deal with the unique status of literary property rights which, unlike other forms of property rights, were secure only in as much as they promoted the public well-being and only for a finite period. Cooper recognized the possible benefits of such a situation: he writes in *Notions,* "There is no lethargy of ideas in this Country. What is known to one, (under the usual limits of learning) soon becomes the property of all" (87). This statement represents the enthusiastic praise he gives his country throughout most of his fictional travel narrative, but it also hints at what would become a standard argument against strengthening copyrights in America. In a democracy, what right had authors to exercise a monopoly over their work and ideas? Shouldn't anyone be able to appropriate and share them? The language of the Constitution and the law that followed it in 1790 were not reassuring for authors on this point: there were no provisions pertaining to translations or derivative works or for establishing copyright agreements with other countries. There was only a very narrow window within which writers could control and sell their works.

Faced with prominent obstacles to success as an author, Cooper used every means at his disposal, including his texts, to justify his profession to his audience. Because of his frequently antagonistic relationship with the press later in his career, critics have long viewed him as a tireless proponent of his ideals, refusing to compromise even when it meant damaging his literary career. While there is no doubt about Cooper's steadfast support for his principles, when it came to issues of copyright, he was keenly aware of the tension between his rights as an author and the frequently invoked rights of his readers. He was the first author to negotiate copyright with his publishers and with his public in the midst of an emerging discourse of authorship and literary property rights that tended to pit writers against these very constituencies.

Cooper grasped quite early on the nature of the debate that was unfolding: those opposed to copyright law often cited a fear of granting monopoly power to authors and large publishing firms, robbing the reading public of access to affordably priced books. At issue were the individual rights of the author within a democratic society. Were copyrights intended for the benefit of authors or America? Was literary property to be treated the same as other types of property? Why should the author have more rights than the type-setter, the binder, or the publisher, all of whom were necessary to produce a book in the marketplace? Like the American authors who came after him, Cooper had to conceive of authorship as a profession not antithetical to democratic principles, but instead sustaining and sustained by them. As a result, his treatment of property in his texts often supports the arguments he and other authors were making for stronger copyright laws throughout his career. While one may find evidence of Cooper's negotiations throughout many of his novels, including the oft-examined *Leatherstocking Tales,* they are perhaps most evident in those works in which he seems to be most directly addressing his readers and the state of contemporary American society: *Notions of the Americans, A Letter to His Countrymen, Home as Found,* and *The Littlepage Manuscripts* (the so-called "Anti-Rent Trilogy"). These texts have received less critical attention than other well-known works, and, when they are examined, tend to be either dismissed for their relative lack of artistry or treated primarily as transparent statements of Cooper's political beliefs or social preferences.[2] Reading them in light of Cooper's views on copyright law and within the context of the emerging discourse of literary property rights demonstrates how Cooper's professional interests are central to these works.

A common thread in these texts is property, and, as numerous critics have pointed out, property is seldom simply property for Cooper. In a typical statement, Cooper writes in *The American Democrat,* "As property is the base of all civilization, its existence and security are indispensable to social improvement" (169). He never considers or discusses property simply in terms of possession, but rather always links it to broader principles of individual rights and democratic society. Therefore, when we consider Cooper's reference to his works as "mere articles of trade," we should not read his statement as "merely" marking the commodification of his artwork. We must see in it his recognition that in the profession of authorship, literature and property were not inseparable, that the author's rights were now property rights, and, as such, fundamental to society. Of course, Cooper already had to know that, whatever his view of the subject might be, the law described a distinctly different notion of literary property. The author not only had to contend with a law that did little to protect his rights, but also with a public perception of those rights that ranged from apathy to outright hostility.

While debates over copyright would continue throughout the nineteenth century, they were in their infancy when Cooper began writing, and he appears to have had limited knowledge of the complexities of copyright law when he published his first novel, *Precaution,* in 1820. As the book was nearing completion, he wrote to a correspondent: "I shall write under the name of 'Edward Jones' to the English publisher and get you to make out an assignment to him of the right for Great Britain (if it can be done) as also to forward my copies and letter" (*Letters* 1: 62). He may have known little about how to protect his literary property overseas, but he clearly was aware of the necessity of doing so, just as he was aware of the possibility of cultivating an international audience. As he prepared to publish his second novel, *The Spy,* he was once again anxious to look after his copyrights, even if he did not know exactly how this might be done: "You would much oblige me by inquiring of the *trade* in London," he wrote another acquaintance, adding a list of questions which included "Whether the Copy right of a book can be secured in both Countries? What is necessary to secure a copy-right, in England only?" (74). This friend enlisted the assistance of Washington Irving, who was at that time the most successful American author in England, not only because of his skill, but also because his protracted residency provided him with contacts and a working knowledge of British publishing. Advice was not forthcoming, however, and because of Irving delayed bringing the novel to the British publisher Colburn, an unauthorized edition appeared before Cooper could arrange to have it published.[3]

As Cooper's career progressed, he learned more and more about the difficulty of controlling copyright. Shortly before leaving on a trip to Europe, he wrote to a British publisher: "Perhaps I may be able to secure a Right in England for the next book," adding,

> I see by our papers, that 'Pilot' has been printed by some adventurer or other—Is there no way of stopping this? We are about to alter our law, and I hope to make it more liberal to Foreigners—Verplanck (the Author) is in Congress, and chairman of the Committee—He is a friend, and indeed, connexion of mine, and has written me on the subject—As I shall go to Washington in a few days, I hope to be in time to throw in, a hint to that effect—There are some strong Literary Men in both Houses at present, and as the President is a good deal of a Scholar, I am in hopes a more liberal policy; than heretofore will prevail. (*Letters* 1: 128)

When we consider Cooper's earlier statements, we can see how far he came over the course of a few years. The losses he suffered as a result of "pirates" overseas, as well as his negotiations with publishers, seem to have demonstrated to him the advantages of tending to his interests in person and awakened a sense of activism. He was primarily concerned with his own business affairs, but he was also equally aware of the gaps in American law, suggesting a fairly rapidly acquired knowledge of the publishing trade. Cooper's belief in Verplanck was not misplaced: the Congressman was a staunch champion for the amendment that finally passed in 1831 granting authors copyrights for an extended duration and increasing the intellectual property protected. Verplanck would later continue to advocate for an international copyright as part of the American Copyright League. If Cooper was in fact in contact with Verplanck regarding the copyright bill being considered at this time, then he was in a position to be informed regarding the prospects for new legislation at this time.

While this letter reveals Cooper's growing knowledge of copyright law, it also demonstrates the combination of conscious self-interest and altruistic concern for international writers that would become a standard feature of the rhetoric American authors used when advocating for changes in the copyright law. This combination of concerns is evident in Cooper's earliest and most developed statement on copyright. After meeting Sir Walter Scott in Paris, the two men discussed how much Scott had lost as a result of literary piracy in America. Cooper, apparently eager to help, wrote a letter to his publishers Carey and Lea, asking them, "Cannot the force of Public Opinion be made to act in this case?" (171). It is significant that he already recognized that the argument over literary property was, in fact, one that would be determined by public opinion, years before the debate began appearing in numerous newspapers and magazines.

In advocating for what he called a "sacred" right (171), Cooper also advanced an argument for literary property rights that suggests the conflict between the individual and society that would become a standard part of the debate over international copyright law and a central feature of several of his novels. He urged his publishers to act in support of international copyright, writing, "I very well know that it would be said such a provision would raise the price of books, and that it would be creating a monopoly in favor of the large dealers—Monopoly is always a safe cry in a popular Government—But <is> are not all Laws of Rights Monopolies?" (172). Implicit in his question is the notion that, when compared to the "popular" will of the majority—a will that is asserting itself in the demand for cheap books— an author's ownership of his or her text, strictly speaking, was a kind of monopoly. Rather than refute such claims, Cooper takes the somewhat dramatic step of suggesting that all individual rights, because they may be to some extent exclusionary, represent kinds of monopolies. His belief that individual rights were therefore vulnerable to "demagogic" accusations of elitism and exclusion would later become even more fervent upon his return to America.

Copyright was more than a matter of the individual versus the majority for Cooper, however. He saw the stakes as potentially even higher. Cooper writes,

I readily grant that so long as we can be content to import our ideas, we may receive them at a cheaper rate under the present law, but then is it not wise to <ask our?> enquire into the prudence of giving <up> such a large portion of the Press, into foreign hands, especially in a government that receives not only all its <impulses> power, but its daily impulses from popular will, and consequently popular opinion. (173)

Other authors, including Samuel Clemens, would argue that reading cheap books from abroad would cheapen the American character because of the moral character of these books, particularly the novels. Cooper alludes to something far more insidious here: because we live in a democracy ruled by popular opinion, we put ourselves into jeopardy by allowing that opinion to be guided by the works of foreign authors.

Throughout his approximately seven years in Europe and even more so upon his return, Cooper saw an odd and dangerous combination of a basic lack of self-reflection on the part of the United States on one hand, and an inappropriate and ill-founded idealization of all things European on the other. Literature, and by extension the copyright laws meant to protect and encourage it, was for Cooper one of the causes of and cures for the problem.

Although he felt that a great deal was at stake, he also seems a bit naïve in his letter to Carey and Lea, asking the pair who had themselves been doing brisk business in pirated British works to call on their fellow publishers to "respect a Right, which ought to be far more sacred than it <can> could be made by any legislative enactments" (171). As David Kaser points out, "Most of the works published by the firm during its seventeen-year history were reprints" (115). The publishing firm had even been one of the first to employ a British agent to select works appearing in London and send them by the fastest means possible for republication in the United States (19). Soon after, Carey and Lea found themselves racing their competitors to get their books to press and to market first, and the most heated of these races involved the works of Sir Walter Scott.

While Cooper mentions none of this in his letter, a comparison of the letter that he sent with apparent drafts of it indicates that he was likely aware of his publishers' activities and may have modified his remarks accordingly. In one of the fragments, Cooper explicitly offers himself as an agent to mediate the interests of both author and publisher: "You will perceive that I constitute myself a protector of your rights, as I am duly commissioned to act on the part of the Author—I stand between you as a mutual Friend" (*Letters* 1: 175). In the letter he sent to Carey and Lea, Cooper backs off from his position as mediator for both parties, perhaps because of his discomfort in championing the publishers as well as the author.

Similarly, in another portion of the fragment, Cooper considers the possibility that a publisher would take advantage of an exclusive right to publish Scott by charging high prices—the kind of monopolistic price controls so feared by opponents of international copyright law: "(But should there exist, in the Republick, <a single> one of those Moral Vampyre [s], who are ever ready to prey on their fellow creatures, the Arm of the Law will be uplifted to restrain him)" (175–6). Cooper's turn of phrase here indicates his opinion of publishers who sought to gain unfairly from their public, but this striking phrase was excluded from the final letter. It is possible that his awareness of the practices of his own publishers and of his own tenuous position between them and Scott convinced him to modify his tone in addressing this issue.

As James Franklin Beard points out, Carey and Lea made no more than a polite response to Cooper, promising to send Scott a set of his works printed in America "that he may see how he looks on this side of the water" (qtd. in *Letters* 1: 183). This empty gesture was surely not what Cooper had in mind. Carey and Lea's *Cost Book* indicates that they published 12,250 copies of Scott's *Life of Napoleon* without making any payment at all to the author (Kaser 48). By comparison, a few months later they published 6,500 copies of Cooper's novel *The Red Rover,* paying $315 for the copyright to do so (52). This expense outweighed many other costs in producing the work. In light of these financial realities, it is hardly surprising that Carey and Lea were not particularly disposed to agree to Cooper's request that they advocate for a change in the present law. And although he also sought the support of his friends in New York[4], no headway was made in changing public opinion; in fact, other than some legislation affecting copyrights of individual citizens, Congress would wait five years to consider changes to the copyright law.

LETTERS FOR HIS COUNTRYMEN

Because copyright was so connected with ideas that Cooper felt were of vital importance to the United States, he did not let the matter drop, even when it became apparent that he could make no headway for Scott. In his first work to address his view of his country explicitly, *Notions of the Americans,* published while he was still traveling in Europe, he returns to the subject of copyright law, this time in a book that presents itself as a piece of travel writing from a European bachelor being led by an American on a tour of the

United States. The narrator recounts his experiences in letters written to friends back home.

Early in the text, Cadwallader, the bachelor's American guide, explains his lack of interest in the works of British travel writers by evoking the notion of "foreign influence" present in Cooper's letters to his publishers. In a lengthy note, Cadwallader tells his charge,

> Destitute of a Literature of our own, but rich in the possession of that which we derived from our ancestors, we were content to submit our minds to the continued domination of writers on whom it was believed that 'the mantle of Elijah' had rested, in virtue of their birth-right. So far as Europe was concerned, for many years after the peace of 1783, the great mass of the American people, saw with English eyes, and judged with English prejudices. (542)

Occasionally more critical of the United States than most of his American readers were accustomed to, *Notions* is still overwhelmingly optimistic and effusive in its praise. That praise is evident here as Cooper suggests that the period of American dependency on British culture is a thing of the past. Cooper reinforces this opinion by having the bachelor, based upon his observations of the country, repeat it: "By all that I can learn, twenty years ago, the Americans were perhaps far too much disposed to receive the opinions and to adopt the prejudices of their relatives, whereas I think it is very apparent that they are now beginning to receive them with a singular distrust" (342). He denies the more striking paranoia of his letters that suggest that the lack of international copyright will promote American dependence on foreign opinion. Just as he appears to have removed those phrases most critical of his publishers from his correspondence, here he seems to have muted his critique of the American reading public in a book written with that public in mind.

Yet Cooper is still the cultural critic in these pages, and, even as he downplays his fears of foreign influence, he cannot deny the crippling effect of literary piracy on the young book trade in America:

> Solitary and individual works of genius may indeed be occasionally brought to light under the impulses of the high feeling which has conceived them, but I fear a good, wholesome, profitable and continued pecuniary support, is the applause that talent most craves. The fact that the American publisher can get an English work without money, must for a few years longer, (unless legislative protection shall be extended to

their own authors,) have a tendency to repress a national literature. No man will pay a writer, for an epic, a tragedy, a sonnet, a history, or a romance, when he can get a work of an equal merit for nothing. I have conversed with those who are conversant on the subject, and I confess I have been astonished at the information they imparted.

A capital American Publisher has assured me that there are not a dozen writers in this Country whose works he should feel confidence in publishing at all, while he re-prints hundreds of English books without the least hesitation. This preference is by no means so much owing to any difference in merit, as to the fact that when the price of the original author is to be added to the uniform hazard which accompanies all literary speculations, the risk becomes too great. (346–47)

This passage demonstrates that, despite the variety of rationales Cooper offered for writing this piece of American travel literature, one of his goals was clearly to bring the attention of his fellow citizens to domestic problems that he felt were important. Copyright law, because of the effect he felt it would have on American literature, was one of these problems. In discussing how a fair copyright law might aid in the development of native talent, Cadwallader, the American spokesman, speaks in the "business-like" tone that marks Cooper's own approach to literature. Cooper confronts directly the common claim that "fame" should satisfy the true artist by suggesting that it is primarily the desire to make a profitable living that motivates authors. In encouraging American literature, copyright is both a matter of principle and practicality.

It is notable that, once again, he modified his arguments for copyright law, just as he shifted his language in drafting his letter to Carey and Lea. Instead of the fear that British opinion might unduly influence American readers, Cooper suggests that the important consequence of the present law is that it discourages publishers from taking risks on American authors. While one might argue about the effects of reading British literature, there was no denying the practical obstacles that publishing practices posed to new authors. The switch in the thrust of Cooper's argument indicates his awareness that the question of copyright was one of public opinion, and might be his best effort to appeal to the reason of his readers.

Despite what appears to be a conscious effort to be impartial while at the same time remembering his American audience, *Notions of the Americans* failed to meet Cooper's expectations. In the years that followed, his authorial fortunes were to fluctuate widely, although the dominant trend of his career was steady decline punctuated by occasional artistic and professional successes. Following the passage of the 1831 amendment which expanded the initial term of copyright from fourteen to twenty-eight years, copyright largely fell out of the public and legislative radar until 1836. For Cooper, however, it remained a symptom of what he felt was wrong with his country. This accounts for his repeated references to issues of literary property in what would become the rather notorious *Letter to His Countrymen* in 1834.

Cooper returned to the U.S. in 1833 with both anticipation and some pessimism. While he had managed to keep his spirits up even as he received gloomy accounts of American society from his friends (Grossman 90), he was repeatedly dismayed by critical response to his novels and to what he felt was his heroic defense of the honor of his country. To cite only one example, Cooper became embroiled in a dispute in France regarding the cost of running a democracy. He took great pains to refute claims that America's form of government was the most costly, and, in return for his trouble, was treated with derision by many critics who accused him of sticking his nose into international affairs beyond his level of expertise.[5] His *Letter to His Countrymen* is a lengthy public response to these and many other accusations, and, as it is the first work Cooper published prominently featuring his name, it represents an apparent attempt to speak directly to his readers without the mediation of a narrator or a romantic plot.

It is not a tactful performance; indeed, the gloves were off in the letter. For example, Cooper revives his earlier accusation of America's subservience to British opinion:

> The practice of quoting the opinions of foreign nations, by way of helping to make up its own estimate of the degree of merit that belongs to its public men, is, I believe, a custom peculiar to America. That our colonial origin, and provincial habits, should have given rise to such a usage, is sufficiently natural; that journals which have a poverty of original matter, should have recourse to that which can be obtained not only gratuitously, but by an extraordinary convention, without loss of reputation, and without even the necessity of a translation, need be no mystery; but the readiness with which the practice can be accounted for, will not, I think, prove its justification, if it can be shown that it is destructive of those sentiments of self-respect, and of that manliness and independence of thought, that are necessary to render a people great, or a nation respectable. (3–4)

This rhetoric foregoes his more moderate tone in *Notions* and echoes his more strident letters from nine years earlier. Cooper once again suggests that deference to foreign opinions is to be expected from a former colony, but, unlike in his travel narrative, here he argues that it is not just an issue of the past. The lack of international copyright, which Cooper refers to here as an "extraordinary convention," is the root of the problem.

To make his case, Cooper cites the criticism of his own novels, particularly his most recent work *The Bravo*. The critics, he argues, are being swayed by French writers angry over the role he had played in the "Finance Controversy." He even suggests that American editors have simply published poor translations of mean-spirited French critics without any acknowledgment, and a large part of his *Letter* is devoted to a close reading of one such essay, delineating phrases and sentence structures that Cooper feels are decidedly French. One of the pieces of evidence Cooper offers testifies to his knowledge of the various pirated editions of his work that were being distributed without his permission:

> That it came from France, was evident enough to me at a glance. The critique contains a fling at these words in the title-page of the book, viz: 'The Bravo, a Venitian story.' Now, the words, 'a Venitian story,' form no part of the true title of the work. They are an unauthorized interpolation of the European booksellers, and are not to be found in the American, or the only authentic edition. Besides this fact, which was almost the first thing that caught my attention, the edition of M. Baudry, Paris, is quoted by name. This edition is spurious, and abounds with blunders, having been, in part, printed from uncorrected sheets, obtained from another country. (20–21)

American readers are getting "foreign" opinions written in response to editions of his book that he did not approve. Here the lack of international copyright intersects with the insidious influence of the foreign press on American opinion. Not only are American readers being asked to accept the opinion of a foreign critic without knowing the origin of the criticism—or so Cooper strongly felt—but the criticism itself is based upon an unsanctioned, unedited copy.

Given the popularity of reprinting in the American publishing business, both in books and newspapers, it is not surprising that professional writing seemed progressively more unpalatable to Cooper. The *Letter* presents itself as Cooper's farewell to his audience; in its conclusion, he suggests that his decision is based on his belief that his public is unable to appreciate the literature he writes: "The American who wishes to illustrate and enforce the peculiar principles of his own country, by the agency of polite literature, will, for a long time to come, I fear, find that *his* constituency, as to all purposes of distinctive thought, is still too much under the influence of foreign theories, to receive him with favor. It is under this conviction that I lay aside the pen" (98). The lack of international copyright not only made it difficult for American authors to compete with popular reprints; in Cooper's mind, it led to a prevalence of foreign opinion that made it impossible for readers to truly appreciate and understand an American book.

In spite of this dramatic farewell to writing, Cooper's attention to the opinions of his readers and his careful refutation of personal charges suggest that he had no wish to burn any bridges. A common perception of the author is that he was always a bold, outspoken critic of America's failings; however, his courage in stating his views should not be mistaken for an utter lack of regard for his readers' perceptions of him. Even in his *Letter,* apparently his final message to his public, he is clearly concerned with how he is viewed by his audience. He seems particularly sensitive to the claim that he has criticized Americans in his works because he is more interested in making a profit overseas than in the United States. Again and again, Cooper sets out to correct this impression. First, he addresses the criticism of his being concerned with profits at all:

> I have been repeatedly and coarsely accused of writing for money, and exaggerated accounts of my receipts have been paraded before the public with views that it is not easy to make. That I have taken the just compensation of my labors, like other men, is true; nor do I see that he who passes a year in the preparation of a work, is not just as much entitled to the fruits of his industry, as he who throws off his crude opinions to-day, with the strong probability that on the morrow circumstances will compel him to admit that he was mistaken. (6–7)

Cooper is responding to a charge that recalls an earlier stage of American authorship, when writing was thought to be more of a pastime; he denies this accusation by replacing the construction of "writing for money" with "the fruits of industry." While one might criticize some for writing for profit, it appears, one would never criticize someone getting paid for his labor. Having these criticisms come from the paid press seems to have been doubly irritating for Cooper. He may consider statements about his pursuit of foreign profits as an attack on his patriotism, but here he is even more concerned with the attack on his occupation. This conflation of issues of economic gain and national loyalty would prove to be a vexing one for authors who spoke out on behalf of international copyright.

Yet if Cooper wants to argue that he is entitled to the profits he earned by his authorial labor, then it is odd that he takes so much time in the letter distancing himself from the charge that he attempted to profit from the overseas sale of his books. He writes,

> A French critic has lately intimated that I have been reaping large emoluments from his countrymen. I have never attempted to sell a copy-right any where but at home. It is true that one contract, written in England and sent to France for my signature, did express the contrary; but I remonstrated against the expression, and never permitted it to be used again. In England, the sheets of what I had written were sold, for the purchaser to do what he pleased with them. The same thing was done for Sir Walter Scott in America, and is constantly practised by other English authors. In France, I sold the sheets for translations, more with a wish to control the time of publication, by acting in concert with the publisher, than with a view to profit. The trifling amount received went to the uses of another. The sheets of three or four books were also sold in Germany, by the same person, and for his benefit. He died before the money for one book was received, and it remains unpaid to this hour. It will be remembered that there were, in all cases, translations previously to these arrangements.
>
> As respects France, a calculation, made on known data, has shown that I paid to the French Government in taxes, during different residences in that country, considerably more money than was obtained from the sales of the sheets of fourteen books. France and Germany excepted, I never had even any indirect connexion with the translations. (57–8n)

Cooper's statement, while literally true, glosses over the fact that, from almost the very beginning, he was thinking about how he might copyright his work abroad. In addition to seeking advice from Irving and others on how to protect his copyrights in England, he was encouraged by Carey and Lea to seek copyrights in other nations: "You should make some arrangement to have your next book translated into Russian, Italian [illegible] If you can then get a good copyright for them all. You will double in fame and fortune" (Carey and Lea, Letter). As Robert Spiller points out, Cooper went to great lengths in 1828 to publish his work himself so that he could send copies to all of his publishers at once, avoiding the race between legitimate copies and pirated editions (*Fenimore* 153). The result of his efforts was the only Cooper novel actually first published in Europe: *The Wept of Wish-ton-Wish,* which first appeared in Florence.

In fact, Cooper tried so many methods of earning a profit from the overseas sales of his book that he found himself in the same position as Irving, fielding letters from American writers hoping to profit from foreign editions of their work. William Dunlap wrote him several times, in a tone that grew progressively more desperate as Cooper failed to reply:

> Having once admitted the hope that the book might through your influence be made to produce something from an European republication, I am flattered by a hope that grows stronger as it grows older [. . .]. My remuneration here will probably not exceed $500—if you can make it yield me anything in addition, I shall be pleased, and so will you—the more the better. Can you secure a copy right in your own name? If so— do it. I hereby make James Fenimore Cooper the sole proprietor of a Book entitled "The History of the American Theatre [. . .]." (*Correspondence* I: 276)

Dunlap's letter illustrates the difficult position of American authors attempting to make a profit from foreign sales of their books, and it demonstrates, at least in Dunlap's opinion, Cooper's expertise in the publishing business. When Cooper first left for Great Britain, he had anticipated gaining greater rights for his books. While the law of the times was to block his hopes, he had learned a great deal. Just as he had looked to Irving for help from his experience, Dunlap now looked to Cooper.[6] His attempt to sign his book over to Cooper in an effort to gain a copyright not only indicates the lengths to which he was willing to go to make a British profit, but also American authors' uncertainty regarding British law.

Given this long-standing interest in international publication, Cooper's emphatic denial of any interest in overseas profits seems unusual. Cooper's intent, after all, is to "tell it like it is" to his countrymen. He must have expected that his readers would not entirely like what he had to say, particularly given the negative response to recent works like *The Bravo*. The criticism of his right to make money and protect his literary property, however, seems to have struck a nerve in 1834. Throughout debate over copyright law, opponents of extending literary property rights of authors held up the "greed" of the author against the needs of the public. In the debate over the 1831 amendment extending the duration of copyright, Senator Hoffman of Massachusetts argued that the law "went to establish a monopoly of which authors alone would reap the advantage, to the public detriment. The people [have] rights to be secured as well as authors and publishers" (*Register* 423). Cooper had accurately predicted this argument in 1826, a fact that must have provided scant comfort when newspaper editors criticized him for making money at the expense of his American readers. This was not only an attack on his patriotism, but on his profession, as well. It is not surprising, then, that Cooper elected to deny altogether his efforts to make a profit overseas rather than to spend all of his time justifying his right to do so. It would be several years before American proponents of international copyright publicly cited their loss of foreign profits as a reason for changing American law.

There is another possible reason for Cooper's denials. In 1834, the American economy suffered tremendously in the wake of President Andrew Jackson's move against the Bank of the United States. The author had publicly endorsed the President's action and denounced the Senate's decision to censure him (*Letters and Journals* 3: 6–7), and he did so again in the *Letter*. During the financial chaos following Jackson's use of executive power to withdraw public funds from the bank, the publishing industry in America was badly damaged. David Kaser provides a concise description of what transpired:

> One by one, other booksellers around the nation went into bankruptcy, and it was an unusual bookseller indeed whose ledgers did not indicate a balance due to the Philadelphia house [Carey, Lea & Blanchard]. [. . .] It was well into September before Henry could write to Miller that business was beginning to return to a state of normalcy and that the firm was once again looking with interest for new books to publish. Carey, Lea & Blanchard had virtually ceased publishing. (55–6)

Given this climate, Cooper must have known how difficult it would be to make a convincing case for his right to sell his books in foreign countries, even if his American publishers had difficulty producing them and his American public was having difficulty affording them. He held back the publication of his *Letter* because of the crisis, as he states in the "postscript" to the letter: "This letter was already written and sent to press, as mentioned in the introductory notice, when the condition of trade caused the bookseller to hesitate about publishing. The writer was also averse to appear before the public at a moment so gloomy, with matter that was necessarily of a personal nature. With this double motive, the pamphlet has been kept back till now" (101).

The economic climate might also explain why he appears so sensitive to charges of greed, even when he does concede that he has a right to make a living from his efforts. Cooper's *Letter to His Countrymen* may have been, as Beard put it, a "masterpiece of miscalculation" (6), further fueling the charges of his critics, but his statements regarding his copyrights and his profession seem carefully weighed to take into account both the historical moment and his audience. The significance of Cooper's statements in his *Letter,* therefore, has little to do with the accuracy of his representation of foreign publishing dealings; rather, the *Letter* is important because it demonstrates how accurately Cooper had predicted the course of the copyright debate and because it shows how vulnerable he was to the charges that could be levied against him within that debate. He would continue to deal with his readers and publishers according to the terms of this argument for the remainder of his career.

HOME AS FOUND

Many copyright historians point to 1837 as the starting date for the debate over international copyright. Such histories tend to ignore earlier private attempts like Cooper's to change the law, instead concentrating on the legislative introduction of international copyright. In 1837, Henry Clay introduced a bill in favor of establishing an international copyright, along with a petition signed by British and American authors (Putnam, *Question* 33). While nothing became of this bill other than its repeated burial and resurrection in committee, it coincided with and helped encourage the public advocacy of authors and other supporters of the measure. The arguments that Cooper had anticipated so long ago now flourished in the press. Writers who supported international copyright took up his position against the unfair claims of monopoly power: "The objection of monopoly may be as well raised against any other species of property of which the law gives a full and perpetual enjoyment, such as lands or chattels, as against this; nay, with more propriety, for the tenure of the former is vastly more exclusive" (Sackett 16).[7] The opposition soon flooded Congress with petitions against international copyright, from tradesmen and "a number of citizens" from a variety of cities and states (US Copyright Office 150–54).

In part because of the uproar against the measure, the Committee on Patents and the Patent Office issued an unfavorable report on the bill in 1838. The report re-affirmed the public nature of copyright: "And the true ground on which the claims to copyright protection are based, considered as a domestic regulation, is that it tends to encourage and reward talent, and to prompt and stimulate genius to those intellectual efforts which, when made public, afford instruction, improvement, and rational enjoyment, by means of which society is benefited" (2). While copyright exists ultimately to serve society, the report continues, the extension of that right to foreign writers would have a profoundly negative impact on the people:

> The number of persons employed in the United States in the various branches connected with book making and periodical publication has been estimated at two hundred thousand, and the capital employed in those branches at from thirty to forty millions of dollars. Some of these branches give employment and support to a great number of women and children. Here are interests too extensive and important to be overlooked. (3)

Not only would the numerous employees in the book business be harmed by international copyright, including all of those helpless "women and children," but the readers, as well. Such language indicates the difficult position in which authors found themselves in the debate: how could an author elevate his or her own rights over those of the children?

While the poorer readers in Great Britain might avail themselves of public libraries, the report argues that Americans rely solely on the low prices of books to furnish them with reading:

> In this country the population is comparatively sparse, less clustered into manufacturing villages, and of course more remote from public libraries. This disadvantage is compensated by the greater number of private libraries, which the cheapness of books enables the industrious farmers, mechanics, and tradesmen to procure, for the entertainment and intellectual improvement of themselves and their families. The multiplication of cheap editions of useful books, brought within the reach of all classes, serves to promote that general diffusion of knowledge and intelligence, on which depends so essentially the preservation and support of our free institutions. A policy which should have a tendency to turn these fructifying streams into more exclusionary channels, would find little justification in what is supposed to be due to foreign authors. (5)

Cooper did not anticipate in the senatorial eloquence which would yield "fructifying streams" back in 1826 when he first took up the issue, but he was correct in suggesting that the cheapness of books would be raised as a prominent argument against international copyright. As the committee's report also makes clear, he was also correct in foreseeing the debate in terms of public opinion, with the resultant opposition between the public and the individual rights of the author. With Congress and the newspapers taking up the case, pitting the authors' rights against the needs of workers and readers, what had largely been a professional concern for the last several years was now a public one.

Though his popularity was waning, Cooper was still a prominent figure in American literature, and he lent his name to the efforts to pass the bill. George Haven Putnam records that Cooper was a member of what he believed to be the first international copyright association, organized in 1837 (*George Palmer Putnam* 33). Because of his influence, it is not surprising that in 1838 *The Knickerbocker* agreed to publish Cooper's response to *Memoirs of the Life of Sir Walter Scott,* a response that included his earlier letter to his publishers on Scott's behalf. The editor remarks of these materials, "We submit them to our readers without comment, farther than to ask attention to the collateral theme of international copy-right, embraced in the letter of Mr. Cooper [. . .]. It gives us pleasure to see the arguments so often advanced in this Magazine, thus ably brought forward and sustained" (*Letters* 3: 323n). Cooper's early grasp of the issues is all the more evident when we consider that arguments being offered in support of international copyright law in 1838 could be "ably sustained" by a letter written twelve years before, long before there was much public discussion of the subject at all.

While none of Cooper's works of this period address issues of copyright as directly as *Notions of the Americans* or *A Letter to his Countrymen,* an examination of what is still considered to be perhaps his most controversial novel, *Home as Found,* reveals that the principles Cooper felt were at stake were still on his mind. More importantly, by examining this novel in the context of the debate over copyright, we can see how the novel serves as another strong statement in support of authorial rights. When the book first appeared, much attention was paid to the parallels between the fictional Effingham's struggle to control the family picnic grounds and Cooper's own arguments with his neighbors over Three Mile Point. This piece of land belonged to Cooper's family and was used as a kind of public park by the people of Cooperstown more and more frequently during Cooper's time abroad. This had gone on with his tacit assent for years, but he brought this practice to an end when he learned that someone had damaged the property and that there was a growing misconception that the land was public property.

While there is no denying the biographical parallel, what is notable is how Cooper frames this dispute in his novel. This argument over property is described in a way that is quite similar to Cooper's understanding of the arguments over literary property. It is first introduced in an exchange between the young Eve Effingham, just returned to America after a lengthy education in Europe, and her more cynical cousin, John. The America Cooper describes is not that of Cadwallader and the traveling bachelor; rather, it is a portrait that literalizes the criticisms he had levied in his notorious *Letter*. Upon their homecoming, the travelers learn much about their country that dismays them. Two changes that particularly vex them deal with the influence of foreign opinions and the threats of demagoguery. Cooper uses the character of Tom Howel, a somewhat comic character marked mostly by his severe anglophilia, to address the former: Eve remarks of him, "I confess a good deal of surprise at finding a respectable and intelligent man so weak-minded as to give credit to such authorities [English papers], or to form his serious opinions on information derived from such sources," to which her cousin replies, "You may be surprised, Eve, at hearing so frank avowals of the weakness; but, as for the weakness itself, you are now in a country for which England does all the thinking, except on subjects that touch the current interests of the day" (91). Tom Howel is at least aware of his prejudice; what is pernicious, Cooper suggests, much as he had a few years before, is the unacknowledged or unrecognized acquiescence to foreign opinion. That such fawning admiration was aided by the free re-printing of British books and newspaper articles is central to Cooper's interest in the issue of international copyright.

As for the threat of demagoguery, the author uses two characters in particular to demonstrate this evil. The first is a newspaper editor, Steadfast Dodge, who traveled overseas with the Effinghams and who largely serves as a foil to his more refined companions, and Aristabulus Bragg, a lawyer who, unlike Dodge, we are told, has some intelligence and might have developed wisely had he been better educated. As it is,

> like Mr. Dodge, he considered everything that represented itself in the name of the public as sacred and paramount, and that so general and positive was his deference for majorities, that it was the bias of his mind to think half a dozen always in the right, as opposed to one, although that one, agreeably to the great decision of the real majority of the entire community, had not only the law on his side, but all the abstract merits of the disputed question. (83)

The danger is not even majority rule *per se;* it is that the mere appearance of a majority, presented by unscrupulous journalists, might undermine the laws that are the product of elected officials, and for Cooper, therefore represent the true will of the people.

In *Home as Found*, as in Cooper's own life, the pressing danger posed by the influence of popular opinion is extra-legal; it threatens to take away an owner's rightful property through mob rule. Edward Effingham has all of the law on his side, but even this is slight comfort. When John informs Eve that a power is threatening to wrest the Point away from her family, she responds, "What power—human power, at least can dispute the lawful claim of an owner to his property? That Point has been ours ever since civilized man has dwelt among these hills; who will presume to rob us of it?" (105). Her cousin replies, "You will be much surprised to discover that there is such a power, and that there is actually a disposition to exercise it. The public—the all-powerful, omnipotent, over-ruling, law-making, law-breaking public—has a passing caprice to possess itself of your beloved Point; and Ned Effingham must show unusual energy, or it will get it!" (105). Some of Cooper's fundamental views on property rights and the threats that they face are here, views that held true for literary property, as well: property ownership is both a legal and sacred right that should be unassailable by human power, and it is vulnerable to a public that acts solely in its own interest, putting the whims of the many over the rights of the few.

Edward Effingham, the family patriarch, has no wish to deny the public access to the land: "I can have no wish to deprive my neighbors of visiting the Point, though I am fully determined they shall not deprive me of my property" (110). Rather than wishing to wield total control—a kind of monopoly, denying the public the pleasures to be taken on his property—he simply wants to maintain his possession and to prevent "injury" to the land. In fact, he is so confident in his right that he is not much concerned at all:

> Though the affair of the Point continued to agitate the village of Templeton the next day, and for many days, it was little remembered in the Wigwam. Confident of his right, Mr. Effingham, though naturally indignant at the abuse of his long liberality, through which alone the public had been permitted to frequent the place, and this, too, quite often, to his own discomfort and disappointment, had dismissed the subject temporarily from his mind, and was already engaged in his ordinary pursuits. (110)

While it can be persuasively argued that Cooper is being more than a little self-serving here, using his fictional character to blunt criticism that he had been miserly and shown an obsessive interest in publicly pleading his case, it is equally important to note that Cooper is also attempting to depersonalize the matter of the Point, rendering it primarily a matter of principle. John

McWilliams has noted this practice in Cooper's writing, and he cites the Point controversy as an example: "Public misuse of Three Mile Point, a tip of land on a small lake in New York, signified sweeping changes in American attitudes toward property law" (12). This was the same tack Cooper took in his *Letter to his Countrymen,* and, while it did not serve him well among his critics, it demonstrates the juxtaposition Cooper saw between his own interests and larger social principles.

These principles were the same for literary property as they were for real estate: the individual owner's rights must be protected from the demands of the public. Edward Effingham's moderate desires are contrasted to those members of the community who seek to take full possession of the Point and view the Effingham's control as impinging upon their rights as the majority. Aristabulas Bragg, the *de facto* mouthpiece for those townspeople in an uproar over the dispute, informs the Effinghams, "the public thinks itself persecuted in this affair" (112), a point echoed by the newspaper editor Steadfast Dodge, who exclaims, "What! shall one insignificant individual, who has not a single right above that of the meanest citizen in the county, oppress this great and powerful community!" (121). Throughout his description of the dispute, Cooper compares the Effinghams' legal right of ownership, carefully documented in wills and deeds, to the unsubstantiated "public right" of the townspeople. The first is depicted as essential to upholding the "country of laws," while the second is shown to be a clear threat to those laws. The fact that the public sees itself as "persecuted" by the Effingham's ownership of the property illustrates Cooper's claim in 1826 that "Monopoly is always a safe cry in a popular government," as well as the dangers that such accusations might pose to the rights of an individual (*Letters* 1: 171).

McWilliams refers to Cooper's method of writing as "synechdocal": "His tales would deal with local struggles or historical events of lesser importance, yet through them Cooper would discuss the most grandly national of issues" (11). He argues convincingly that the author is responding to what can be seen as a larger trend towards a view of property that places the public welfare over the individual's rights:

> The growing political and economic power of manufacturers, cities, immigrant and labor groups was distressing to men of Cooper's social and cultural assumptions. [. . .] In 1835 Chief Justice Taney succeeded Chief Justice Marshall, thus bringing the Supreme Court into an era in which the community's right to general welfare took precedence over the individual's right to property. (187)

Home as Found appears to be the author's critical response to these changes in society. The novel lends itself to readings that concentrate on issues of real estate, readings made even easier after his later "Anti-Rent" trilogy; however, one can also see in his description of the land dispute a commentary on arguments over literary property, for Cooper viewed these two forms of property as being governed by similar principles.

In fact, Cooper portrays an argument in favor of property in *Home as Found* that was employed at least twice during the preceding few years to support authorial property rights. In *The American Jurist* of 1833, one commentator writes,

> We have all heard, if we have not had the occular enjoyment, of the magnificent gardens of Mr. Niblo in New York. These gardens are in the soft and fragrant season of summer thrown open to the public, but they still belong to the enterprising proprietor, who invites visitors only that he may derive pecuniary emolument. Those who are attracted to his establishment, and they are many, may walk there, or sit there, and view its beauties and its grandeur; but they do not venture to cull a single flower or sever a single twig; and if Mr. Niblo should be gravely informed at the conclusion of an evening's exhibition, that his visitors claimed the title to his grounds, it would no doubt surprise him. The case of the author is similar; when he writes and prints a book and sends it out into the world, so far from intending to abandon the profits arising from it, he shows a contrary intention. (J.K.A. 73–4)

A similar argument had appeared in *The American Jurist* in 1829, stating that, while one may have the right to walk through another's garden, one does not therefore have the right to sell the trees there ("Literary Property" 258). Examples such as these were made to refute claims that once authors had chosen to publish their work, they had also yielded their ownership of it. The metaphor of the garden is, of course, a flawed one, as it does not deal with the most difficult issue of literary property: the reproduction of the thing itself. One does not take a flower from the garden; rather, one takes a copy of the garden itself. What is important for understanding *Home as Found* is what the metaphor attempts to explain—that ownership of property does not end when one allows another the use of it.

Supporters of literary property rights were continually drawing parallels such as these to make their case, and Cooper's portrayal of the picnic grounds dispute not only employs the same imagery, but it also turns on the same logic. Edward Effingham concedes that he has allowed visitors to use the park, and he has no wish to stop their use; what he is attempting to do is to maintain possession and control of his property even though it appears to have become "public" property. While the incident is clearly autobiographical, it is also literary in its implications.

The literary nature of these events extends beyond rhetorical and logical formulations, however. By depicting this dispute over real estate in a novel, Cooper makes the argument itself a piece of literary property. Just as the Effinghams printed notices proclaiming their ownership of the Point, Cooper's copyright in *Home as Found* announces both the creation of another piece of property and the limits of the public's access to that property. Like the visitors to Niblo's gardens, readers are now welcome to view the property for a fee. More than simply an ill-advised attempt to get the last word, Cooper's depiction of the property dispute represents an attempt to change the "grounds" of the debate, taking control and possession of both sides.

Unfortunately, the boundaries provided by copyright are not so clear, and they were even less so in Cooper's time. Literature and land remained vulnerable, and this was made painfully clear to Cooper when members of his community reacted to his published warning against trespassing. Much as he depicted in *Home as Found,* several gathered to pass a series of resolutions condemning his action. Unlike in his novel, however, one of the resolutions passed against him urged that any of his works found in a local library should be removed. (Cooper believed that the order had been given that they should also be burned.) In a letter to *The Freeman's Journal,* Cooper addressed this outrage:

> Thus is one question of a right of property to be decided by doing violence to other rights of the same nature; and this indecent and illegal procedure, one equally removed from the duties of good citizens and from all principles of order, reflection, and respect for the will of the people, as that will has been manifested in the laws, is paraded in certain journals, as showing the spirit of the public of Cooperstown! (*Letters* 3: 276)

The threat to his books violated rights of property that were of "the same nature" as those threatened by the public's attempt to usurp his land. Cooper may be able to create literary property, but, as imperfect copyright laws often demonstrated, his control over this property was not guaranteed. Even more vexing for Cooper, these transgressions against his land and literature were proclaimed to be "the will of the people," a will that threatened to trump those laws meant to protect the individual from such public caprice.

This is not to suggest that the Point dispute in *Home as Found* should be read as some sort of allegory for disputes over literary property; indeed, allegory does not address the overlapping arguments and the transformation of a representation of arguments over property into a piece of literary property. What the episode does indicate is how our understanding of this text may be expanded when we recognize how it coincides with Cooper's earlier statements regarding copyright and the debate that was beginning to heat up as he wrote the novel. By reading it only as an unfortunate attempt at self-justification, much as Cooper's contemporaries did, we fail to recognize what he felt was at stake: what mattered most to him, both in his own troubles and in his fictional account, was sustaining the rights of property, in all forms, in the face of accusations of monopolistic control and attempts to elevate the will of the majority over the individual.

Such concerns should not be read as Cooper's alone, as the simple self-interestedness of a genteel landowner. They were at the heart of the on-going debates regarding the profession of authorship in America and the rights of literary property, as Sackett makes clear in his *Plea for Authors:*

> [Authors] have heretofore been considered rather with reference to the comparative smallness of their number, than with a due regard to the influence they exert upon individual and national prosperity. Advantage has been taken of the generous motives which influence the most eminent, to despoil them of the just and natural remuneration of their labours. Instead of the ease, the competence, and the respectability that springs from that competence, in countries constituted like our own, they have been left to the cold charity of the public—a public which, not content with despoiling them of their rights, is mean enough to reproach them with the poverty consequent upon that despoliation. (5)

This counter-poising of authors versus public is illustrated in the nation's earliest landmark copyright case, Wheaton *vs.* Peters, in 1834.[8] The Supreme Court ruled, in essence, that copyright was a privilege granted by the government, not a common-law right, and, therefore, one had to follow all government procedures in order to secure the rights to one's work. Lyman Patterson writes of this decision,

> The striking points about the premises of the majority and the dissenters is that they are polar, one proceeding from the interest of the public, the other from the interest of the individual creator. [. . .] The majority, viewing copyright as a monopoly, were content to protect the

author's property for a limited time under the conditions prescribed the statute. To do otherwise would be contrary to the public interest. The dissenters, on the other hand, seemed to think that the best way to protect the public interest would be to give unlimited protection to the author's property. (211)

Just as the language of the Constitution suggests, the author's right to a "monopoly" over his or her text was limited by the public interest. Cooper became more and more wary of the public throughout his career, and the townspeople he depicts in Templeton, seeking to take advantage of the Effingham's property, were the same people he saw taking advantage of the small number of authors.

ANTI-RENTISM AND THE CONTINUING ARGUMENT OVER LITERARY PROPERTY

Cooper was frequently criticized for his involvement in the Finance and Bank controversies, and that criticism intensified following the publication of *A Letter to His Countrymen*. Nothing matched the intensity of the ridicule he was forced to endure following the publication of *Home as Found*, however. Seizing on the biographical parallels, easy to spot after the public attention Cooper had already received in the Three Mile Point dispute, critics railed about his narcissism. This led to a now-legendary series of court battles as Cooper sued a number of editors, including Horace Greeley, for libel. While he met with some success, the cases dragged on for years, and his reputation consequently suffered from either the contempt or the neglect of the press.

Whether it was because he became preoccupied with his legal troubles or because he became more reluctant to speak out on a subject that would put him once more in conflict with members of the press, Cooper largely stopped commenting publicly on copyright for several years. When one considers the fact that the most common charge against Cooper during the libel suits was that he was greedy, going after publishers to extract paltry financial reward, it is not surprising that he began distancing himself from the cause of international copyright. In 1842, Charles Dickens came to the United States and spoke in favor of international copyright, insisting that authors had a fair right to profit from their work. The critics howled about his avarice. Cooper had long recognized the very public nature of the debate over copyright, and although never one to back away from a fight, by 1842 he seemed reluctant to be poised against his shrinking American audience.

That year, he wrote a letter to *The Evening Post,* taking great pains to refute a claim by Dickens that he had signed a petition in favor of international copyright law, even as he professed to agree with the principles of such a law:

> I have never even seen the petition in question, and conceive it proper to say as much; as I feel reluctant to be publicly held responsible for acts, of the precise nature of which I am ignorant. Had it been thought necessary to consult me in relation to the petition in question, I am far from certain, I should have signed it. I wish for no *international* legislation on any subject; and least of all with England. (*Letters* 4: 302)

Cooper seems aware that he would gain no favor by being associated with Dickens when it concerned copyright.[9] His disdain for England not only echoes his lifelong criticisms of the country, but it also must be read in the context of the criticisms he had himself been facing—that he was too concerned with foreign opinions and profits. Cooper's refutation of Dickens seems to be an attempt to shield himself from the calumny being rained down upon his fellow author.

At the same time, however, he takes time to elaborate his own defense of literary property rights. He avoids those earlier justifications he had offered in favor of such a law: that it would foster American authorship, that it would ensure the rights of the individual, and, most importantly, that it would help free America from the pervasive influence of foreign opinion. Instead, Cooper writes, he favors such a law because it is line with the "golden rule of conduct" (304). He sets forth a largely religious argument:

> As respects property, so sacred is it held by the christian law, that we are commanded not to *covet* even, that of another, much less, to *steal* it. [. . .] It would be easy to show that it is the *interest* of this country, in a worldly point of view, to give every author a right of property in his works; but I go much higher than this. I believe it is bound, in common with all other nations, to extend the same protection to this right of property, as it does to all others. (304)

The strength of his conviction is revealed in the final line of his letter: "As for England and France, or Holland, I would not ask the question as to what they do, one or all; but, in our own case, I would do that which, it strikes me, we are bound to do, in order to bring the legislature of the country up to the level of the progress of the age, and to the revealed law of God" (305). Such sentiments are clearly far removed from all of the previous rationales

Cooper had offered to justify an international copyright law, although they do serve to reinforce what Cooper saw at stake in issues of copyright: where before he had felt it was an issue of intellectual independence, here he seems to feel it is a matter of Christian duty. Not only is this quite different from his earlier stance, it also contrasts sharply with the public appeals of Dickens, who had argued in favor of the law largely on the basis of reciprocity and fairness to British authors.[10]

There are a number of ways to account for this change. It may be an indication of the growing occupation with religion that is characteristic of Cooper's final novels. It also seems to be a natural extension of the prominence Cooper had given property in works such as *The American Democrat*. As McWilliams has argued, the author's later works tend to collapse the distinction between republican principles and property ownership: for Cooper, an American's character is evaluated on the basis of his views regarding property (222). It is not a far step from this conflation of character and property rights to a connection between religious morality and literary property rights. Just a few months later, Cornelius Mathews, a fellow author and a strident and vocal champion of international copyright law, proclaimed, "We are here, between ocean and ocean, to lead a life as pure, to administer examples as great as God grants us strength to render. If we are first to restore to an injured class rights long withheld, to place the author upon his feet, to clothe him in the garment that becomes his station and pursuit—so be it! We can claim no higher honor, no profounder glory, than to have done so" (8). Such appeals to Americans' religious values would become more and more prominent as the debate over literary property rights continued.

Yet we must consider Cooper's appeal to religious virtue in the context of his apparent eagerness to distance himself from the claim that he had signed a petition in support of a new law. His claim in his letter that he feels "reluctant to be publicly held responsible for acts, of the precise nature of which [he is] ignorant" (*Letters* 4: 302) is offset by his immediate pronouncement that he might not sign such a petition at any rate. This proved to be a prophetic statement, for in 1843 Cooper refused membership in the newly formed American Copyright Club. In a letter to Mathews, the secretary of the club, Cooper once again proclaimed his support for international copyright law, citing "principles of common honesty," as well as expediency: "Unless we have a copy right law, there will be no such thing as American Literature, in a year or two. At present very few writers are left" (414). Here are no lofty proclamations of religious virtue; rather, this letter seems closer to the kind of nationalism that typified Cooper's earlier statements on the subject. International copyright is necessary so that America can "have [. . .]

a Literature of [its] own" (414). Such arguments are entirely absent in his letter to the editors of *The Evening Post* written only a few months before.

The reasons for Cooper's eagerness to set the record straight publicly regarding his support for international copyright, his use of a more abstract religious argument and his refusal to join the American Copyright Club, are all hinted at in the conclusion of his reply to Mathews. Cooper writes,

> I beg you to communicate to the club that I would cheerfully join them, did I join any thing, but an issue has been raised that induces me to stand aloof. I ask nothing from the American public, and I owe them nothing. I wish to keep the account square. I am certain the tax-gatherers will not overlook me, and this will be <certain> sure to keep me up to the discharge of all my duties as a citizen. Beyond this I feel reluctant to go. (414)

When we recall Cooper's urging of his fellow members of the Bread and Cheese Club to support this cause in the 1820s, we can see how much had changed for Cooper in twenty years. James Grossman describes Cooper's decision as perpetuating the growing perception of his contemporaries that he was becoming a "misanthrope," the letter representing a "moment of churlishness" (262). However, one must consider the "issue" that Cooper alludes to in this letter. Although his libel suits were just coming to an end, he was still sensitive to the charges made against him in the papers, particularly the charge that he was a "shaver," interested only in extracting money from his opponents.[11] His statement that he "owes" the American public nothing seems to indicate that Cooper felt he had done enough for his country. His reference to the tax collector suggests that the only duties he will perform for his country will be those extracted from him.

Cooper felt that advocating stronger and broader copyright laws was something that should be done for the good of the country: he had been making statements to that effect since 1826. Less than twenty years later, it appears he was no longer willing to negotiate the tensions between his audience and his publishers in pursuing the passage of such a law. In fact, in writing publicly of the matter as primarily an issue of religious duty, Cooper not only frees himself from charges of self-interest, but he portrays the issue abstractly, removing authors, himself included, almost entirely from the matter. Authors, he writes in his editorial, are protected by the same religious principles that protect the horse owner and the carpenter (*Letters* 4: 304). While it was hardly unusual for supporters of copyright to make metaphorical connections to other kinds of property and owners, it was unusual for

Cooper, and his retreat from the pragmatic arguments of the past coincides with his retreat from a more proactive stance in the debate.

In spite of his apparent wish to retreat from the slings and arrows of public opinion, events in New York were moving him once again to take up his pen to address his fellow citizens regarding what he viewed as a fundamental threat to democracy. As in *Home as Found*, this threat took the form of a public attack upon the rights of individual property holders, once again under the banner of supposedly democratic and egalitarian principles. The "Anti-Rent Wars" affected him profoundly, not only because they involved close family friends, but also because they seemed to be the fruition of the seeds planted on his own Three Mile Point.[12] As lease-holding farmers refused to pay their rents and urged the government to grant them ownership of the leased lands, Cooper was dismayed to see law-makers giving in to this vocal segment of the population who claimed to be speaking for the majority, arguing that rent was "undemocratic." While the farmers were happy to see land taken away from their landlords and given to them, they had no problem with owning their own property. Driven by what he saw as the hypocrisy, violence, and public demagoguery of the Anti-Renters, Cooper apparently set aside his pledge to "keep the account square" with his public, and he once more began writing in an attempt to help steer his country in the right direction.

As with the Point controversy in *Home as Found*, the debate over the Anti-Rent movement appears to be fairly far afield from the question of literary property; however, the movement was gaining so much public attention that it is little surprise that the issue was taken up by advocates for international copyright, once again employing the principles so starkly set forth in the debate over real estate in an attempt to render the logic of literary property more clear. In his speech of 1843, Cornelius Mathews proclaimed,

> If I may throw open literary property to all the world, why not all other property? If there may be an allowable agrarianism of ideas, why not of acres and tenements as well? What would be the result if all the farms and estates in America were, to-morrow, made common, we can, in a measure, guess. There would follow, as these very reasoners should know, a grand disruption of society. I have a shrewd notion, that the gentlemen who claim to have thought out the author's book, in common with him, employing him only as secretary of the commission, may be of the very lineage and creed with those who claim as a right one eye of the author's spectacles and one sleeve of his coat. The world has not yet answered to itself in the consequences, for the unjust distinction

it has chosen to make between the property of the head and the hand.
[. . .] The world prospers best when to each man it allots his right and
protects him in it. (9–10)[13]

Mathews' final statement is, of course, quite similar to those Cooper made in
defense of individual property rights, particularly in *The American Democrat,*
where he argued, "It is not known that man exists anywhere without establishing rules for the protection of property" (170). Cooper had long based
the progress of humanity on the defense of property in all its forms.

Mathews makes similarly broad claims regarding the rights of property,
most notably that one should not distinguish between types of property
when considering an owner's rights—"the unjust distinction [. . .] between
the property of the head and the hand." Of course, the Constitution had
long since established just such a distinction, but, in doing so, it made
almost any right to intellectual property vulnerable. Unlike real estate, literary property's protection was circumscribed by the needs of the public. An
attack on international copyright published in 1843 entitled *Considerations
and Arguments Proving the Inexpediency of an International Copyright Law*
seizes on this fact. Its author, John Campbell, argues,

> Now, it is manifest that a law permitting British authors [. . .] to dis-
> pose of the right to print their works in this country, while it would
> impose a heavy tax on the American people, could nevertheless, confer
> upon American authors no benefit worthy of the name. The difference
> being that, although as every one knows, we are flooded with English
> publications, the reprint of an American book in England, is on the
> other hand, an event so rare, as to weight nothing in a general argu-
> ment. [. . .] The rich might, and doubtless would, continue to pur-
> chase at the enhanced price, but what would be the condition of the
> middling and lower classes of our population, whose characteristic, be it
> remembered, is intelligence; and whence do they derive that intelli-
> gence, which so honorably and happily distinguishes them from persons
> abroad in corresponding spheres of life? Why from the circulation, to be
> sure, of every species of knowledge in the cheapest form, put forth by
> rival publishers, striving to supply the intellectual market on the lowest
> possible terms. (5)

Although Campbell appears to be concerned only with curtailing the rights
of British authors (he addresses Dickens, particularly), the dangers that his
argument poses to all literary property rights are clear. His assertion that

international copyright would do nothing for American authors while imposing a "heavy tax on the American people," while misleading, was a common one, and one that authors were continually forced to address.

By the 1840s, not only were writers feeling the pinch of competition from cheap editions of Dickens' novels, but their prospects for success abroad were hampered by the inability to secure rights overseas. Walt Whitman wrote of the dismal state of affairs for American writers in an editorial published in the *Brooklyn Evening Star* in 1846: "The writers of America are more miserably paid than their class are in any other part of the world. And this will continue to be the case so long as we have no international copyright. At this time there is hardly any encouragement at all for the literary profession in the way of book-writing" (*Journalism* 252). Statements such as these and the public remarks of authors like Mathews tried to combat the misperception that American authors had nothing to gain from international copyright, as did organizations like the American Copyright Club; however, at least during the 1840s, Dickens' dispute with the American press over the issue had contributed to making the issue of international copyright seem like a distant one to the average American reader.

Seen in this light, Cooper's refusal to join the copyright club and his public denial of supporting Dickens' cause appear to be, at the very least, extremely unhelpful. Aubert J. Clark, a scholar of the international copyright movement, writes,

> This was a serious blow to those who emphasized the value of copyright protection for a distinctively American literature. [. . .] Oddly enough, Cooper wrote most of the American stories while abroad in Paris, Florence, Rome and Dresden. His works were praised by the great European critics, and influenced more than one generation on both continents. Perhaps years spent abroad, and years spent in splendid isolation on the great Cooper estate of Otsego Hall, influenced Cooper's decision to stay clear of the movement. [. . .] That Cooper said he would join the Copyright Club if he joined anything did not help much; he still remained aloof. (74–75)

Clark unfairly questions Cooper's motives, misrepresents his status at this time (how could anyone who was aware of Cooper's frequent public trials, financial worries, and rigorous publishing schedule describe him as living in "splendid isolation"?), and effaces Cooper's long history of support for international copyright. Cooper's refusal does invite scrutiny, however. More than many authors of the time, he was aware of the difficulties of publishing abroad and the losses that a popular author could suffer as a result of international piracy; a public statement to this effect might have been helpful in countering claims like Campbell's.

In fact, Cooper was used as an example in a written *Reply* to Campbell's attack on international copyright. In 1844, Thomas Adamson wrote,

> 'Thus, Irving's and Cooper's novels,' continues John Campbell, 'are published at two dollars, while those of James and Bulwer are sold at one fourth the price—and so on how far soever the comparison may be extended.' Any boy in the street would laugh at the wild absurdity of such a misstatement as this. It is perfectly well known to every body, John Campbell included, that all of Cooper's late works have been sold at twenty-five cents a vol. (11)

Adamson refutes the point that American novels are more expensive because of their copyrights, thereby strengthening the argument that authors were being hurt by the lack of international copyright, but his comment also demonstrates how far Cooper's star had fallen since the 1820s, when his books sold for two dollars each. Because of his long career, Cooper was uniquely positioned to set the record straight regarding how his livelihood had suffered. On the other hand, his reticence also appears to justify his earlier declared disinterest in foreign profits. Whatever the true explanation for it, the author's refusal to join the American Copyright Club undermines the commonly held view that he was always willing to risk his reputation in support of his beliefs. Like all authors, he was balancing his own beliefs and professional interests with the views of his readers.

The charge that American authors would benefit little from international copyright was perhaps the easiest to refute, even if Cooper refused to do so. The more sweeping argument made in Campbell's text, and the more potent because of its appeal to the public welfare, was that the circulation of inexpensive texts was essential to the intellectual well being of the American citizenry. This claim seems to be supported by the constitution's "limited Times" clause and divides authors from their readers, the "intellectual market" seeking only inexpensive wares. Campbell quotes approvingly the following statement from another international copyright opponent: "Now we can prove that so long as copyright exists, a book will have a limited circulation, because it will be published at a comparatively high price; for however harshly the word may sound, copyright is a 'monopoly;' and like all other monopolies, its tendency is to keep the commodity at a high price, and thus restrict its diffusion" (qtd. in Campbell 8). As we have already noted, the charge of monopoly was a particularly damaging one. Books, in this view, were not like farms, as Mathews tried to argue, but were instead more of a "public possession" granted to authors for only a short duration before being "diffused" throughout the marketplace. Whereas a farmer's possession of his property might not be thought of as a monopoly, an author's possession of his or her text was.

The Committee on Patents and the Patent Office report of 1838 also argued for the unique qualities of literary property, stating,

> [L]iterature itself is only valuable as it tends to improve and bless mankind. It should not, therefore, be confined to exclusive channels, but diffused and spread throughout the whole mass, as a medium of intelligence, of refinement, of correct taste, pure morals, sound principles, and elevated sentiments; shedding upon the whole face of society the beams of light and knowledge and intellectual improvement. (5)

How could one argue for the exclusive possession of something so clearly meant to benefit the majority? Why should only the wealthy enjoy these valuable possessions?

Because the issue of copyright law became substantially more visible at the same time that the Anti-Rent riots were fomenting in New York, it is natural that Mathews would draw on arguments employed in them in an attempt to explain the justice of an international copyright. Similar rhetoric had been employed by another advocate in 1838: "In spite of the interested cry of 'No monopoly,' as applied to literary productions, any limitation of their author's property in them is as grossly unjust as would be the cutting down of a freehold estate to a lease for a term of years" (Sackett 16). However, just as copyright proponents were trying to abolish the "distinction between head and hand," writers like Campbell were trying to keep that line bright. The Anti-Rent riots, in their own way, were blurring that line even further, questioning even the rights of landowners to their property. The "grand disruption of society" that Mathews had warned would follow if all property were treated the way literary property was treated was unfolding on the large estates in New York. As McWilliams puts it, for Cooper, "New York Anti-Rent Wars indicated a national catastrophe" (12). In the face of this new "catastrophe," Cooper would turn once again to fiction to employ an array of tactics in defense of individual property rights.

In writing *The Littlepage Manuscripts*, Cooper offers both an emotional and systematic defense over the course of three novels, depicting the fate of a society that elevates the circulation or "diffusion" of property over the rights of its owners. From the beginning, he had conceived of the *Manuscripts* as a trilogy, with the final volume offering "an exhibition of the Anti-Rent commotion that now exists among us, and which certainly threatens the destruction of our system" (*Letters* 5: 7). As with *Home as Found*, Cooper did not limit his arguments to the immediate question of anti-rentism, however; rather, he used it as a fictional vehicle from which to defend his broader views of property rights. As the Mathews speech indicates, the question of anti-rentism and international copyright could be viewed as matters of similar principles.

Cooper took up this defense in his works, and it is fitting that in one of the few favorable reviews of the first novel, *Satanstoe*, appearing in *The Merchant's Magazine, and Commercial Review*, the sub-title was given as the *Title-Page Manuscripts* (House xxxii). This error reminds us that each time Cooper wrote a novel addressing issues of property, he was simultaneously creating a new piece of literary property and granting himself "title" over it. As with *Home as Found*, the distinction between the subject matter and the book that contains it collapses. The novels are prolonged examinations of questions of title, but, as objects of literary property, they are themselves subject to questions of ownership and control. In this regard, the conceit that they are manuscripts is also important. Manuscripts had always been accepted as unquestionably the property of their owners. It is only in their publication that title comes into question. Rather than announcing himself as author/owner, Cooper presents himself only as the books' editor. In the Preface to *Satanstoe*, he writes, "Every chronicle of manners has a certain value. When customs are connected with principles, in their origin, development, or end, such records have a double importance, and it is because we think we see such a connection between the facts and incidents of the Littlepage Manuscripts and certain important theories of our time, that we give the former to the world" (3).

In "giving" these texts to the world, Cooper avoids the somewhat problematic positioning of himself as an editor dispensing with another author's property. These are not texts that are being pilfered; they are gifts. As "author," the book's narrator Corny Littlepage proclaims his intention to write his memoirs and to assign the same task to his son and grandson: "Perhaps, by the end of the latter's career," he writes, "they will begin to publish books in America, and the fruits of our joint family labours may be thought sufficiently matured to be laid before the world" (7–8). Cooper, as editor, is merely following the wishes of his author, and what is more, he is performing a service for the country, providing readers with a glimpse of a history from a time when "scarcely such a thing as a book of memoirs that relates to a life passed within our own limits, and totally without light literature, to give us simulated pictures of our manners and the opinions of the day" (7). The book is presented as pre-dating not only the destructive Anti-Rent riots, but also the very development of American literature itself and the arguments over property rights. *Satanstoe* thus does not present itself directly as a polemic on property ownership; rather, it is intended to be a historical portrait of American life prior to the Revolution.

Kay Seymour House has suggested that Cooper's choice of presenting himself as editor gives him "the advantage of having two voices in one book" and allows him to avoid the danger of being confused with his creation, as he had been in *Home as Found* (House xxi).[14] While both of these statements are true, House fails to point out another advantage Cooper gains from this practice: he distances himself from the more extreme positions taken by his narrators, even when he agrees in principle. Often, Cooper presents himself as the voice of moderation, apologizing for the more apoplectic exclamations of his characters.[15] He addresses this directly in his preface to the second novel, *The Chainbearer:*

> It is thought by a portion of our readers that the first Mr. Littlepage [. . .] has manifested an undue asperity on the subject of the New England character. Our reply to this charge is as follows: In the first place, we do not pretend to be answerable for all the opinions of those whose writings are submitted to our supervision, any more than we should be answerable for all the contradictory characters, impulses, and opinions that might be exhibited in a representation of fictitious characters, purely of our own creation. (227–28)

This would appear to be one more negotiation with his audience. His defense not only advances his conceit of editorship, but it also allows for the fact that it is a conceit; whether the work is fiction or journal, Cooper's disclaimer is equally applicable. Aware of how certain positions would appear to his readers, he took purposeful steps when presenting his views to avoid the kind of condemnation that befell authors like Dickens. By positioning himself as editor and setting the first text prior to the Revolution, Cooper distances himself from the controversy he intends to discuss, despite his statement in *Satanstoe*'s preface, "We conceive no apology is necessary for treating the subject of anti-rentism with the utmost frankness" (4).

His editorial stance should not be seen as diminishing his conviction, however. As with all questions of property rights, Cooper saw the Anti-Rent movement as profoundly dangerous to the nation. He writes, "the existence of true liberty among us, the perpetuity of the institutions, and the safety of public morals are all dependent on putting down, wholly, absolutely, and unqualifiedly, the false and dishonest theories and statements that have been boldly advanced in connection with this subject" (4). Just as Mathews employed a parallel between agrarianism and literary piracy to demonstrate the moral principles that underlie international copyright, Cooper saw in the Anti-Rent movement a current of ideas that would undermine the foundation of the country, a foundation that he asserted again and again was based upon the protection of individual property rights.

Despite the stakes set forth in the preface, *Satanstoe* is, as critics have pointed out, something of an idyll, a return to a time even more bucolic than that portrayed in *The Pioneers,* although there are early indications that trouble lies ahead. McWilliams has described it as "a world in which all is given and reliable" (312), and Robert Emmet Long has argued that the novel "looks back on an earlier, more innocent world with nostalgia and longing" (146). Corny Littlepage, although somewhat irritated by the efforts of more recent inhabitants to change the name of his beloved home, has little reason to doubt the security of his holdings. The property of Satanstoe itself is from the very beginning a secure family possession: "As my father, Major Evans Littlepage, was to inherit this estate from his father, Capt. Hugh Littlepage, it might even at the time of my birth be considered old family property, it having indeed been acquired by my grandfather, through his wife, about thirty years after the final cession of the colony to the English, by its original Dutch owners" (9). Corny's father enters into a deal with a family friend to expand the family holdings even further by purchasing land from the Indians, a purchase that we are told is made with strict honesty and fairness, even if, as the narrator admits, $250 worth of merchandise is a small price to pay for 40,000 acres (53)! The remainder of the novel details the adventures that befall the narrator as he sets out to survey the property, including getting involved in the battle of Ticonderoga, rescuing his fiancée from the frozen waters of the Hudson, and staving off an Indian siege at the home of his future father-in-law.

The only evidence of lasting trouble on the horizon is the character of Jason Newcome (who, unlike the Littlepages, is a "newcomer"), a Connecticut schoolteacher who arrives to take up duties in Satanstoe and subsequently finds several opportunities to amuse the narrator with his mistaken pronunciations and unpolished, prudish ways. While Newcome attempts to portray himself as an honest, plain man, the narrator expounds upon what he views as the central feature of Newcome's character:

For property, he had a profound deference, so far as that deference extended to its importance and influence; but it would have caused him not the slightest qualm, either in the way of conscience, or feeling, to find himself suddenly installed in the mansions of the patroons, for instance, and placed in possession of their estates, provided only he fancied he could maintain his position. The circumstance that he was dwelling under the roof that was erected by another man's ancestors, for instance, and that others were living who had a better moral right to it, would give him no sort of trouble, so long as any quirk of the law would sustain him in possession [. . .] I have mentioned this propensity of Jason's, at some little length, as I feel certain [. . .] it will be seen that this disposition to regard the whole human family, as so many tenants in common of the estate left by Adam, will lead in the end to something extraordinary. (287–8)

The foreshadowing allows Cooper to portray the Anti-Rent controversy as the inevitable result of a long-standing misapprehension of property rights and the laws that are meant to protect them. The criminal deeds of Newcome's descendents in the novels that follow do not represent specific misdeeds in the Anti-Rent disputes, but symptoms of a larger societal ailment.

The passage also shows Cooper's frustration with what he saw as the Anti-Renters' hypocrisy: they had no qualms with property laws and rents provided they served their own interests. Only when these laws meant that they had to pay the money they owed did they rise up in protest. In *Satanstoe,* Cooper shows us a world where benevolent landlords paid fairly for property (even if the price is ridiculously low) kept in the family for generations, where those same landlords pay large sums out of their own pockets to ensure the success of their tenants and settlements, and where the seeds of evil are sown quietly, in seemingly benign attempts to replace traditional names and customs and to pay established property owners less than their due. *The Littlepage Manuscripts* may be read alternately as a crescendo or a descent: the problems posed by those who fail to respect property rights are magnified as Cooper's rhetoric hardens; the sins committed by the Newcomes grow worse as society devolves into a mob riled and ruled by demagogues. The novels portray a fall from grace precipitated by piracy. Even as Cooper was apparently withdrawing from the public battle over literary piracy, he was writing a series of novels that ridiculed many of the arguments of copyright's opponents.

The second novel in the series, *The Chainbearer,* reveals that Corny Littlepage's son took his edict to heart and kept a journal of his own times. The novel is set in the 1780s, and Mordaunt Littlepage, who fought bravely in the Revolution, sets out to examine the family's patent that, after years of expense to the owners, has finally improved to the point where he decides to seek some return on the investment. He enlists the help of an old family friend, Andries Coejemans, "The Chainbearer." This man carries chains to survey patents and measure property, a profession, Cooper tells us, which requires "honesty," "a practical eye," and the skills of both a woodsman and a hunter (232). While Mordaunt is nominally the protagonist of the novel, Chainbearer, like Natty in *The Pioneers,* is the hero of the piece. The two characters share several qualities, most notably their rustic features, but Chainbearer is a firm defender of property rights. McWilliams has argued convincingly, "Chainbearer, a fictional descendant of the Leatherstocking, has fully endorsed the principles of Judge Temple" (319). His adventures with Mordaunt provide endless opportunities for both characters to speak on the principles of property and the rights of its owners, particularly when they run afoul of a shameless squatter, "Thousandacres," and his family. Jason Newcome reappears as well, scrambling to maintain his lease and secretly dealing with the squatters.

The novel is replete with declarations on the moral principles of ownership, many recalling previous arguments Cooper made regarding property. For example, Mordaunt explains the importance of property to a Native American companion, Trackless, in familiar terms:

> Now, all the knowledge and all the arts of life that the white man enjoys and turns to his profit, come from the rights of property. No man would build a wigwam to make rifles in, if he thought he could not keep it as long as he wished, sell it when he pleased, and leave it to his son when he went to the land of spirits. It is by encouraging man's love of himself in this manner that he is got to do so much. (283)

Only the prospect of continual possession motivates civilization's advance, Mordaunt argues, and the Native Americans lost their land because of the Americans' greater knowledge, all of which can be traced back to property. Rather than challenging such a claim, Trackless supports the Littlepages' ownership of their land, since they purchased it from his descendants. In this way, the Native American is recruited as a supporter of property rights and as living evidence of Cooper's argument: a Native American who respects property is more civilized than the squatter who does not. For the author, humankind advances because it is motivated by property and profit. As he wrote in his letter to *The Evening Post* in 1842,

> While nations are coarse, uncultivated and ignorant, copy-rights are of
> little value, and this is the reason why the appreciation of this species of
> property has not kept even pace with the appreciation of that which is
> more connected with the physical indulgencies. But literary property is
> now of value in all civilized communities, and, on every rule of expedi-
> ency, justice, and amity, it is as much entitled to be protected, as houses,
> lands, and merchandize. (*Letters* 4: 303)

Cooper's argument is a direct refutation of the claim made by international
copyright opponents who claimed that anything strengthening or expanding
of literary property rights would have the opposite effect, limiting the diffusion of knowledge among the citizenry.

Only the vibrant oppositional viewpoint provided by the squatter
Thousandacres prevents *The Chainbearer* from reading like a one-sided
assault on literary straw men. The squatter and his family are cutting down
trees on Mordaunt's land for lumber, and he proclaims, "My sweat and labor
be in them boards; and it's as good as sap, any day. What a man sweats for he
has a right to" (349). Although the narrator observes dryly that a thief could
work up a pretty good sweat, as well, his observations become increasingly
shrill and unpersuasive as Thousandacres makes his case. Grossman effectively re-states this argument: "The boards they have made from the timber
they have cut have their own sweat and labor, their flesh and blood, in them.
No chainbearer, carrying chains willingly as the servant of the rich to measure the earth, can rob them of what must be theirs because it is part of themselves" (210). Such arguments do, as Grossman points out, have a "grim
authority" (210). Even Cooper's editorial voice recognizes the squatter's
insight, although the recognition is clearly intended to mark the novel's
commentary on current events. Thousandacres notes the political power of
his view:

> I hold to liberty and a man's rights, and that is no reason I should be
> deflected on. My notions be other men's notions, I know, though they
> be called squatters' notions. Congressmen have held 'em, and will hold
> 'em ag'in, if they expect much support, in some parts of the country, at
> election time. I daresay the day will come when governors will be found
> to hold 'em. Governors be but men a'ter all, and must hold doctrines
> that satisfy men's wants, or they won't be governors long. (412–13)

Cooper's editorial reply notes, "Thousandacres speaks here like a veritable
prophet" (413). The comment is intended to direct the reader to the Anti-Rent

uprising in New York, of course, but it applies equally to the debates over literary property: changes to the copyright law were exceedingly long in coming.

Again and again, the failure of Congress to act can be ascribed to the perception that the public-at-large either opposed changing copyright law to make it more beneficial to authors or were largely apathetic. Such sentiment was particularly evident by 1845 when Congress had been repeatedly flooded with petitions against international copyright over the years each time the subject was broached. At the same time, Dickens had become an ineffective spokesperson for the cause, unlikely to gain sympathy when compared to the construct of the poor farmer forced to purchase his books. As one critic remarked following Dickens' visit,

> [H]ow did these intelligent farmers of the far west, obtain the pleasure and reap the advantage of perusing the productions of our gifted guest? By purchasing his Copyright works—every one a guinea? Not at all; charged at that price, our backwoodsmen and their families too, would have remained as ignorant of the beauties of Boz, as they are of English Copyright books, of great, if not of equal merit, though not reprinted in this country, and consequently beyond their reach. (Campbell 6)

The copyright debate was framed in such a way as to pose the elitist English authors against the humble "everyman" of the United States. Few congressmen were willing to see themselves cast as supporting the British.

Thousandacres could as easily be speaking for the poverty-stricken reading public of the time as for the anti-renters. When asked if he has ever attempted to defend his claim to a piece of property in the face of opposition, he answers,

> We all like to be on the right side, if we can; and some of our folks kind o' persuaded me I might make out, once, ag'in a reg'lar landlord. So I stood trial with him; but he beat me, Mr. Mordaunt, just the same as if I had been a chicken and he the hawk that had me in his talons. You'll never catch me trusting myself in the claws of the law ag'in, though that happened as long ago as afore the old French war. I shall never trust to law any more. It may do for them that's rich, and don't kear whether they win or lose; but law is a desp'rate bad business for them that hasn't got money to go into it right eend [sic] foremost. (351)

While those with more liberal sentiments might sympathize with Thousandacres' views of the legal system, this is clearly not Cooper's intention. He therefore employs Chainbearer as his primary voice in arguments with the squatter rather than the aristocratic Mordaunt, most notably in a mock-trial scene that critics have noted seems to be an echo of Natty's trial in *The Pioneers*. When Thousandacres proclaims, "My creed is, that a man has a right to hold all he wants, and to want all he holds," Chainbearer answers, "Got help t'e men, t'en, t'at haf to carry chain petween you and your neighpors, T'ousandacres; a man's wants to-tay may tiffer from his wants to-morrow, and to-morrow from t'e next tay, ant so on to t'e ent of time! On your toc-trine, not'in' would pe settlet, ant all woult pe at sixes and sevens" (388). Chainbearer wins the debate, if not the trial, and it is one of Cooper's most convincing portrayals of the property argument. Rather than employing an elite landlord versus a lowly squatter, he presents a more level pairing, two voices that, rather than look down upon each other, debate the question openly. The author's attack on anti-rentism is generally viewed as unsuccessful because the tone of his novels, particularly as it is manifest in his narrator in the final volume, makes both the speaker and the argument unattractive. In *The Chainbearer*, he avoids this mistake by creating two characters drawn from Natty Bumppo, his most attractive artistic achievement.

It is a sign of Cooper's pessimism, then, that the dispute between the two men ends in violence. Chainbearer is shot in the back by Thousandacres. The deed allows Chainbearer to seize the moral high ground decisively, a fact that Cooper makes clear by having Thousandacres shot as well, apparently by Trackless, avenging his friend. The squatter's family is subsequently scattered, fleeing the law, while the humble Chainbearer is revered. The novel ends with Mordaunt's final observation on the character of his friend: "That he was not superior to the failings of human nature, need not be said; but so long as he lived, he lived a proof of how much more respectable and estimable is the man who takes simplicity, and honesty, and principle, and truth for his guide, than he who endeavors to struggle through the world by the aid of falsehood, chicanery, and trick" (460). Whatever the strengths or failings of these two characters, their passing is mourned by the reader, as well, who is left to watch the novel move towards its inevitable marriages, punctuated by a few more speeches on the evils of squatting and the true benefits imparted by leases and landlords. Although the novel does not close with the same sense of nostalgic optimism that imbues *Satanstoe*, property is still secure and misdeeds pertaining to property are punished.

Cooper has received his share of criticism regarding his relative silence on the issue of copyrights in the 1840s, but one cannot read *The Littlepage Manuscripts*, particularly the latter two volumes, without being overwhelmed by the attention he pays to property rights. He narrowly avoided writing a novel-length diatribe in *The Chainbearer* by returning to the honest simplicity of Natty Bumppo, even if he completely transformed the values of his greatest character to do so. The final novel, *The Redskins; or Indian and Injin,* on the other hand, is little more than a sustained rant. The author always made it clear that his primary intention in writing the *Littlepage Manuscripts* was to expose the false principles underlying the Anti-Rent movement, and, in his final volume, he goes to great lengths to accomplish his goal. Most notably, he skips a generation of Littlepages to reach the 1840s. (Apparently, the intervening son was no great journal writer.) In setting forth his views once again in his preface to *The Redskins,* he returns to his attack on the rhetoric of the Anti-Renters:

> The discriminating reader will probably be able to trace in these narratives the progress of those innovations on the great laws of morals which are becoming so very manifest in connection with this interest, setting at naught the plainest principles that God has transmitted to man for the government of his conduct, and all under the extraordinary pretense of favoring liberty! [. . .] It would be idle to deny that the great principle which lies at the bottom of anti-rentism, if principle it can be called, is the assumption of a claim that the interests and wishes of numbers are to be respected, though done at a sacrifice of the clearest rights of the few. That this is not liberty, but tyranny in its worst form, every right-thinking and right-feeling man must be fully aware. (461)

In writing of the justice of international copyright nearly twenty years earlier, Cooper had foreseen the opposition and written, "Monopoly is always a safe cry in a popular Government—But <is> are not all Laws of Rights Monopolies?" (*Letters* 1: 172). In the Anti-Rent movement, Cooper sees the worst effects of such a view of individual rights in a democracy coming to fruition.

The novel sets out to expose this popular tyranny. The current Littlepage, Hugh, is traveling abroad with his uncle when he reads of the anti-rent troubles that endanger the various estates that their families have accumulated over the years (always legally, of course). After multiple pages of dialogue regarding the injustice of it all, they set out for America. Learning that it may be dangerous to return to their settlement openly, they disguise themselves as traveling salesmen from Germany and enter incognito. This gives them ample opportunity to hear the anti-rent argument first-hand and to refute it through innocent sounding questions whose real audiences are each other and the reader. Stretching plausibility to the breaking point, they find Trackless still alive, as well as a loyal slave who has lived with the Littlepage family for generations. These men are, we are told, at least 120 years old and exist primarily to offer living examples of proper regard for property and respect for the older patrician families of New York; Hugh refers to them as "monuments of the past" (527). In the novel's climax, the Littlepages are saved from anti-renters disguised in calico as "Injins" by the appearance of actual Native Americans who have stopped by on their return from Washington to convince the aged Trackless to join them.

This contrast is meant to demonstrate the truly reprehensible nature of the "Injins," who possess none of the honor of their Native American models. Near the conclusion, one of the criminal leaders, Seneca Newcome, whose family heritage has led him to become a fervent anti-renter, attempts to burn a farmhouse down, and order is restored and violence abated by the appearance of the sheriff who, single-handedly, is able to convince the unlawful anti-renters to disperse. McWilliams is surely correct when he suggests we distinguish "the artistic blunders of Cooper's tale from the principles it seeks to support" (325). Indeed, the plot often seems to serve only as a vehicle by which Cooper can give his characters space to make arguments in defense of property and the landed gentry.

Even his editorial voice fails to soften the criticisms offered by his narrator; instead, it seems as though Cooper cannot help but pile on: "Mr. Hugh Littlepage writes a little sharply, but there is truth in all he says, at the bottom. His tone is probably produced by the fact that there is so serious an attempt to deprive him of his old paternal estate, an attempt which is receiving support in high quarters" (521). Dekker argues that such disclaimers are entirely insufficient: "Hugh Littlepage is Cooper's *beau idéal*, Cooper's own advertisement for the advantages of the great landed wealth; so far as this novel is concerned, Cooper must stand or fall by the way his narrator behaves. Moreover, it is very hard to believe that Hugh Littlepage does not mirror Cooper's own feelings" (*James Fenimore Cooper* 234). Whether or not we share Dekker's notions of Cooper's authorial responsibility, it is impossible to deny that the tone of the novel is much more strident than in the previous works, and Cooper's editorial maneuvers fail to distance him from the sentiments of his narrator.

There is little new in *The Redskins;* he distills the arguments that he has been making far less obtrusively in the previous two novels and in works such as *Home as Found,* and he sets them before the reader with a vengeance. Gone is the persuasive tone of Chainbearer, and in his place is the sanctimoniousness of the landlord. "His propaganda," Grossman notes, "is of the sort that convinces only the rabid partisans on his own side" (213). After yet another conversation with an anti-renter while incognito, Hugh proclaims,

> It is time that the American began to see things as they are, and not as they are *said* to be, in the speeches of governors, Fourth-of-July orations, and electioneering addresses. I write warmly, I know, but I feel warmly; and I write like a man who sees that a most flagitious attempt to rob him is being tampered with by some in power, instead of being met, as the boasted morals and intelligence of the country would require, by the stern opposition of all in authority. Curses—deep, deep curses—ere long, will fall on all who shrink from their duty in such a crisis. (567)

While the narrators of the previous novels allude to the possible disasters that might befall the United States if the views of Newcomes became commonplace, none approach the kind of apocalyptic tenor of Hugh Littlepage. The tone shows Cooper's passionate feelings regarding the Anti-Rent movement and the principles that he felt fueled it, but that same passion hijacks the novel and renders it simply a diatribe.

Perhaps because of Cooper's polemical style in these works, critics have failed to see how these novels fit into larger debates over property. Those for and against international copyright appropriated the arguments of the Anti-Rent movement. The parallels between land and literary property, between individual rights and the needs of the public were employed throughout the 1840s in speeches, pamphlets, and editorials. Cooper was clearly aware of this debate, as he had been throughout his career, and he understood the arguments well. While his refusal to join the American Copyright Club in 1843 is often noted by critics, such attention fails to acknowledge Cooper's previous efforts on behalf of international copyright and his letter to *The Evening Post* supporting the cause even while denying any alliance with Dickens in the matter. Nothing has been said of how *The Littlepage Manuscripts* extend Cooper's defense of literary property.

In this trilogy, Cooper provides a thorough, if not always persuasive, defense of the principles that he suggested were at stake whenever literary property was considered. At the same time, he draws his readers into a mode of exchange that sustains the arguments he makes in the novels. The novels are his property, and those readers who purchase them engage in the kind of lawful behavior he calls for on the part of leaseholders. Those who read his novels are, in effect, "renters," gaining access to his fiction without taking permanent possession of it. Cooper not only depicts the evil results of disrespect for property rights, but he also attempts to enact an ideal process of ownership and exchange by creating literary property whose unique quality is its ability to be owned and exchanged simultaneously. Those who would seek to pirate his work or purchase pirated copies become, in effect, the "anti-renters" he so harshly criticized in his novels. The trilogy, therefore, is both representative and performative, much more than the "polemics of a local struggle" (336), as McWilliams labels *The Redskins*. There is no denying that the primary concern of Cooper's trilogy was the Anti-Rent movement; however, by understanding how the discourse of literary property rights was informed and shaped by the dispute in New York, we can see that Cooper did not turn away from the movement for international copyright or change his views regarding the importance of authorial rights during the 1840s. By writing the history of the Littlepages' struggle to maintain their property in the face of public pressure and populist appeal, Cooper created what can be seen as his most sustained defense of the rights of authors.

COOPER'S LITERARY ESTATE

The Littlepage Manuscripts received very little attention in the press at the time of publication.[16] The books themselves make a somewhat melancholy spectacle: published as paperbacks, Cooper's name is misspelled "J. Fennimore Cooper" on the front cover of *Satanstoe,*[17] while the back cover has a prominent advertisement for "MRS. ELLIS'S HOUSEKEEPING MADE EASY." The misspelling of Cooper's name was repeated on the cover of *The Chainbearer,* and the back cover trumpets in bold face, "CHEAP BOOKS." In negotiating for the publication of these books in Great Britain, Cooper had been informed in fairly plain terms of how far his status had diminished. His British publisher at the time, Richard Bentley, wrote,

> With regard to your own Works on reviewing the sale of your later productions, I find I must confine myself in future to an impression of 750 copies. And this limit is the more necessary when the subject is not at once completed—continuations never being so saleable as single works. This number of copies will not enable me to offer you (with every desire to give you the full market value for your Works) more than £250 for your next work in 3 volumes. Should I hereafter be encouraged to print more, I shall be most happy to increase the price. (*Letters* 5: 8)

Cooper felt quite betrayed by this, and although he agreed to the proposed arrangement with Bentley, he began looking for another publisher.

At the same time, he was still writing more books and turning some of his older titles to account. Never an author to jealously retain his own copyrights, Cooper was continually negotiating to sell rights to his work. He wrote to his wife, Susan Cooper, in 1845, "I have discovered that the old books are worth something, and have actually sold the right to print 250 copies of each for $200. These books are likely to produce me two or three hundred a year, in future. I have been offered to day $1200 *in cash* for the right to print these books, Afloat and Ashore included, for the next ten years. I have offered to accept at *five* years" (12–13). Cooper was not at all sanguine about his prospects or his accomplishments as an author. In reply to a request for advice in 1846, he wrote,

> I am very sorry to say that my pecuniary benefits, in this country, amount to nothing worth naming. I own so much literary property, and so many plates, that in the whole they amount to something, though far less than you would suppose. The cheap literature has destroyed the value of nearly all literary property, and after five and twenty years of hard work, I find myself comparatively a poor man. [. . .] My last bargain with B & S. [Burgess & Stringer] was a complicated one, including the use of plates of no less than three old books, besides the new one.
>
> [. . .] I make no doubt you can do much better, as the press is a solid phalanx against me, and I am unpopular with the country, generally— Indeed, were it not for the convenience of correcting proof sheets, I would not publish in this country at all. I have a work in contemplation, that will be secured here, to cut off the profits of pirates, but which I do not mean to publish in America, at all, any farther than may be necessary to secure the copy right. If they will not pay, they ought not to read. (131)

Cooper was always mindful of his audiences abroad, but his first concern had always been his American readers, as he had proclaimed vehemently in *A Letter to His Countrymen* and as so many critics since have emphasized. His letter demonstrates how much his views changed towards the end of his career. He presents himself as something of a victim of "cheap literature," a sufferer from the lack of international copyright. This explains his determination to "cut off the profits of pirates" and suggests that despite his despondency, he was still willing to resist the negative impulses he saw as resulting from the excesses of the publishing trade.

Perhaps the most disturbing element of this letter, however, is the image it presents of Cooper hoarding a crumbling literary estate. We have already described how he had been at once creating property even as he wrote about, becoming a significant "title-holder." Earlier proponents of copyright had argued that an author was like the property owner who allowed others to stroll through his or her garden, provided they did no damage and did not take what did not belong to them. Cooper himself had both depicted and enacted this exchange in *Home as Found,* portraying the Effinghams as property owners who were willing to provide access to their land in exchange for just consideration. Here the author seems determined to lock the gates, or at the very least charge a heavy toll. His words almost confirm the worst fears of copyright opponents—that copyright would cut off avenues of learning from those who could not afford to buy books: "If they will not pay, they ought not to read." Cooper portrays American readers as "anti-renters," seeking to exploit his literary property unfairly. If his earlier allusion to his works as "mere articles of trade" marks Cooper's professionalism, then his words here seem to present the dark side of that profession. He may not have given up on authorship, but he certainly seems to have given up on his American readers.

Of course, this letter might simply represent a moment of profound pessimism. In fact, following the publication of *The Redskins,* he went on to publish five more novels; however, his lack of faith in his literary holdings might have done him considerable damage. After successfully publishing a handsome collection of the works of Washington Irving, George Palmer Putnam approached Cooper in 1849 about doing the same with Cooper's works. Unfortunately, the large number of Cooper's works which were already available in cheap editions, and the complexities of Cooper's copyrights, with different editions owned by different publishers, made such a collection nearly impossible. As Beard has noted,

> In his modesty and his eagerness to bargain for a few hundred or a few thousand dollars, Cooper colossally underestimated the value of his literary property and permitted Stringer and Townsend to gain control. Had he been willing and able to entrust this extensive property to Putnam, who sought to pay Cooper at the rate he paid Irving, the novelist could have left his family a far more substantial competence. (*Letters* 6: 6)

In his apparent belief that American readers did not value his works, Cooper undervalued them, as well. He ended up selling his copyrights of his older works to Stringer and Townsend for $3,500, noting, "This sale is of the last importance to us all, and quite equals my expectations. It is a good bargain for both parties" (192). It is difficult not to believe that, in the end, it was a much better bargain for the publishers. Cooper also signed over his copyrights to *The American Democrat* and the revised *The History of the Navy* to Caroline, his second daughter: "To have and to hold the said copyright, with all the benefit, profit, and advantage thereof to the said Caroline M. Phinney, her executors, administrators and assigns, in as ample and beneficial a manner to all intents and purposes as I the said J. Fenimore Cooper might have had or held the same if this present assignment had not been made" (Contract). In writing of this transaction to his wife, he wrote, "I am glad Cally is picking up a few crumbs from my table" (*Letters* 6: 226).

While Cooper was thinking less and less of his own works, he was dedicated to the establishment of a literary estate for his daughter Susan. He dealt with publishers on her behalf,[18] and even took out her copyrights in his own name (*Letters* 6: 196). His interest in her success seems to have reawakened his interest in the question of copyright. He arranged for the publication of her book, *Rural Hours*, with his old British publisher Bentley in 1850. When Cooper wrote him regarding its publication and prospects for success, the publisher lamented, "Almost every American book is now pirated by the infamous dealers in stolen goods here; and there literally appears to be no chance for an American book. Surely, surely it must be worth while to preserve this market for American literature, which could be done immediately by y[ou]r Congress granting a similar right to us Britishers" (178). This did no more than confirm what Cooper had already known, having written his daughter several months before to tell her, "The unfortunate state of the copy right law may prevent your receiving much remuneration, though it must produce something" (*Correspondence* 2: 672). In responding to Bentley's plea, Cooper wrote, "There is not the slightest probability of Congress' giving your authors any rights here. The mistaken step of attempting to coerce would of itself prevent any thing of the sort. An author, in America, is a creature very little thought of or cared for" (*Letters* 6: 156).

Shortly after writing this letter, Cooper received the following from Putnam, who was an extremely active proponent of international copyright throughout his lifetime: "I beg to enclose a memorial for international copyright, which I trust you will honor with your signature. If a proper effort is made it is probable this measure may be carried. Your name would have great weight and presume you will have no objection to it" (Letter to James Fenimore Cooper). Despite Cooper's apparent pessimism and his low regard for his own influence, not to mention his reluctance to engage the issue publicly a few years before, he signed the memorial Putnam sent him, and Charles Sumner presented it to Congress in 1852 (US Copyright Office 170). Cooper's name is the first signature on the memorial, which includes the signatures of

Bryant and Melville, as well, and which asks Congress to "enact a Law for the benefit of American literature which shall give to British Authors and Publishers the same right to the control of their literary property in the United States that the Law of England offers reciprocally to the authors and publishers of this Country" (qtd. in Cameron 112). It is tempting to believe that Cooper's new commitment to the cause of international copyright was inspired by his concern for his daughter's success; indeed, Bentley made it sound as if literary piracy were the only thing stopping her success in England: "In consequence of the nefarious proceedings of pirates all American works have proved latterly lamentable failures; and I regret to say that 'Rural Hours' has not paid its expenses" (*Letters* 6: 274).

He found his daughter's failure hard to believe, but he nevertheless responded to the publisher almost exactly a month before his death:

> I can not be misled by parental affection for my opinion is made up from as honest and natural an expression concerning this book, as I have ever known touching any work whatever. Here I leave you, for to say the truth, I am not in a condition to carry on any controversy whatever, just now.
>
> After saying this, you may be surprised at my adding that I should like to address a letter to you for publication on the subject of the copy-right law,—and if you answer me encouragingly I will do so at once and possibly it may be found of use in settling this important question. (282)

Cooper apparently never wrote the promised letter. If he had, one can imagine what it might have said. Although he may have been moved to action late in life by fatherly concern, it is just as likely that his life-long interest in the question of copyright was stirred once more. Throughout his career, in his novels and in his correspondence, he defended the rights of literary property as essential components of American democracy. For him, the question of copyright touched on the rights of the individual versus the majority, the ability of the United States to develop its own literature, the undue influence of foreign opinion, and basic principles of fairness and honesty. If he was occasionally reluctant to offer his support publicly, or if he underplayed his own interest in international copyright, then it was because he understood how the debate over literary property might put him at odds with his readership and how his critics would use his support against him. He understood this almost from the beginning of his literary career, long before he was fully familiar with the technicalities of copyright law and long before the debate over authors' rights became public.

Critics have viewed Cooper as an author who was willing to express his views boldly, sometimes even recklessly, without regard for the opposition of newspaper editors or readers. This is an over-simplification. While there is no denying the courage of his convictions, Cooper was involved in far more subtle negotiations with his public and his publishers than our traditional views of him allow. His texts represent a ceaseless effort to justify the principles of literary property rights, even while they sometimes also indicate the difficulty American authors faced in portraying copyright as a matter of public interest. In texts like *Home as Found* and *The Littlepage Manuscripts,* we see how the discourse of literary property rights is evident in Cooper's fiction and how these works offer defenses of authors' rights even as they appear to be uniquely focused on landowners' rights. He continually sought to demonstrate that property rights did not constitute the tyranny of the one over the many; rather, for him, those very rights were what allowed the majority to prosper, by inspiring individuals to excel and by preventing majority rule from becoming oppression. In working to make this case, Cooper was one of the first American authors to argue that literary property rights were not simply a matter of economic justice for the individual, not simply connected to "mere articles of trade," but fundamental to a sound democracy, as well.

Chapter Two

Harriet Beecher Stowe and Sentimental Possession

PROPRIETY AND PROPERTY

Before the publication of *Uncle Tom's Cabin* in 1852, many arguments in favor of copyright centered either on English authors or on the necessity of expanding copyright protection in consideration of the "widows and orphans" of deceased writers. More abstract notions of moral principle were often divorced from particular American authors, and proponents addressed literary property through metaphorical comparisons with other forms of property. This was in part because of the prominent role British authors played in sending their petition to Henry Clay in 1837, prompting the introduction of the first international copyright legislation in Congress. Supporters and critics of increased copyright protection had long presented the issue of literary piracy as one of fairness to foreign authors: Cooper's letter to Carey and Lea on behalf of Scott is a good example. This formulation had, however, done significant damage to the cause of international copyright in the US, as indicated by the largely negative response to Dickens' pleas on behalf of his literary property rights in the 1840s. It was difficult to make American readers and publishers, and, consequently, legislators, take much of an interest in the well-being of foreign authors who seemed to be doing just fine in their own countries.

In 1845, George Palmer Putnam attempted to set the record straight in his work *American Facts,* suggesting that American authors were as likely to suffer from the lack of an international copyright as their foreign counterparts: "The transplanting of American magazine articles into English periodicals, frequently in so disguised a shape that the exotic loses its identity, has become an ordinary occurrence. Some works of fiction, in their new names and English dress, would scarcely be recognized by their own fathers" (85). Although various supporters of international copyright attempted to make the argument that changes in the law would benefit American literature, they were hard pressed to make a convincing case that they were affected by the law as it stood. Indeed, Cooper was unwilling even to confess an interest in overseas profits publicly, let alone make an uproar about losses he may have suffered.

While copyright was an issue that had long engaged the attention of American writers, for most of the early part of the century these authors were on the periphery of the debate as it had been structured, more often acting as British surrogates than as agents with their own interests. This was in part a function of how copyright law addressed the act of publication. As McGill points out, "On going-into-print, an author surrendered his perpetual right to his manuscript for a limited right in a printed text" with the result that "linking property rights in texts to a distinction between handwriting and print did much to place copyrights in the hands of publishers" ("Duplicity" 41). Few would dispute that an author owned his or her handwritten manuscript. What was less clear was the extent to which an author who consented to allow the work to be multiplied could still claim exclusive control and ownership, hence the employment of metaphors such as the private garden opened to the public. Copyright supporters argued that just as Mr. Niblo could offer admission to his New York gardens for a fee without surrendering possession, so too could an author sell "access" to his or her work in the form of copies without relinquishing ownership.

Because this question became central upon "going-into-print," as McGill points out, publishers were at the nexus of the copyright debate. Authors like Cornelius Mathews were active on behalf of copyright for many years, but publishers were just as likely to take the lead in both sides of the debate, as Henry Carey, the Putnams, and the Harpers demonstrate. James Barnes observes that publishers increased their involvement in the 1840s, when the effects of the depression of 1837–43 at last began to wane and the manic reprint competition for a time began to recede with the arrival of more stable economic times (79).[1] Because authors were only occasionally successful overseas, publishers seemed to be among those with the most to lose or to gain in terms of copyright law, particularly in terms of international copyright. As one speaker put it, remarking on Stowe's success in 1852, "I have heard eminent *litterateurs* say, 'Pshaw! the Americans have no national literature.' It was thought that they lived entirely on plunder—the plunder of poor slaves, and of poor British authors" (qtd. in Hedrick 234).[2] Until the 1850s, even the most popular of American writers seemed to have less at stake in the problem of reprinting than the publishers.

All of that changed with the unprecedented sale of *Uncle Tom's Cabin*. Here was a novel that was popular the world over, that sold not hundreds or thousands of copies but hundreds of thousands of copies. While earlier authors like Cooper had suffered from unauthorized printings overseas, no author prior to Stowe made so much money for so many others. As Barnes notes, "Occasionally the reprinters would strike it rich as they did in 1852 with *Uncle Tom's Cabin* [. . .]. Within just a few years one million copies had been sold, dwarfing the sales of any contemporary work on either side of the Atlantic" (154). American authors' losses in Great Britain rose to greater prominence, and G. P. Putnam's earlier arguments regarding British pirates were suddenly easier to accept. As one writer for the *London Illustrated News* wrote, "the whole race of English booksellers, with few exceptions worth mentioning, are greater literary pirates than the Americans.

[. . .] The book trade goes on swimmingly; and the English public have cheap 'Uncle Toms'" (qtd. in Barnes 154). American authors were finally prominent in discussions of copyright, and Harriet Beecher Stowe's success put her firmly in the center of the debate over literary property rights.

In figuring texts as products of labor, writers and legislators on both sides largely employed either images derived from laborers and craftsmen— farmers and carpenters are common examples—or wealthy estate holders like Mr. Niblo. Within such metaphorical extensions, women were effaced, appearing only as the dependents of male authors, forced to live with men who were frequently described as indifferent at best in seeing to their finances, legally unable to leave their only assets, their texts, to their families upon their deaths. Stowe's success reversed such characterizations, clearly putting her into the position not only of breadwinner, but also of protector of property. As the most successful American author to emerge so far, she had significant interest in controlling the rights to her works.

Stowe faced many of the same problems that confronted Cooper: to practice her profession, she had to face critics who questioned her right to make a living through writing. She also had to negotiate the intricacies of copyright law, which had only become more complex since Cooper's early years of success. It was no longer enough simply to publish a book first in Great Britain to secure its copyright there; by 1854, an author had to be physically present in English territory when the book appeared (Winship 102). Stowe often traveled to Great Britain and to Canada throughout her career in an effort to ensure her rights abroad. And while she was forced to negotiate the same tensions with her readers and publishers that confronted other authors, she faced additional challenges. One was the relationship between her professional practice and her critiques of slavery and the market system. She was, on the one hand, attacking formerly accepted property rights in the name of democracy and equality, while on the other she was attempting to protect her own literary rights, rights that had also been attacked as undemocratic. She faced a difficult personal negotiation, as well. As a married woman writing in the 1850s, she did not have the power to sign contracts or to own her own property; therefore, whenever she chose to enforce her rights, she required her husband Calvin's consent and assistance.[3] As her correspondence indicates, this was not always readily granted.

Beginning with the success of *Uncle Tom's Cabin*, these negotiations are reflected in her work, particularly in *Dred*, the novel that followed *Uncle Tom's Cabin*, as well as her later novels *The Minister's Wooing* and *Oldtown Folks*. Stowe's status as a female author, and a phenomenally successful one, put her in a problematic relationship to the issues of democracy and copyright law: her rights were already significantly compromised, and the profits from her first novel made her susceptible to the same charges of greed and hypocrisy leveled against Dickens, another author whose fortune had been made from his portrayals of the suffering of the lower classes.

Stowe negotiated these tensions in a number of ways: privately, she negotiated with Calvin Stowe regarding what books she could write and when. Because she needed him to accompany her to England to sign copyright agreements, she required his consent. When it was not forthcoming, she sought other ways to write her books and protect her copyrights. Professionally, following what she interpreted as Calvin's failures in the bargaining for *Uncle Tom's Cabin*, she negotiated with her publishers herself, carefully attending to the dates of publication of her works to ensure their protection. Publicly, she depicted herself not as a laborer *per se*, but as a vehicle of inspiration and, foremost, as a wife and mother. She presented herself as coming to authorship almost accidentally, only expecting to make the occasional few dollars. Most importantly, she used her novels to depict a sentimental system of property ownership, what Lori Merish has dubbed "sentimental materialism," that would justify her own careful protection of her literary property and at the same time discourage her readers from purchasing cheap pirated copies of her books. As Merish points out, Stowe's sentimental portrayals render authorship itself, the creation of property, one more domestic activity. Some of her negotiations were more successful than others, yet all reveal the impact that the discourse of literary property rights had on her work.

In Melissa Homestead's examination of copyright and *Uncle Tom's Cabin*, she notes that by the time Stowe published her novel, she was already an experienced writer (121). She had published a short geography in Cincinnati in 1833 and a book of short stories entitled *The Mayflower* in 1842 (Stowe, *Life:* 65, 103). Homestead suggests it may have been this experience that prompted her to take out a copyright on *Uncle Tom's Cabin* even before it ran as a serial in *The National Era* (121). Despite her experience, and despite what appears to be an extra measure of precaution, Stowe was clearly caught off guard by the immense success of her novel. Calvin Stowe had made the arrangements for its publication with J. P. Jewett, and, as Joan Hedrick notes, "Calvin [. . .] had less practical sense than Harriet, and he had let Jewett talk him out of his original proposal—20 percent of the sales—by arguing that they would *make more* by taking 10 percent and allowing Jewett to invest the difference in advertising" (223–24). Harriet clearly came to doubt the wisdom of this bargain, for she later wrote to Jewett asking, "Were you correct in persuading me & Mr Stowe that a ten percent contract on books that sell as mine have is better for us than a twenty percent one?" (qtd. in Hedrick 224). Her statement demonstrates her second thoughts and suggests that she had a greater role in the negotiations than one might guess, questioning Jewett's wisdom in persuading her and her husband to accept the bargain.

It is difficult to determine how much influence Harriet truly had during the negotiations; matters are only made more unclear by a manuscript Calvin wrote entitled "Statement of Facts, by C. E. Stowe, in regard to the publication of Mrs. Stowe's work entitled 'Uncle Tom's Cabin.'" There is no indication of what prompted Calvin to write this document, although it is possible that it was intended to answer Harriet's concerns. She herself wrote of her participation in the contract, "I did not know until a week afterward precisely what terms Mr. Stowe had made, and I did not care. I had the most perfect indifference to the bargain" (qtd. in Stowe, *Life* 159). It is also possible that Calvin's statement was written at the request of Jewett, who was perhaps eager to give Harriet assurances that he had not cheated her. Throughout the text, Calvin emphasizes his active role in drafting the contract, noting at the last,

> There was no collusion what ever, and no improper means of any kind used, in making the bargain; but every thing [inserted "as far as I know,"] was conducted in a manner perfectly open and fair, and if I made a poor bargain for myself, it was wholly my own fault. I did the best I knew how for myself, and Mr. Jewett did the best he knew how for himself; but I have no reason to think there was any unfairness on either side. (Stowe, "Statement of Facts")

Calvin's reference to making a bargain "for himself" highlights both his involvement and his view of his role in the contract negotiations. Despite his apparently total control of the Stowe side of the deal and Harriet's own claims of indifference, it is difficult to believe that Harriet was left totally in the dark. When publishing *The Mayflower* ten years earlier, Stowe had written to her husband,

> I shall get something from the Harpers some time this winter or spring. Robertson, the publisher here, says the book ('The Mayflower') will sell, and though the terms they offer me are very low, that I shall make something on it. For a second volume I shall be able to make better terms. On the whole, my dear, if I choose to be a literary lady, I have, I think, as good a chance of making profit by it as any one I know of. (Stowe, *Life* 103–4)

This does not suggest an author who would be uninterested in negotiating the terms for publication of her book, particularly since it was already clear during the serialized publication that *Uncle Tom's Cabin* would be an immense success.

A more likely explanation for Stowe's reluctance to acknowledge any role she may have had in the contract for her novel is her concern for the public perception that she was interested in the profits to be made from the book. Hedrick suggests that, despite her misgivings regarding the contract, Stowe did not take the issue to court because "[s]he may have had glimmerings of the figure she would cut in the press, and her public image was worth more to her than she stood to gain from Jewett" (224). She was conscious of her image even in the first few months following the success of *Uncle Tom's Cabin*, as an oft-quoted letter she wrote to a London correspondent demonstrates. She represents herself as a "little bit of a woman," compelled to write by the encouragement of friends and by financial necessity. Of her payments for her hit novel, she writes, "Having been poor all my life and expecting to be poor the rest of it, the idea of making money by a book which I wrote just because I could not help it, never occurred to me" (Stowe, *Life* 202). Her statement contradicts her admission only a page earlier that she had originally taken up writing to earn extra money, but the more pressing note she strikes here is of accidental success: she only wrote the book because she "could not help it," not because she anticipated making a profit.

Here, her claims are not so different from Cooper's thirty years earlier when he denied any pecuniary motivations in writing his first novel. Stowe faced a different challenge, however. Having cast herself in the role as spokesperson for "the lowly," she was vulnerable to charges of hypocrisy and self-interest for the rest of her career. Homestead argues that her relative powerlessness as a married female writer in some senses shielded her from this criticism: not only was she unable to sign her own copyright agreements, but the susceptibility of her work to piracy was used by proponents of stronger copyright laws to cast her in the position of a victim, a woman unfairly wronged and swindled:

> Even though the law placed clear limits on the power of the author, those limits did not prevent Stowe and her similarly self-effacing female peers from succeeding commercially on an unprecedented scale. Indeed, those limits may, paradoxically, have enabled the commercial success of Stowe and her female peers by allowing them to appear both to be powerless and self-effacing *and* to exploit fully the circumscribed possibilities of the market. (165)

Yet Stowe's self-effacement did little to shield her from public criticism as she attempted to increase her profits, and it is difficult to see how her lack of legal agency provided much of an advantage when it came to protecting her literary property and forwarding her career; indeed, her inability to sign agreements on her own behalf frequently limited her opportunities during the 1850s.

IN THE COURTS OF LAW AND PUBLIC OPINION

Stowe's ambition and her interest in protecting her literary property are evident even in the letter that is often cited by scholars as revealing Stowe's construction of her humble authorial persona. She writes, "Mr. Bosworth in England, the firm of Clarke & Co., and Mr. Bentley, have all offered me an interest in the sales of their editions in London. I am very glad of it, both on account of the value of what they offer, and the value of the example they set in this matter, wherein I think that justice has been too little regarded" (Stowe, *Life* 202).[4] Stowe's awareness of the state of the publication of American works in England indicates her interest in "this matter" even as she presents herself as a relative neophyte, "agreeabl[y] surprised" at the profit she is making. Her professional self-interest emerges even as she disclaims it, and her reference to "justice" towards American authors echoes those same sentiments expressed by other supporters of international copyright law.

Despite her attempts to manage her public image, it is not surprising that her efforts to protect her literary property inevitably made her an object of public scrutiny, even when such efforts required the active participation of her husband. Such was the case when Philadelphia publisher F.W. Thomas published an unauthorized German translation of *Uncle Tom's Cabin* in

1853, and Stowe filed suit in federal court. Homestead, who has studied the case extensively, has found that the case was in fact brought by Calvin Stowe, with Harriet as a co-plaintiff; this was because, as Homestead writes,

> Under the common law principle of coverture, as a married woman Stowe had no independent legal identity. When a man and woman married, the woman was 'covered' by the man: their union resulted in the creation of a single legal subject, and that subject was the husband. Stowe's only access to the forum of the court was through her husband, and although she claimed copyright in her own name, the property she acquired immediately became her husband's. Her *husband* signed the publication contract with John P. Jewett, and her *husband's consent* to be co-plaintiff was a necessary prerequisite for asserting her claim against Thomas. (125)

Stowe's legal status has serious implications not only for her attempts to control her property, but also for her portrayals of property relations within her novels. Rather than serving as a shield from criticism, it more often forced her to adjust her plans to conform to Calvin's wishes. This can be seen in a letter Calvin wrote to her while she was on her first trip to Great Britain in 1853. Indeed, many of his letters touch on Stowe's business affairs. He writes, "If you wish the 1000 pounds at Alexander's transferred to your order please tell me so; but I thought in consequence of your *autographs* it might be best to let it be with me; and Alexander understands that he is to pay nothing to my order without a private letter from me informing him that I have given such an order, & minutely describing it" (Stowe, Letter, 17 June 1853). Calvin uses Harriet's fame as a way to justify his participation in managing the family finances, even as he played a steadily smaller role in bringing money into the household.

Stowe was continually pressured to balance her own desires and wishes against those of her husband. The evidence of these negotiations can make for painful reading; Calvin wrote the following to Harriet as she traveled abroad:

> You ask why I *"reproach"* you, & say you never *"reproach"* me. It is very true that you never do—that you are always most forbearing & magnanimous. And it is never *in my heart* to *"reproach"* you. [. . .] You must take into consideration your celebrity and my obscurity, & the fact that I have ambition as well as other people; and that if my love for you were not very deep & sincere & wholehearted, our relative positions acting

on my sensitive, irritable & hypochondriach nature, might be productive of still more offensive & painful results. (Stowe, Letter, 2 March
1857)

While Calvin had encouraged Harriet to pursue authorship from the very
beginning of her career, her newfound success was a source of tension
between them, and it appears she always had to keep in mind not only his
legal sway in her dealings, but also his emotional reactions to her career. In
both public and private life, her authorial autonomy was constrained by her
marriage, and Calvin's management did little to dim the public spotlight on
her actions. Her position as co-plaintiff in the Thomas case did not protect
her from the scrutiny of the press; as author, she was the public figure,
regardless of the fact that she did not have even the limited powers of ownership that were granted single women and men in her profession.

As the case went to trial, Harriet Beecher Stowe was publicly offered up
as an example of all that was wrong with copyright and authorship. In 1853,
Henry Carey, a publisher and staunch opponent of international copyright
specifically and any extension of authorial power generally, attacked Stowe in
his *Letters on International Copyright.* He wrote,

> The whole tendency of the existing system is to give the largest reward
> to those whose labors are lightest, and the smallest to those whose labors
> are most severe; and every extension of it must necessarily look in that
> direction. The 'Mysteries of Paris' were a fortune to Eugene Sue, and
> 'Uncle Tom's Cabin' has been one to Mrs. Stowe. [. . .] and yet a single
> year should have more than sufficed for the production of any one of
> them. (36)

Such criticism recalls the view that authorship should not be a money-making profession as much as a genteel pastime. This idea persisted during the
antebellum period, particularly when it might benefit publishers seeking to
cut costs. As one editor for *Brother Jonathan* put it in 1842, "The man who
would be literary must earn his living first—pursue an honest occupation . . .
His necessities thus provided for, literature may be to him the most delight-
ful and ennobling amusement. . . . We want no . . . purely literary men. . . .
There is no room in a republic for any such diploma pedants." (qtd. in Fink
65). No author who truly valued the republic would think of making a living
from his or her writing.

Carey's complaint builds on this notion in two ways: first, he argues
that the amount of reward far exceeds the amount of labor, and second,

authors who compose fictions are apt to be more greatly benefited than those scholars who amass knowledge for its own sake, who do the painstaking research that is so often pilfered by popular authors. He feels that extension of copyright law only furthers this inequity:

> In confirmation of this view, I here ask you to review the names of the persons who urge most anxiously the change of system that is now proposed, and see if you can find in it the name of a single man who has done any thing to extend the domain of knowledge. I think you will not. Next look and see if you do not find in it the names of those who furnish the world with new forms of old ideas, and are largely paid for so doing. The most active advocate of international copyright is Mr. Dickens, who is said to realize $70,000 per annum from the sale of works whose composition is little more than amusement for his leisure hours. In this country, the only attempt that has yet been made to restrict the right of translation is in a suit now before the courts, for compensation for the privilege of converting into German a work that has yielded the largest compensation that the world has yet known for the same quantity of literary labor. (37)

As we saw with Cooper in the 1840s, the comparison with Dickens, who failed utterly in swaying public sympathy towards international copyright and the plight of authors, served as a particularly harsh condemnation of any author's principles. Carey continues his attack on the true merit of literary work, referring to Dickens' authorial labor as "little more than amusement for his leisure hours." By linking Stowe's labor to Dickens' and his compensation to hers, Carey portrays her attempts to halt Thomas' publication of his unauthorized translation as one more example of authors trying to get more profit than they deserve. Carey is correct in asserting that her case was unprecedented; while those in support of copyright protection might view Stowe's efforts as a ground-breaking step in defense of literary property, Carey points out that this was the "only attempt that has yet been made to restrict the right of translation," a step of unmitigated gall, casting Thomas as the one whose rights Stowe is attempting to restrict.

As with Dickens in the 1840s, critics of Stowe and her immense success were quick to note the apparent contradiction between the values she seemed to advocate in her work and her own commercial pursuits. Perhaps the most biting of these critics was George R. Graham, who published two stinging critiques of Stowe's novel in February and March of 1853 in *Graham's Magazine*.[5] The first, entitled "Black Letters; or Uncle Tom-Foolery in

Literature," is a more general indictment of abolitionist literature, with Stowe receiving a good deal of attention. Graham notes what he saw as at least metaphorical hypocrisy underlying the circulation of abolitionist novels in the marketplace: "those who 'would not have a slave to till their ground,' use him pretty severely in the press-room" (209). Although he devotes a great deal of space to criticizing the grievous stylistic faults of the novel and one other like it (*The Cabin and the Parlor*), he returns to his central concern once more at the conclusion of his article. He writes,

> We have taken up the "Cabin literature" for the purpose of saying frankly what we think of the whole business—for it is a *business,* and nothing more. We have spoken temperately and critically of the books, indignantly and perhaps warmly of the spirit which pervades them, and we say by way of emphasis, that we despise the whole concern—the spirit which dictated them is false. They are altogether speculations in patriotism—a question of dollars and cents, not of slavery or liberty. [. . .] Many of the persons who are urging on this negro crusade into the domain of letters, have palms with an infernal itch for gold. [. . .] He would be an explorer worthy of all honor who could stumble upon a truth which they [sic] would not sacrifice for shillings. (215)

The passage begins with a criticism of the novelists' complicity with market culture: they are part of a business, and, if the first metaphor is to be believed, it is a business which prospers off of slavery as much as Southern slaveholders do. This undermines the books' messages, rendering them acts of financial speculation rather than statements on behalf of freedom. Furthermore, Graham uses this representation of Stowe's motives to question implicitly her claims of divine inspiration, stating, "the spirit which dictated them is false." Finally, in a construction similar to Carey's, Graham remarks upon authors' greedy exploitation and use of knowledge (in this case, "a truth,") that should benefit and belong to all of humanity. The word "shillings" would seem to be a subtle dig at English authors and perhaps readers, a criticism which would not be surprising given Graham's claims that *Uncle Tom's Cabin* owed a great deal of its popularity to British critics who lavished praise on the novel simply to trumpet England's abolition of slavery and to claim moral superiority over the United States (210).

In a final attack on the hypocrisy that Graham sees in these novels and their authors, he suggests that their success comes at the expense of African-Americans living in the North:

> [L]et us see the amiable publishers and writers and most valorous
> moralists, who are hurling stones at their brothers of the South, do a lit-
> tle something from the great wealth thus achieved, for the *free negroes of*
> *the North*. Many of these bold reformers control influential presses, but
> we do not see Sambo educated by them to set their type, carry their
> papers, drive their presses, or keep their books. (215)

While he does not remark upon any issues of copyright directly, statements
such as these resonate with arguments already discussed: while authors prosper, others are left in ignorance and poverty. While democratic principles
may appear to be championed, they are in fact merely manipulated by those
wishing to increase their profits.

It is not surprising that in republishing his *Letters on International*
Copyright in 1868, Carey would still single out Stowe's *Uncle Tom's Cabin* for
particular attack and lodge criticisms that put one in mind of Graham's critique. For example, Carey returns to the argument he made fourteen years
before—that Stowe's labor is not worth the large reward she received: "The
late Governor Andrew's services were surely worth as much, per hour, as
those of the authoress of 'Uncle Tom's Cabin,' yet did he give five years of his
life, and perhaps his life itself, for far less than half of what she had received
for the labors of a single one" (6). In addition to attacking the magnitude of
Stowe's profits, Carey also questions the value of her novel as a work of abolition. John Andrew was governor of Massachusetts during the Civil War and
is remembered for his work in championing the formation of African-Amer-
ican regiments in the Union army, including the 54th Massachusetts (Malone
279–81). By comparing Stowe's work as an abolitionist novelist with Governor Andrew's work as a public official, Carey clearly aims to diminish her literary contribution as well as criticize the profit it brought her.

Carey seems fixated on the relative value of Stowe's writing, but he
saves some of his harshest criticism for the hypocrisy he finds in the abolitionist sentiments of copyright proponents. Since he had earlier selected
Stowe for particular scrutiny in this regard, it seems likely that she is one of
the "Eastern authors" to whom he now refers:

> The day has passed, in this country, for the recognition of either perpetu-
> ity or universality of literary *rights*. The wealthy Carolinians, anxious that
> books might be high in price, and knowing well that monopoly privi-
> leges were opposed to freedom, gladly co-operated with Eastern authors
> and publishers, anti-slavery as they professed to be. The enfranchised
> black, on the contrary, desires that books may be cheap, and to that end

> he and his representatives will be found in all the future co-operating
> with the people of the Centre and the West in maintaining the doctrine
> that literary *privileges* exist in virtue of grants from the people who own
> the materials out of which books are made; that those privileges have
> been perhaps already too far extended; that there exists not even a
> shadow of a reason for any further extension; and that to grant what now
> is asked would be a positive wrong to the many millions of consumers, as
> well as an obstacle to be now placed in the road towards civilization. (13)

Both Graham and Carey, the former writing before the Civil War and the
latter adding the above passage soon after it, make a strikingly similar point
regarding the claims of sympathy for African-Americans and the apparent
willingness to deprive them of an opportunity for education and employment. Both accuse authors of seeking profit at the expense of the less fortunate. Carey's distinction between the "literary *privileges*" of authors and the
rights of "enfranchised" blacks seems strategic. Authors would be hard-
pressed, as they always had been, to argue that their "right" to exclusive control over their literary property should come at the expense of the "many
millions of consumers." Stowe, who was the first author to go to court in an
attempt to stop a translation, was thus vulnerable both to Graham's charges
of profiteering and to Carey's later charges of hypocrisy.

When Graham published his editorial, however, many of his readers
were ardent fans of Stowe, and a month later he seems to have been compelled to write a response to "some very bitter attacks" lodged against him for
his earlier statements, despite his claim that the magazine had gained over
three thousand subscribers since the previous issue ("Editor's Table" 365).
Graham repeats his charge that *Uncle Tom's Cabin* is first and foremost a
money-making scheme and reiterates his own support for African-Americans
while demanding that his critics demonstrate their own. He writes,

> Uncle Tom has served its purpose—it has made an excitement and—
> *money!* but *we* must be excused from falling down and worshiping so
> false and mean a thing [. . .]. To all valiant MacDuffs, who write for
> *praise* and *dollars,* we say 'Lay on!'—if you will only spend *a little* of
> your money in helping to raise the condition of the free Negroes of the
> North, we shall bear your abuse patiently and *try to think* you sincere!"
> (365, 366).

There are many issues at work in Graham's editorial, not the least of which is
his apparent support for the Compromise of 1850 and his feeling that books

such as Stowe's were injuring "our common country" by enflaming Northern sentiments against the South and slavery (365). At the same time, his constant referral to the free African-Americans in the North is uncomfortably close to Southern apologists who responded to *Uncle Tom's Cabin* by citing the hardships of Northern blacks. However, what is most striking is his unceasing attention to the amount of money the novel had earned. This is inextricably linked to the novel's politics and puts the authenticity of its enterprise into question: "the *strong, money-making side for a publisher now, is the anti-slavery side*" (365).

Other reviewers, though less critical of Stowe's motives, describe the novel's success in terms that suggest a similar contradiction between the novel's call for liberation and its startling profitability. Calling the book's success "an epidemic," a critic for the New York magazine *The Literary World* writes of how the novel's popularity is fueled through cheap pirated editions in London: "The publisher of this cheap edition, having already pocketed the handsome sum of four thousand pounds, is cheering himself with the prospect of some ten thousand more. He keeps some four hundred men, women, and children constantly occupied in binding the work" ("Uncle Tom Epidemic" 355). Similarly, a critic for *Putnam's* writes, "The publishers have kept four steam-presses running, night and day, Sundays only excepted, and at double the ordinary speed, being equal to sixteen presses worked ten hours a day at the usual speed. They have kept two hundred hands constantly employed in binding Uncle Tom, and he has consumed five thousand reams of white paper" ("Uncle Tomitudes" 98). Uncle Tom is personified, and not only is he constantly being "bound," his voracious consumption is forcing "two hundred hands" to work non-stop in binding him. His white slaveholders figure as the consuming and consumed "white paper" that defines his existence in the marketplace. He seems at once victim and victimizer in the publication process, as *The Literary World's* reference to the "men, women, and children constantly occupied in binding the work" makes clear. The long hours and harsh labor practices suggested by both of these reviews indicate that the novel's success is far from liberatory, no matter the author's intentions or the message of the work itself.

Despite attempts to define her public image, Stowe could not avoid being implicated in the industrial excesses underlying the commodification of her text. In ruling against her attempt to stop Thomas' publication of his German translation, Judge Grier not only articulated her role in the "paper-binding" of Uncle Tom, but he also suggested that, once she had put her characters up for sale, she had sacrificed proprietary rights to them:[6]

> The distinction taken by some writers on the subject of literary prop-
> erty, between the works which are *publici juris* [public property], and of
> those which are subject to copyright, has no foundation, in fact, if the
> established doctrine of the cases be true, and the author's property in a
> published book consists only in a right of copy. By the publication of
> Mrs. Stowe's book, the creations of the genius and imagination of the
> author have become as much public property as those of Homer or Cer-
> vantes. *Uncle Tom and Topsy are as much publici juris as Don Quixote and
> Sancho Panza.* All her conceptions and inventions may be used and
> abused by imitators, play-rights and poetasters. *They are no longer her
> own—those who have purchased her book, may clothe them in English dog-
> gerel, in German or Chinese prose. Her absolute dominion and property in
> the creations of her genius and imagination have been voluntarily relin-
> quished.*[7] All that now remains is the copyright of her book; the exclu-
> sive right to print, reprint and vend it, and those can only be called
> infringers of her rights, or pirates of her property, who are guilty of
> printing, publishing, importing or vending without her license 'copies
> of her book.' A translation may, in loose phraseology, be called a tran-
> script or copy of her thoughts or conceptions, but in no correct sense
> can it be called a copy of her book. (*Stowe v. Thomas* 207–8)

Grier interprets the law in such a way as to refuse the distinction between a
book that has become public property and work that has been copyrighted.
In a sense, all published works become public property. Copyright, in his
decision, protects only exactly that—the right to make exact copies; while he
concedes that Stowe may have once had "absolute dominion and property"
in Uncle Tom and Topsy, she has now yielded that dominion through publication. He suggests that it is Stowe's own decision to commodify "the creations of her genius and imagination" by making the work available for
purchase in the first place that makes that work vulnerable to piracy. She is
the one who first exposes Uncle Tom and Topsy to the marketplace, putting
them into play as objects of exchange; once that is done, she can do little to
protect them from translation or adaptation by those who purchase them.

As Homestead points out, this decision highlights an uncomfortable
contradiction between the abolitionist ideals Stowe champions and her
defense of her literary property rights:

> By making Tom and Topsy the emblems of Stowe's 'creations and con-
> ceptions,' Grier brings to mind the classic trope of the (male) author's
> book as his child—a child produced out of his brain rather than from a

woman's womb. [...] Grier's use of the metaphor slides into a substitu-
tion of Tom and Topsy as characters for the work as a whole as her
brain-child. Uncle Tom and Topsy are thus figuratively transformed
into Stowe's children, and Stowe, their 'mother,' has willingly subjected
those children to abuse by selling them. (150)

Grier's depiction of a transactional logic close to what Stowe rightly depicts
so harshly in her novel seems seriously to call into question the justice of
her publishing enterprise. If, as Homestead suggests, Stowe is rhetorically
positioned as a mother selling her children, then it would seem that her
status as a female author made her vulnerable to a particularly harsh form
of criticism.

Grier's language also brings to mind other conceptions of authorship,
most notably authorship as "invention," a formulation that hearkens back to
copyright's early association with patent law. Stowe's attorneys, as well as
other copyright advocates, argued that copyrights protect the ideas and conceptions of authors as well as the precise forms those ideas take. While Grier
employs the language of invention, he explicitly rejects any comparison: "as
the author's exclusive property in a literary composition or his copyright,
consists only in a right to multiply copies of his book, and enjoy the profits
therefrom, and not in an exclusive right to his conceptions and inventions,
which may be termed the essence of his composition, the argument from the
supposed analogy is fallacious" (*Stowe v. Thomas* 207). In fact, Grier suggests
that writing a good translation often "requires more learning, talent and
judgment, than was required to write the original" (207). Regardless of the
question of talent, Grier's decision does little to grant authors credit for or
property in their ideas.

One more image he employs requires notice. In addition to invoking
and then dismissing the analogy between the author and inventor, he also
employs the image of the author as a landowner, whose "absolute dominion
and property" is yielded upon publication. As we have already seen, this was
a common analogy. If one recalls the earlier instances of its use, however,
particularly that of literary property and gardens, one sees that Grier is
offering a severely limited interpretation. According to his logic, the famous
Mr. Niblo cited by copyright advocates in the 1830s would forever lose all
control of his garden once he granted admission to the public.

While Grier's decision was a blow to authors' rights, denying protection of works from unauthorized translation, it also suggested that authors
would need to take rather extreme measures to protect their property; they
would, in fact, have to keep their work entirely to themselves, not sharing it

with anyone. Even more problematic for Stowe's abolitionist message than the suggestion that she has sold her literary children is the idea that if an owner would protect her property, she must cling to it steadfastly. Only the author who never let his or her work see the light of day could maintain control over it. Grier writes that, upon publication, "The author's conceptions have become the common property of his readers, who cannot be deprived of the use of them, nor their right to communicate them to another clothed in their own language, by lecture or by treatise" (*Stowe v. Thomas* 206). Stowe was vulnerable to charges of hypocrisy because the kind of ownership she sought for her texts was too easily elided with defenses of slavery. Her property was not simply literature; it was literature of slaves. As Judge Grier made clear, what she was attempting to control was Uncle Tom and Topsy: these characters were her possessions. She may love them and wish to protect them, but such protection depended on her maintaining ownership of them.

In contrast to Stowe's determination to retain possession of her novel, Grier's decision suggests two alternative interpretations, neither of which places Stowe in a flattering light. On the one hand, Grier offers a type of "literary abolitionism," abolishing Stowe's "absolute dominion and property" in Uncle Tom and Topsy and allowing the characters to circulate and to "work" for others. On the other hand, Grier notes that, upon publication, Stowe's characters become "common property"—not free, but susceptible to appropriation by multiple owners for multiple purposes. Because of the nature of her literary property—"slave" literature—Stowe's attempts to protect her copyright suggested several unpalatable parallels to the subject of her novels.

These parallels were more than a matter of analogy, as is made clear in an 1856 letter from a friend, who wrote, "I have made 'Old Tiff's' acquaintance. *He* is a verity—will stand up with Uncle Tom and Topsy, pieces of negro property you will [be] guilty of holding after you are dead. Very likely your children may be selling them" (qtd. in Homestead 160). Phrased in these terms, Uncle Tom and Topsy could only be "free" and Stowe's "guilt" assuaged if they were made freely available to work for other publishers, playwrights, and translators. Like the slaves sold by uncaring masters, however, her texts and characters become vulnerable to bowdlerization and abuse once out of her "loving" control, as the innumerable trinkets that emerged following the success of *Uncle Tom's Cabin* demonstrate. Grier's decision left writers with two unappealing choices: they must either exercise total control over their literary property by refusing to publish manuscripts, or they must stand by while their work is changed and sold again and again by others.

These legal arguments emerged several months after Stowe published her novel, but property rights were clearly on her mind even as she wrote the book. Homestead argues of *Uncle Tom's Cabin,*

> Through its exploration of Tom's status as both person and property and particularly through its examination of Tom's relationships to his various 'owners,' both human and divine, the novel explores Stowe's anxious questions about the possible appropriation and exploitation of her slave characters, as well as the conflicts between Stowe's maternal values and her authorial proprietorship. If we read Tom as a figure of literary property, then each of his owners represents a possible model of authorial proprietorship. (154)

By drawing on Grier's decision and examining the parallels between Stowe's relationship as author with her characters to the master/slave relationships in the text, Homestead suggests that she was exploring several alternative modes of ownership in an attempt to articulate one "in accord with the novel's maternal critique of the marketplace" (154). Despite her attempts, Homestead argues, "the novel just as often exposes the limitations of authorship and Stowe's complicity with the market" (154). Homestead quite convincingly examines *Uncle Tom's Cabin* in terms of its portrayals of ownership and its relationship to the discourse of literary property. As an already published author, Stowe would certainly have been aware of the debates over copyright. Stowe's later works demonstrate how she negotiated not only the contradiction between her role as property owner and her role as abolitionist, but also her status as a successful female author attempting to protect her rights within a discourse that questioned them. What one discovers is that while Stowe clearly did not cease publication in order to maintain absolute control of her works, she did go to greater and greater lengths to protect them.

STOWE'S LITERARY TRAVELS

In the years between 1849 and 1854, the status of British copyrights for foreign authors was quite uncertain as a pivotal case, *Jefferys v. Boosey,* worked its way through the British legal system. Although the case itself dealt with an Italian opera, it had serious implications regarding the rights of any foreigner to a British copyright.[8] The rights of foreigners were first upheld, then denied, then upheld, and then, in the final appeal in 1854, the House of Lords ruled that "only if a foreigner travelled to Britain and remained there long enough to witness the publication of his work was he entitled to copyright protection.

Otherwise he could neither claim a copyright himself nor sell the right to a British subject, including a publisher" (Barnes 172). This decision had immediate implications for Stowe. After the success of *Uncle Tom's Cabin,* she had traveled to England and to Europe. When she returned to America, she wrote an account of her journey in the form of an epistolary travel narrative entitled *Sunny Memories of Foreign Lands,* published in 1854. The *Jefferys v. Boosey* decision left her British publisher with little recourse in protecting rights to the work, as the following advertisement makes clear:

> In ordering copies of this work, the public are respectfully requested to specify the Author's Editions; as, in consequence of a recent decision in the House of Lords, finding that Foreign Authors had no LEGAL protection for their works in this country, the Author has no redress except such as is afforded by public discrimination in purchasing Authors' editions.
>
> On their part, Mrs. STOWE's Publishers have taken care to print such Editions of the present work as can satisfactorily compete with any that can be brought against them. (qtd. in Barnes 173)

There was nothing to do but ask the readers to purchase the authorized edition. The honor of consumers provided little protection, and author and publisher alike watched with dismay as unauthorized reprints flooded the British market (173).

When she turned to writing *Dred,* Stowe had learned much from her experiences publishing *Uncle Tom's Cabin, A Key to Uncle Tom's Cabin,* and her recent travelogue. She was now keenly aware of the difficulties of protecting her literary property, and she took new steps to protect it. To protect her rights in Great Britain, she made arrangements to have the book published there first, going so far as to set sail before the work was even completed, writing throughout her journey and during her first days in London.[9] Composing and publishing a novel in this way took careful planning and timing, as Stowe's correspondence with her publishers reveals. Her instructions to Phillips and Sampson Low regarding the production of the novel are clear and precise: "I wrote 25 pages ms, yesterday & 20 day before & send herewith 40. Shall write fifty more to day & to morrow [. . .]You must not put any more in any paper till you hear from me in England. The two last weeks before the book comes out let these two chapters go in the Era & Tribune & you will hear from them quick" (Letter to Mr. Phillips). One gets a sense of how preoccupied Stowe was with her copyrights from the comments of her sister Mary, who wrote in a letter home,

> *Mrs Stowes new work was published* & the first copy sent to her—I
> believe however I mistake in saying *published* that will not be the right
> term till Tuesday—only a few copies are bound for special purposes—
> such as getting copy right which cannot be done until the work is com-
> pleted—The prospect for a sale is considered very good in this country
> & if Mr Low does not have to go to law for the protection of his copy
> right will be very profitable. (Perkins, Letter)

Her sister's familiarity with the procedures and the steps being taken to secure
the copyright for *Dred,* along with other correspondence between Stowe and
her husband, give us an indication of Stowe's attention to the issue.[10]

Indeed, she garnered praise for her efforts from fellow author and histo-
rian William Prescott, who wrote, "I congratulate you on the brilliant success
of the work, unexampled even in this age of authorship; and, as Mr. Phillips
informs me, greater even in the old country than in ours. I am glad you are
likely to settle the question and show that a Yankee writer can get a copyright
in England—little thanks to our own government, which compels him to go
there in order to get it" (qtd. in Stowe, *Life* 312). Prescott had reason for his
admiration. He had also gone to great lengths to protect his copyrights,
including writing to Charles Sumner in 1843 for advice in deciphering
American copyright law and learning how he could gain a British copyright
without jeopardizing his American rights. Prescott evidently had friends in
high places, for Sumner subsequently sought the advice of Supreme Court
Justice Story (Sumner, Letter). This intersection of an author with both the
legislative and judicial branches of the federal government provides some
insight into the complexity of antebellum copyright law and also highlights
the trouble authors had guaranteeing their rights.

Stowe did succeed in getting a British copyright, and, whenever she
could, she set out on the road to protect that right for her subsequent novels. Following the completion of *The Minister's Wooing* in 1859, she set sail
once again for London, writing to Lady Byron, "It is to publish this work
complete that I intend to visit England this summer" (qtd. in Stowe, *Life*
343). As she had with *Dred,* she also sought to coordinate her trips with her
publishers whenever possible. This most often meant taking up short resi-
dencies in Canada. When she had completed *The Pearl of Orr's Island,* she
wrote to the British publishers of *Agnes of Sorrento* in 1862: "To secure the
copy right of Messrs Sampson Lowe in The Pearl of Orr's Island I shall
reside in the British dominions from the fifteenth to the twenty second of
April—On any of these days if you feel disposed to make use of Agnes of
Sorrento in book form you will have a chance of securing a copy right"

(Letter to Messrs Smith & Elder). In order to succeed during this trip, Stowe also had to closely coordinate the American publication of her works. She was fortunate to find a publisher in James Fields who was willing to aid her in her efforts.

As she strove to complete both *Agnes of Sorrento* and *The Pearl of Orr's Island,* her ability to protect the rights of both novels in Great Britain figured prominently into her publishing plans, as the following letter to Fields makes clear: "I have been figuring on the time as you have appointed it & have concluded that I could not finish up both works & get them to England so as to have them print & have ready to issue on the 1st of April It is too much risk to say so—Will you publish on the 1st of May & let me put the *English* date at the seventeenth of April" (Letter to James T. Fields). With the stakes so high and the window for securing protection so narrow, careful planning was essential, as was travel to Canada. The prospect of such a trip was not appealing to her; she wrote to a longtime friend, "I have been pressed and overdriven [. . .]. Next I have to go to Canada and spend ten days or a fortnight securing copyright. Not a pleasant journey, but we shall try to make the best of it" (qtd. in Fields 291). Although she never returned to Great Britain, Stowe traveled to Canada once again in 1869; her grandson Calvin Stowe's brief description lends some insight into the exact nature of the trip: "In April, 1869, Mrs. Stowe was obliged to hurry North in order to visit Canada in time to protect her English rights in 'Oldtown Folks,' which she had just finished" (Stowe, *Life* 404). Her efforts to secure copyright demonstrate how the legal conditions dictated not only the publication of her novels, but her personal actions, as well. She was forced to travel regardless of her desire or her health, and she had to push herself to complete works in time to publish them while residing in Canada. She was "pressed and overdriven," but the rules of copyright nevertheless necessitated such action.

Of course, her ability to take such trips depended not only upon her determination; she also had to negotiate familial obligations. We have already referred to the exchanges Harriet had with Calvin regarding her success. Because Calvin's signature was required on her copyright agreements, his reluctance to travel could have a direct impact on her career and her ability to write and publish the novels she wished. When the family traveled to Great Britain in 1856 to secure copyright for *Dred,* Calvin once again returned to the U.S. on his own. While abroad, Harriet considered writing a novel dealing with the European aristocracy and class system. When she wrote to her husband regarding the idea, he first presented himself as reluctant regarding the project because of his concern for her reputation, and he employed his power as signatory to influence Harriet's plan:

If any thing worth the journey can be ready in London by the middle of April, I can go there & attend to it, & right home again. The sea always does me good. But your next work ought to be more carefully & leisurely written than your last one, & I don't believe you can have anything ready that will be worthy of your reputation till my summer vacation in August, & I am very willing to go to London then, *if it will pay*—not otherwise.

There is one very grave caution about writing on the subject you propose. As you stand before this country you must not *even seem* to countenance any kind of wrong, oppression or hardship on the poor abroad which you would condemn at home, and the oppressive institutions of the old world should meet with no more quarter at your hands than the oppressive institutions of the new. Could you [added—"with this view"] write to your own and the public satisfaction? [. . .] Think of this, & let me know in your next whether it would be possible to have anything ready by April, or whether everything could not be better secured by our taking a trip together to Montreal or some other Canadian city in August. (Letter, 2 Feb. 1857)

Calvin's point regarding Stowe's emerging reputation and the accompanying danger inherent in a perceived inconsistency is not without merit, given the way critics seemed poised to jump on any perceived hypocrisy. It is impossible, however, to ignore his clear reluctance to make another trip to Great Britain any time soon. His emphasis on financial reward as a condition of his willingness to travel indicates his true feelings, as he already seems predisposed to doubt the prospects for her proposed novel. On the whole, one doubts his gesture towards acquiescence: "The sea always does me good"; there is little indication that Calvin was eager to take in the salt air.

When Harriet still seemed determined to continue with the project, Calvin wrote again, this time expressing concern for her health and chiding her for her spending habits: "I can not bear the thought of your attempting another book this Spring. If you were to write yourself into paralysis or imbecility, what would become of us all? Come home and make arrangements to *save money* instead of *earning it,* for you know a *penny saved is a penny earned,* and the labor much less" (Letter, 23 Feb. 1857). When this did little to dampen his wife's enthusiasm to begin another novel during her travels, Calvin wrote yet again, setting forth even more explicitly his unwillingness to take part in her project: "Write your book as fast as you please, and then come here & spend June & July in finishing it; & in August, if necessary, I will go to London to secure the copy right. I have no fancy for going this coming April, it's of no use, & you needn't expect it" (Letter, 23 Feb.-

March [?] 1857). While there is no way of knowing if Calvin's obstinacy was to blame, Harriet never wrote the projected novel.

Back in the states, whenever foreign travel seemed impossible, Stowe was innovative in looking for other ways to write the books she wanted to write and still manage to secure her copyrights. The most striking example of this innovation came in 1860, shortly after she had returned from her third trip to Great Britain. As on previous trips, Calvin had left for home before her, and Harriet compensated by adjusting her plans. After her return home, she wrote a letter to Elizabeth Gaskell, a British author she had befriended during her travels, proposing a unique collaboration designed to allow Stowe to write the work about Italy that she had been contemplating and allowing both women to profit from copyrights secured in their respective countries. The letter reveals a great deal regarding Stowe's thought process in regard to copyright law, the relationship between her professional life and her personal life, and her pure audacity in approaching Gaskell:

> Mr. Lowe has written me that you seemed favorably inclined to entertain a project for a sort of partnership with me in a work on Italy—
>
> It had been my intention to get such a work out <without> before leaving England, but I found the state of my family to be such that I could not leave them any longer—*Home* became in my eyes worth a thousand books—& to get there a month sooner worth any sacrifice Also, I wanted to prepare my materials a little more at my leisure—I was ready to give up my chance of an English copy right but my publishers was disappointed at this and pushed [?] to cast about for some means to secure it. The idea of joint authorship had been proposed to me and it then occurred to me that you had been to Italy
>
> [. . .] Could we not in some way unite our forces without interfering with each others individuality secure copy rights mutually in our respective countries and divide the profits [. . .]
>
> As the work must *appear* first in England and the copy right *here* can be secured without any other formality than merely the recording of a printed title page—the editorial and [?] arranging duties will devolve on you—(Letter to Gaskell)

One cannot help but think of Stowe's earlier intended project that she had been forced to abandon when Calvin did not agree to travel to help protect the copyrights. Harriet had always enjoyed her trips to Europe during the 1850s, but Calvin had not, and it is likely that he played a role in what appears to have been a sudden decision to return home.[11]

Regardless of the cause, Stowe's letter shows once again the difficulties she faced managing her literary business, particularly the protection of her copyrights, and her role in her family. Her proposed alliance with Gaskell reveals her determination not to allow domestic matters to interfere with her authorial pursuits as they had in the past, and it also demonstrates how much weight Stowe gave matters of copyright protection in determining what books were to be written. Stowe never wrote the proposed work—perhaps Gaskell was reluctant to take total editorial responsibility for the project[12]—although she did write *Agnes of Sorrento,* securing copyright for the novel through her trip to Canada. Stowe's literary journey was also a literal journey, as she used her proceeds from earlier novels to travel whenever she could to protect her rights.

THE MISTRESS OF CANEMA

Stowe's understandable preoccupation with her property rights offers an explanation for something that has long vexed readers of her second "antislavery" novel, *Dred.* Since the book's publication in 1856, readers and critics alike have struggled to account for the fact that for more than 200 pages, more than a third of the novel, the protagonist is not the insurrectionist from whom the work gets its title, but is instead a young northern-educated slaveholder named Nina Gordon. The title character is completely absent, and, when he is finally introduced, Nina dies of cholera before ever interacting with him, long before the novel's conclusion. Playwrights who dramatized the text during the 1850s—with no feedback or permission from Stowe, of course—either eliminated Nina completely or granted her an escape from death that the author denied. More recently, literary critics have devised their own strategies for dealing with Nina: some, like Alice Crozier, have ignored or diminished her importance almost completely, focusing instead on Harry Gordan, Dred, and the potential for violent rebellion in the novel. Others, including Hedrick, cite the speed with which Stowe wrote the book and suggest that her anger at the beating of Charles Sumner prompted her to abandon her sentimental heroine in exchange for the more dynamic Dred. Theodore Hovet, for his part, has argued that Nina's prominence is not a structural flaw at all, but is in fact an integral part of a "master narrative" that organizes the entire text, a narrative that is "the story of humanity's fall and redemption" (ix).

Nina does pose a problem for the book, and this is because of the problem book-*keeping* poses for both Nina and for Stowe. Stowe's difficulties protecting her literary property rights following the success of *Uncle Tom's Cabin* are reinscribed in the property relations depicted in *Dred.* The Grier case suggested that authors only maintain control of their property by clinging to it tightly, preventing any circulation of their texts. Stowe understandably rejected this construction of her profession and her rights. In Nina Gordon, she presents a heroine whose major challenge is learning to control her property, including her slaves, in a responsible fashion. Introduced to the reader as a coquette with little regard for managing her plantation or romantic life, Nina is gradually empowered and learns to take control of both; in the process, she attempts to practice an ownership that is both legal and moral, based as much on sympathetic attachment as on Southern slave law.

As critics like Gillian Brown and Lori Merish have demonstrated, Stowe does not undermine proprietary relations in her work as much as she attempts to redefine them as, in Merish's words, "bonds of love, the product of natural sentiments and intimate attachments" ("Sentimental Consumption" 19), what Merish describes as "sentimental ownership." Stowe's representation of Nina's sentimental ownership seems to offer a defense of her proprietary rights. Such a defense, however, reveals the uncomfortable relationship between her arguments for abolition and her attempts to protect her literary property: it undermines her abolitionist sentiments even while it offers a view of literary proprietorship that Stowe would return to in later works. In *Dred,* Nina only makes sense when viewed not as an abolitionist figure, but instead as both the empowered author and the enlightened reader. She comes to view her property in terms of sympathy and affection, disdaining to see it circulated in a crass manner. Other slaveholders—her brother, for instance—look for nothing more than a good bargain: Stowe pits responsible ownership against immoral trade.

This is why Nina, even as she grows to support abolition, does not release her slaves; rather, she holds them closer than ever, an act that is presented as her final moral accomplishment. As Nina comes closer to achieving this end, however, Stowe drifts further and further away from her stated goal of "revealing to the people the true character of that system" of slavery (*Dred* 30). Even as Nina begins to doubt the justice of slavery, she does not renounce any legal or moral ownership, no matter how kindly or well intentioned it may be. The novel and its message are thus caught in a dilemma. Stowe must undermine either Nina's responsible and sentimental exercise of her property rights or the abolitionist message itself. Refusing to do either, Stowe kills off her heroine and focuses instead on Dred and the violence she had long emphasized was at the heart of the slave system. If, as later critics have pointed out, Stowe appears to be ambivalent regarding Dred, it may be because he represents property that is without any attachment and stands as a refutation of the arguments for benevolent ownership that seem to occupy much of the rest of her novel. Unlike other slaves depicted in the novel, like the loyal Tiff, Dred denies utterly the justice of ownership in a way that Nina never does. Stowe's own ambivalence is evident in the fates of both her protagonists.

Nina Gordon first appears as a character naively unconcerned with how tenuous her economic and personal stability are. In the first chapter, "The Mistress of Canema," she returns from school engaged to three different suitors, trailing a large assortment of trinkets and boxes, stating in the opening line of the novel, "Bills, Harry?—Yes.—Dear me, where are they?—There!—No. Here?—O, look!—What do you think of this, scarf? [sic] Isn't it lovely?" (31). The chapter's title provides an ironic commentary on the heroine, for it quickly becomes clear that the young woman is mistress of her plantation in name only. Harry is a slave who effectively runs Canema and manages Nina's finances, and, unbeknownst to her, he is her half-brother. The emotional obligations this situation entails is only one of several examples in the novel of the entanglements of sentimental and proprietary relationships. Nina, who cannot keep her bills or her beaus straight, seems unprepared to deal with any of these concerns. When Harry questions her about the fairness of her course with her suitors, she makes light of his inquiry. He presses her, stating, "some time or other you must marry somebody. You need somebody to take care of the property and place," (38), to which Nina replies,

> 'O, that's it, is it? You are tired of keeping accounts, are you, with me to spend the money? Well, I don't wonder. How I pity anybody that keeps accounts! Isn't it horrid, Harry? Those awful books! Do you know that Mme. Ardaine set out that 'we girls' should keep account of our expenses? I just tried it two weeks. I had a headache and weak eyes, and actually it nearly ruined my constitution.' (38–9)

The passage explicitly links Nina's gender—she is one of the 'girls' who must learn to keep accounts—with her physical incapacity to manage her own expenses. The scene literalizes in Nina's frail body Stowe's own constitutional inability to manage her literary property, emphasizing her own legal weakness as both an author and a woman.

Unlike Stowe, however, Nina has nearly complete legal right to her property; only a disinterested uncle has some say, and he declines to get involved in any way. The situation particularly vexes her alcoholic brother, Tom, who complains, "All left to you and the executors, as you call them; as

if *I* were not the natural guardian of my sister!" (192). Nina is free from
negotiating with her male family members. While her legal title is clear,
however, she must overcome her own particular constitutional weakness.
Stowe emphasizes the difficulties facing her: "The duties of a southern
housekeeper, on a plantation, are onerous beyond any amount of northern
conception. [. . .] Our reader has seen what Nina was on her return from
New York, and can easily imagine that she had no idea of embracing, in
good earnest, the hard duties of such a life" (64). Her practical education
begins quickly. After dismissing all of her suitors save Edward Clayton, a
slaveholder who views himself as a guardian to his slaves, Nina faces the first
test of her control over her property. When her brother Tom returns to the
plantation, he takes an interest in Harry's wife, who belongs to a neighbor,
and proposes to buy her for himself. Nina announces that she will buy the
woman to protect her, and when Harry suggests that she really doesn't have
the money available, she proclaims,

> I'll sell everything I've got—my jewels—everything! [. . .] I'm not
> quite so selfish as I've always seemed to be. [. . .] Only you be off. You
> can't stand such provocation as you get here; and if you yield, as any
> man will do, at last, then everything and everybody will go against you,
> and I can't protect you. Trust to *me*. I'm not so much of a child as I
> seemed to be! (198)

Nina's plan further reveals the entanglement of emotional and monetary interest, granting her possession not only of her half-brother, but his
wife, as well. The scene also reinforces her power as owner; not only can
she purchase the woman, but she is now her brother's protector, though
eighteen years his junior. Stowe emphasizes Nina's newly-asserted power:
"Nina gave her orders with a dignity as if she had been a princess, and in all
his agitation Harry could not help marveling at the sudden air of womanli-
ness which had come over her. 'I could serve *you*,' he said, in a low voice,
'to the last drop of my blood!'" (198–9). Despite the courtly language of
this passage, one cannot ignore the nature of the characters' relationship.
Harry is loyal to Nina out of his love for her, marked by their "blood" relation, and, while it is also clear that she is concerned for him, this moment
signifies the beginning of Nina's transformation from a "spoiled child" to a
princess, marking her development into a slaveholder with both legal and
sentimental ownership of her slaves. Nina begins to overcome her constitutional weakness in a way that Stowe, as an author and a married woman,
could not.

The bonds between Nina and Harry are clearly products of both legal and sentimental fashioning and are evident when Harry tells his sister, "You have always held my heart in your hand! That has been the clasp upon my chain!" (199). Although Nina, "after a moment's thought" (199), tells him she will file the papers to free him, she never does so. Her response is quite different from that of Mr. Marvyn, a Northern slaveholder depicted in Stowe's 1859 novel *The Minister's Wooing*. In that novel, the benevolent slaveholder, upon learning that the family's favorite servant desires her liberty, reacts immediately: "'Well, Candace, from this day you are free,' said Mr. Marvyn, solemnly" (104). Despite a similar familial attachment, Nina cannot bring herself to act so decisively. As the novel continues, she learns more about how sentiment intersects with slavery, rather than seeing how emotional bonds make slaveholding untenable. She visits Anne Clayton, Edward's sister: "A queen she really was on her own plantation," Stowe writes, "reigning by the strongest of all powers, that of love" (392). After speaking with Anne and observing her plantation's operation, Nina exclaims, "[Y]ou are not nominally like me, but really housekeeper! What wonderful skill you seem to have!" (393). Nina recognizes Anne's trusting relationship with her slaves as a skill, a method of management. The true housekeeper, the scene seems to suggest, creates an emotional bond to strengthen control of her or his property.

Although Anne and her brother both educate their slaves and grant them religious instruction, and although their neighbors disapprove of them and eventually drive them off, there is no denying the fact that they are still slaveholders. Despite frequent allusions to abolition, none of the slaveholders in the novel moves unequivocally to free his or her slaves—a curious omission in an "anti-slavery" novel. Anne remarks to Nina, "I think Edward has an idea that one of these days they may be emancipated on the soil, just as the serfs were in England. It looks to me rather hopeless, I must say" (397). Her words prove prophetic. When Clayton and his sister are threatened with mob violence near the end of the novel, a friend remarks, "Your plans for gradual emancipation, or reform, or anything tending in that direction, are utterly hopeless; and, if you want to pursue them with your own people, you must either send them to Liberia, or to the Northern States" (664–5). Instead of sending his slaves north or to Africa, Clayton buys land and moves them to Canada with him where they become his "tenants" (672). He feels too responsible for their well-being, it seems, simply to grant them liberty in the United States.

Nina Gordon does not live long enough to consider moving or freeing any of her slaves, including Harry. Instead, when cholera strikes her plantation, she achieves the perfect management and control she had envied in Anne Clayton. When the disease first appears, her aunt begs her to leave. Nina replies, "[P]erhaps you had better go; but I will stay with my people. [. . .] I think it would be very selfish for me to live on the services of my people all my life, and then run away and leave them alone when a time of danger comes" (457). Throughout the scenes describing the progress of the disease, she refers to her slaves as "my people." Once again, the language is clearly meant to express the emotional attachment that Nina now feels for the slaves that she had long been indifferent to, living off their services; however, as in her exchanges with Harry, the language also reminds the reader of her position as owner, a position only strengthened by her new-found emotional attachment.

Stowe goes to great lengths to compare Nina's sentimental management of her plantation with the purely commercial ambitions of other slaveholders. When Tom takes over Canema after her death, his approach is dominated by his interest in profits: "His habits of reckless and boundless extravagance, and utter heedlessness, caused his cravings for money to be absolutely insatiable; and, within legal limits, he had as little care how it was come by, as a high-way robber" (587). There are, Stowe suggests, some forms of property ownership that are better than others. Nina owns "her people," but her possession allows her to protect them from the unscrupulous plans of people like her brother. Tom seeks possession only insofar as it brings him power; his inability to control Harry vexes him because it thwarts his domination: "[W]hat stung him to a frenzy, when he thought of it, was, that every effort which he had hitherto made to recover possession of Harry had failed" (589–90). There are different kinds of slaveholders in *Dred*; they are distinguishable not by the degrees of their possession, which is total, but in their differing motives and sympathies.

These distinctions suggest several parallels with authorship. Stowe sought to protect her property and her creations from the infringement of "pirates." These same publishers sought to protect their right to property not because of a bond of affection, but because they sought to use the property to financial advantage. Of course, both Stowe and the "pirates" could profit from the work, just as Nina, despite her love for Harry, profited from his management of her estate. Stowe claimed that she had written her first novel without an eye toward making a profit; her suit against Thomas's publication of the German translation of *Uncle Tom's Cabin* seems to belie this claim. As Homestead writes, "Stowe was not concerned, however, with stopping publication of the Thomas translation merely to protect an abstract or symbolic right, but with protecting the market for her *own* translation. She had a clear economic interest in preventing Thomas from publishing his German translation as her affidavit filed in the suit makes clear" (135). The economic motives of both Stowe and Thomas were similar, a fact which undermines any attempt to view Stowe simply as the caring author/creator.

Just as any attempt to differentiate between Stowe's motives and Thomas' are undermined by Stowe's financial interest in protecting her property, Stowe's attempts to draw a bright line between slaveholders like Tom Gordon, his sister Nina, and the slaveholding Claytons fail when she simply cannot separate the sentimental bonds she describes from systems of ownership. Expressions of affection are invariably laced with language representing power and control. When Clayton rushes to the plantation during the height of the cholera epidemic to find Nina, she tells him, "[Y]ou must let me take care of you. Don't you know that I'm mistress of the fortress here—commander-in-chief and head physician? [. . .] Come, let me lead you off, like a captive" (475). She had envied Anne's skill as a housekeeper, and, where Anne was a queen on her plantation, Nina is now truly "The Mistress of Canema," with power over all who come within her "fortress." Richard Boyd describes this transformation in Nina's relationship with Clayton succinctly: "This 'new' Nina [. . .] acts toward Clayton in a fashion more akin to that of a benevolent slave owner than an ardent lover" (25). This is the climax of her development. At the beginning of the novel she was light-hearted about her possessions and her suitors; now she has true command of both. It is at this point she succumbs to cholera, dying less than ten pages later, beseeching Clayton to "take care of [her] poor people" (482). Even with her last breaths, she asserts the ownership she has come to embrace.

After her death, Nina is quickly forgotten and Dred becomes the most prominent character in the novel. The comparison is striking; Dred is a character that exists beyond society and the domestic "fortresses" of slaveowners, benevolent or otherwise. Unlike Nina's half-brother Harry, Dred never resigns himself to his captivity and never forms attachments with others: "He joined in none of the social recreations and amusements of the slaves, labored with proud and silent assiduity, but, on the slightest rebuke or threat, flashed up with a savage fierceness, which, supported by his immense bodily strength, made him an object of dread among overseers. He was one of those of whom they gladly rid themselves; and, like a fractious horse, was sold from master to master" (274). Dred is unlike any of the other slave characters Stowe describes in the novel: while it is clear that Stowe finds something noble in his "unsubduable disposition" (274), her depiction is also marked by the frequent use of the term "savage" to describe his personality.

At the same time, his indomitable will ironically accentuates his slave status: Stowe likens him to a horse, being frequently traded. Harry and Tiff, like Uncle Tom before them, show their humanity through their loyalty and their emotional attachments. Dred, despite a marriage that is given little description, does not exhibit this same capacity. He is, instead, a riddle, or, to be more precise, an obscure textual artifact; upon his first appearance, Stowe's narrator "reads" him in striking detail. She writes, "The perceptive organs jutted like dark ridges over the eyes, while that part of the head which phrenologists attribute to the moral and intellectual sentiments, rose like an ample dome above them. [. . .] If any organs were predominant in the head, they were those of ideality, wonder, veneration, and firmness" (261). The narrator's approving phrenological interpretation is once again qualified by the observation that Dred's eyes "betokened habitual excitement to the verge of insanity" (261). Much later in the novel, Clayton reinforces Dred's nature as both a text to be read and as a possible lunatic by comparing him with "old rude Gothic doorways, so frequent in European cathedrals, where scriptural images, carved in rough granite, mingle themselves with a thousand wayward, fantastic freaks of architecture" (632). Dred may represent scripture, but only in a twisted, obscure fashion. He is a text that appears to defy reading at the same time that he denies ownership, sentimental or otherwise.

The fates of Dred on the one hand and the Uncle Tom-like slave Tiff are revealing. Dred dies at the hand of Tom Gordon, still waiting for the Biblical sign that would usher in the revolution against his oppressors. Tiff accompanies the white children in his charge, technically his "owners," to the North, where he miraculously survives a shipwreck and lives to see them grow to be healthy and happy adults. Tiff escapes and lives "happily ever after" as a result of his refusal to rebel against the sentimental bonds of his slaveholders. The dismal swamp represents Stowe's nearest approach to a radical politics of liberation, but she undermines this radical potential by finally placing her authorial weight behind the more passive, and ultimately more commercial, forms of sentimental attachment displayed by Nina, the Claytons, and Tiff and the children. Nina's story is a progression towards perfect proprietorship, a responsible acceptance of legal and sentimental power. Such a story proves untenable within the framework of a novel intended to undermine the system of slavery. No matter how pure Nina's motives, her love for "her" people and their love for her are continually entwined with her ownership of them: the sentimental attachment cannot be separated from the legal one, as her possession of her brother Harry demonstrates. While Nina's death removes the most prominent representation of such possession, the escape of the Claytons with their slaves suggests Stowe's discomfort with the more radical alternatives.

Rather than a stirring call for slave rebellion or an unambivalent defense of abolition, her portrayal of sentimental ownership offers a defense of her attempts to protect her literary property by suggesting what Merish calls "a (paradoxical) model of 'consensual,' spiritually redemptive property relations seemingly compatible with America's democratic ideals" (*Sentimental Materialism* 137–8). Property should be cared for and cherished, Stowe suggests, not stolen or purchased cheaply for instant gratification. Ownership in itself is not wrong; irresponsible management and uncaring, reckless appropriation of other people's property, on the other hand, are. Responsible possession improves character and strengthens connections between people. Nina Gordon, unfettered by the kind of legal obstacles Stowe faced, is able to practice that perfect sentimental proprietorship that was denied to Stowe as an author. While Stowe may have aspired to such ownership as an author attempting to "protect" her property, her authorial actions did nothing to undermine the logic of slavery. Likewise, her depictions of Nina and Clayton fail to advance her abolitionist goals. As Lisa Whitney remarks, "In *Dred* every white adult, no matter what his or her position on slavery, participates in the system as an oppressor" (560). Nina's death would seem to indicate Stowe's awareness of the self-defeating logic of her novel, but Dred's death and the fates of the Claytons and Tiff leave the novel without a satisfactory alternative that would indict sentimental property ownership. When Stowe moves away from focusing on abolition in her novels, her depictions of sentimental possession serve her much better. In *Dred,* however, her inability to separate the sentimental bonds between people from the bonds of owner and objects ultimately lead her into a swamp more dense and self-defeating than any contrived for her creations.

BOOKS AND "ALL THINGS SACRED"

Dred was not the critical or commercial success that *Uncle Tom's Cabin* was, but it was enough to cement Stowe's literary reputation. She was now a household name, and copies of her books and samples of various Uncle Tom paraphernalia were widely available for purchase. Although Stowe could do little to control variations of her novels, such as plays and translations, she could control the form the novels themselves took upon publication, and this was very important to her. In particular, following the publication of *Dred,* she wanted her books available in a more attractive, more permanent format. She wrote to her publisher in 1859, "I would like to ask you also definitely[,] Are you ready to put up Uncle Tom uniform with any other works so as to commence the sale of *sets*—I know not why 'Stowes works' should not stand by the side of Hawthorne Lowel [sic] & others next Christmas—please write me about it.—if so I will take instant steps to prepare it with the introduction I spoke of" (Letter to Mr. Philips [sic]). She became more and more interested in the physical presentation of her novels, asking her publisher James T. Fields in 1862, "Will you get up New Years & Christmas Editions of the Pearl & Agnes?" (qtd. in Austin 273). After Fields presented her daughter with a set of Hawthorne's works bound in white as a wedding gift in 1865, Stowe asked for sets of her own work bound in the same fashion (284). This concern for handsome and uniform editions is clearly a bid for authorial legitimacy. Having her novels found on the shelf alongside an author like James Russell Lowell, an established critical and popular success who also served as her editor at times in *The Atlantic Monthly*, would elevate her professional standing.

Stowe's interest in producing durable, attractive volumes shows her awareness of her own reputation and her belief in the value of her books. At the same time, however, her desire to see her novels published in a uniform set indicates an attempt to define her works as more than popular ephemera: their publication in this format would give them greater legitimacy in the literary marketplace and make the books themselves weightier artifacts in family households. Stowe's vision of these works being available for Christmas purchase highlights her desire to imagine them being brought home as gifts for family members, items that could be treasured and passed on from one generation to the next.

The creation of books that could be cherished as material artifacts, as much for their beauty as their content, is a crucial part of what Merish has described as the extension of sentimental affection to objects, animating possessions with human emotion: "The domestic 'romance of the object' figured in Stowe's writings—the sentimental construction of the home as an animating, humanizing domain that transforms insensible 'objects' into sensible, hybridized 'animated objects'—shaped, I have suggested, the consumption of diverse commodities during the antebellum period—including the consumption of novels" (*Sentimental Materialism* 163). In first *The Minister's Wooing* and then again in *Oldtown Folks*, Stowe employs a rhetoric that emphasizes the emotional value of objects in the household, including books. This rhetoric emphasized the caring for and the cherishing of objects more than the purchasing of them.

Throughout many of Stowe's later novels, there is great attention paid to the possession of objects, while very little is said of their purchase.[13] This represents a shifting of attention: in her overtly anti-slavery novels, she makes a clear contrast between the possession of slaves such as Harry and the sale and exploitation of those slaves. The sentimental possession which she describes sets forth what Merish has described as "a (paradoxical) model of 'consensual,' spiritually redemptive property relations seemingly compatible with America's democratic ideals" (137–8). Again, such a model does not so much undermine property relations as redefine them, preserving the right to private property by reconfiguring it as an act of emotional investment, redeeming both the owner and object. In later novels, Stowe's attention shifts even more noticeably towards descriptions of the domestic sphere and the care and maintenance of cherished objects. Such a value of ownership would aid Stowe as an author in a number of ways. Pirated texts were notoriously cheap; to take advantage of newspaper postal rates, many of these were not even bound until regulations were tightened somewhat in 1845 (Barnes 23). These novels were not really suited for being cherished or passed down from one generation to the next. Also, there was the suggestion that novels that had been printed through inappropriate means would demean their owners: by setting forth a scheme of moral ownership, Stowe shifts the debate from expediency to sentiment; this put her in line with Cooper and others who were arguing that copyright was necessary to protect the moral character of Americans. Stowe also suggests that moral ownership means close governance of property; Stowe's works redefine possessiveness as sentimental care.

In *The Minister's Wooing* and *Oldtown Folks*, both set in an idyllic New England past, Stowe portrays a society where possession is by and large undisputed, even as it pertained to slaves. While slavery was still abominable, when practiced in New England, it nearly amounted to adoption:

> [T]here were from the very first, in New England, serious doubts in the minds of thoughtful and conscientious people in reference to the lawfulness of slavery; this scruple prevented many from availing themselves of it, and proved a restraint on all, so that nothing like plantation-life existed, and what servants were owned were scattered among different families, of which they came to be regarded and to regard themselves as a legitimate part and portion. (Stowe, *Minister's* 66)

The practice appears to be so benevolent that when one owner offers emancipation to his most loyal slave, she gladly accepts her freedom, but then quickly reasserts her willingness and desire to stay in the household and continue working as she always had.

Stowe contrasts this warm relationship in its domestic setting with the unacceptable trafficking of slaves and the accompanying harsh surroundings of the slave trader: "In a small, dirty room, down by the wharf, the windows veiled by cobwebs and dingy with the accumulated dust of ages, he sat in a greasy, leathern chair by a rickety office-table, on which was a great pewter inkstand, an account-book, and divers papers tied with red tape" (90–1). The implements of trade are accent marks for the room that suffers from a demonstrable lack of domestic care. The concern for profit, the attention to exchange rather than possession, brings neglect to one's possessions as demonstrated by the "greasy" chair, the "rickety" table and the over-all atmosphere of filth pervading the room. The same lack of domestic care is apparent in the trader's home; while it is elegant, it is not comfortable: in the parlor, "[h]eavy mahogany chairs, with crewel coverings, stood sentry about the room" (92). Absent an owner's care for anything beyond the aesthetic value of owning "none but the best" (92), objects become merely ornaments, "sentries" that reign coldly, rather than meaningful tokens. If the slave trader has an affectional life at all, his home offers no hint of it.

In contrast to the slave trader's opulence, the home of the heroine, Mary Scudder, is envied and enjoyed by characters ranging from seamstresses and French nobility to Aaron Burr. The slave trader's wife notices the difference between her elegant home and the simple cottage of the Scudders: "She mentally contrasted the neat little parlor, with its white sanded floor and muslin curtains, with her own grand front-room, which boasted the then uncommon luxuries of Turkey carpet and Persian rug, and wondered if Mrs. Katy [Scudder] did really feel as cool and easy in receiving her as she appeared" (29). Mrs. Scudder's ease comes in part from her natural elegance, but Stowe suggests it is also the result of the care for prized possessions; the treasuring of a few prized objects eliminates the desire for the constant acquisition of new objects:

> The old trunk stood with its histories, its imprisoned remembrances,— and a thousand tender thoughts seemed to be shaken out of every rustling fold of silk and embroidery, on the few yearly occasions when all were brought out to be aired, their history related and then solemnly locked up again. Nevertheless, the possession of these things gave to the women of an establishment a certain innate dignity, like a good conscience; so that in that larger portion of existence commonly denominated among them 'every day,' they were content with plain stuff and homespun. (20)

Ownership becomes the metaphoric equivalent of a good conscience through the emotional investment of the owners. The fineries owned by the Scudders are prized for their nostalgic value rather than their expense.[14] The joy that the family receives from possessing these artifacts is enough to eliminate any desire for further acquisition. Significantly, Stowe is not simply comparing the poor with the rich, as the slave trader's wife does. The Scudders, we are told, possess "quite a catalogue of brocade satin and laces" (20). It is no fault to own nice things; it is *how* they are acquired and owned that makes the difference.

One must treasure all of one's possessions, Stowe argues, because even the most trivial object has the potential to become one's only emotional link to a loved one. She writes,

> So we go, dear reader,—so long as we have a body and a soul. Two worlds must mingle,—the great and the little, the solemn and the trivial, wreathing in and out, like the grotesque carvings on a Gothic shrine;—only, did we know it rightly, nothing is trivial; since the human soul, with its awful shadow, makes all things sacred. Have not ribbons, cast-off flowers, soiled bits of gauze, trivial, trashy fragments of millinery, sometimes had an awful meaning, a deadly power, when they belonged to one who should wear them no more, and whose beautiful form, frail and crushed as they, is a hidden and a vanished thing for all time? [. . .] You are living your daily life among trifles that one death-stroke may make relics. One false step, one luckless accident, an obstacle on the track of a train, the tangling of the chord in shifting a sail, and the penknife, the pen, the papers, the trivial articles of dress and clothing, which to-day you toss idly and jestingly from hand to hand, may become dread memorials of that awful tragedy whose deep abyss ever underlies our common life. (120–1)

All objects, even the most inconsequential, have the potential to be transformed into "relics" of inestimable value. Rather than contrasting the material and spiritual worlds, Stowe suggests that they "mingle," each investing the other with significance. The passage is remarkably expansive in extending emotional investment to objects; indeed, if one took it literally, one might feel disinclined to dispose of anything at all for fear of throwing out some "sacred" memorial of a loved one. While apparently concerning itself with the latent worth of "trifles," the effect of the passage is to eliminate the very notion of trifles. To the attentive owner, all objects potentially serve as traces of the past that must be cared for and preserved. While appearing to endorse humble living—by comparing Mrs. Brown's conspicuous opulence with the Scudders' simplicity, for example—Stowe in fact offers a compelling argument for the purchase of expensive objects built to last. If one must treasure all of one's belongings, is it not better to possess beautiful finery, lovingly preserved and cared for, than it is to be left with "cast-off flowers, soiled bits of gauze," and "trivial, trashy fragments of millinery"? The more impermanent the object, the greater risk one runs of having no link to one's history.

This emotional economy is not simply applied to clothing and furniture. Books serve prominently as indications of character and as objects of sentimental value. In Mary Scudder's room, "[a] quiet, maiden-like place," "small enough for a nun's apartment," there is a library that demonstrates how books can become more than mere objects: "A small table under the looking-glass bore the library of a well-taught young woman of those times. 'The Spectator,' 'Paradise Lost,' Shakspeare, and 'Robinson Crusoe,' stood for the admitted secular literature, and beside them the Bible and the works then published of Mr. Jonathan Edwards" (19). Stowe emphasizes the timelessness and acknowledged artistic and educational value of these texts by comparing them with a more racy popular novel also present in the library: "Laid a little to one side as if of doubtful reputation, was the only novel which the stricter people in those days allowed for the reading of their daughters" (19). Mary is far too refined and religious a character to possess a book of such potentially immoral content, but Stowe explains away this possible transgression: "the book, as we have said, remained on her table under protest,—protected by being her father's gift to her mother during their days of courtship" (19–20). The book is valuable because it is more than a book; it bears the traces of her absent father. More than an object of romantic exchange, it represents the romance itself. It quite literally has "sentimental value."

Books serve a similar function in Stowe's later New England novel, *Oldtown Folks*. The narrator's father, an aspiring scholar with few material means, pours all of his emotional and material capital into books: "Through many a self-denial, many an hour of toil,—studying his Latin grammar by night in the paper-mill, saving his odd pennies, and buying book after book, and treasuring each one as a mine of wealth,—he went on, till finally he gained enough of a standing to teach" (17). Each book gains value from the time and care put into its purchase and the subsequent attention given it once possessed. Given this sentimental investment, it is not surprising that books become the narrator Horace's only inheritance (29).

His father's longing to go to college had been the subject of much head-shaking in the family, but his love of learning and books is not uncommon in the family. Horace's grandmother, the model of compassionate matriarchy, is of like mind. Horace tells the reader, "My remembrances of her are always as a reader. In her private chamber was always a table covered with books; and though performing personally the greater share of the labors of a large family, she never failed to have her quiet hour every afternoon for reading" (28). For a modest Calvinist family, the grandmother's profusion of books is noteworthy, not just for the evidence of learning and recreation—which we are assured have done nothing to distract the grandmother from her duties—but for the fact of accumulation. Books, like other artifacts, are granted access to the comfortable environs where the family spends the most time and thus take on greater significance. Characters in Stowe's novels do not simply read novels; they keep them close in private chambers, passing them on to the next generation. The narrator comments, "The books on her table came in time to be my reading as well as hers" (309).

The ideal matron, the author suggests, would meld reading and books seamlessly into her domestic routine. Reading and homekeeping are not antithetical: "Now the kitchen was my grandmother's own room. In one corner of it stood a round table with her favorite books, her great work-basket, and by it a rickety rocking-chair, the bottom of which was of ingenious domestic manufacture, being in fact made by interwoven strips of former coats and pantaloons of the home circle" (59). The items in this kitchen are literally woven from the fabric of family, the chair incorporating apparel worn by the inhabitants. Similarly, all the objects here described, including the rocking chair, are simultaneously woven into the fabric of the family, collapsing the distinction of "text" and "textile." The "favorite books" beside the "great work basket" mark the books' place in the domestic economy. And, Stowe suggests, reading and housework are not as far apart as they might appear. The narrator remarks later of another well-read woman,

> Her conscientiousness pervaded every nook and corner of her domestic duties with a beautiful perfection; nor did she ever feel tempted to think that her fine mental powers were a reason why these homely details should be considered a slavery. Household cares are a drudgery only when unpervaded by sentiment. When they are an offering of love, a ministry of care and devotion to the beloved, every detail has its interest. (376)

That books as well as chores can be "pervaded" with sentiment, making the former "favorites" and the latter "a ministry of care" through proper emotional investment is the cornerstone of Stowe's sentimental materialism.

Miss Mehitable, another older woman in Oldtown, possesses a similar affinity for books, which, as in the grandmother's kitchen, become objects that denote comfort:

> To me her house was always full of delightful images,—a great, calm, cool, shady, old-fashioned house, full of books and of quaint old furniture, with a garden on one side where were no end of lilies, hollyhocks, pinks, and peonies, to say nothing of currants, raspberries, apples, and pears, and other carnal delights, all of which good Miss Mehitable was free to dispense to her child-visitors. (63)

As with the grandmother, one gets the sense that Miss Mehitable's home has gained its warm atmosphere from the fact that it is a place where things are *kept,* including books. The age of objects in Stowe's novels is almost always in direct relationship to their sentimental value, and some objects, particularly books, gain from their profusion, as both women possess an abundance of them. To ensure that the emphasis on the age of the house and its belongings (it is "old fashioned" with "quaint old furniture") does not suggest lifelessness, Stowe couples the description of the inside of the house with garden imagery. Rather than a musty place full of musty things, Miss Mehitable's residence is both "calm" and "cool," as well as full of abundant life, blossoming with fruits and welcoming the visits of children.

As she had in *The Minister's Wooing,* Stowe employs comparison to demonstrate that one can possess objects in the wrong way. Primarily, one errs by either owning property for display rather than daily use—remembering that "use" is also connected with "care," both of which serve to connect the object more closely with the owner—or by owning property *only* for its use value and failing to appreciate its potential emotional worth. Stowe emphasizes the "homey" quality of the grandmother's kitchen by comparing it to Aunt Lois's parlor. The aunt's excessive concern for "propriety" indicates her failure to understand the importance of emotional investment through use and care:

> We had our best room, and kept it as cold, as uninviting and stately, as devoid of human light or warmth, as the most fashionable shut-up parlor of modern days. It had the tallest and brightest pair of brass andirons conceivable, and a shovel and tongs to match, that were so heavy that the mere lifting them was work enough, without doing anything with them. It had also a bright-varnished mahogany tea-table, over which was a looking-glass in a gilt frame, with a row of little architectural balls

on it; which looking-glass was always kept shrouded in white muslin at
all seasons of the year, on account of a tradition that flies might be
expected to attack it for one or two weeks in summer. But truth compels me to state, that I never saw or heard of a fly whose heart could
endure Aunt Lois's parlor. It was so dark, so cold, so still, that all that
frisky, buzzing race, who delight in air and sunshine, universally
deserted and seceded from it; yet the looking-glass, and occasionally the
fire-irons, were rigorously shrouded, as if desperate attacks might any
moment be expected. (59)

The contrast between this parlor and places like the grandmother's kitchen
and Miss Mehitable's home is almost comedic in its intensity. The grandmother keeps her books and her workbasket close at hand—her employment
of them evident in the afternoons of reading and in the carefully hand-
repaired furniture—but the parlor is rarely used. In fact, it defies use. The
tools for the fire are nearly too heavy to lift, and the looking-glass, which
might appear glamorous with its gilt frame, cannot be employed or even seen
because it remains enshrouded. While the objects themselves are described as
being "bright," the effect of the room is precisely the opposite. Both the
grandmother's kitchen and Miss Mehitable's house offer warmth and comfort, attracting frequent visitors, but the parlor won't even attract flies.

While objects that are kept for no purpose save ostentatious display
provide no comfort, Stowe suggests that the ownership of objects simply for
use, without any emotional investment, is equally wrong-headed and can
serve to sour relationships between people. This is evident in Stowe's
description of Miss Asphyxia, who takes in the orphan Tina. She is, according to the narrator's description, a "working machine" (87), nearly indefatigable in her labor. Miss Asphyxia does not extend human feeling to objects;
rather, she views all things, young girls included, as objects with only one
purpose: work. Once again, Stowe takes this to an almost comic extreme:
Miss Asphyxia views all flowers as "blows," trifles that are only useful when
dried (91). In her system, Tina is rendered merely an object: "She regarded
her exactly as she did her broom and her rolling-pin and her spinning-
wheel,—as an implement or instrument which she was to fashion to her
uses" (107). Although she has, in her own words, "as pretty a piece of property, and as well seen to, as most any round; and all I've got—house and
lands—is my own arnin's, honest, so there!'" (201), Stowe makes it clear that
her possessions do not bring peace or comfort. Asphyxia's very name affirms
how her view of the world has choked off any life that might have flourished
on her hard-earned land.

There are a number of similar examples portraying the importance of emotional investment in objects, notably books, but one brief passage deserves particular attention. In a description of the New England ministry, the narrator takes a moment to mention an example of their "many forms of literary labor" (378). The "specimen" that the narrator singles out looks like a clear case of piracy: "it is recorded of the Rev. Mr. Taylor of Westfield, that he took such delight in the writings of Origen, that, being unable to purchase them, he copied them in four quarto volumes, that he might have them for his own study. These are still in the possession of his descendants. Other instances of literary perseverance and devotion, equally curious, might be cited" (378). While one might expect that Stowe would be disinclined to praise such piracy, the language of the passage indicates that those same qualities that make the reverend's behavior "curious" are also endearing. The care with which Rev. Taylor copies these documents, an act which is, on the one hand, an almost humorous kind of "literary perseverance," and on the other is a measure of "devotion," seems to excite Stowe's admiration. What he produces are heirlooms, objects of his own delight that are now passed down through the family.

Stowe draws a fine yet clear line regarding acceptable literary piracy. The cheap texts produced by most illicit reprinters would rarely survive through generations, and they certainly did not require the same kind of time and effort to produce. They entailed little financial or emotional investment on the part of either the publisher or producer. While these cheap books, despite the scarce sentimental appeal they might offer to the refined home, might be all that some people can afford, Stowe here presents another option for the oft-mentioned "poor farmers" that made frequent appearances in discussions of literary property rights. If people really cannot afford to purchase books, Stowe seems to say, they can, in fact, still acquire them without loss of virtue, although the process is remarkably tedious. It is difficult to imagine hand-copying *Dred,* for example. Still, if one wanted truly to *possess* a book, with all of the emotional investment that the word implied for Stowe, this would be the course one would take if one truly could not afford an authorized edition, or, better yet, a handsomely bound holiday edition. Only then could one possess a text that would live on, a sacred relic of the life and relationships that had been built around it.

THE SENTIMENTAL(IZED) AUTHOR-OWNER

Throughout her New England novels, Stowe emphasizes the emotional connection between objects and owners. Books serve particularly well as vehicles for the kind of sentimentality that fuels what becomes, in Merish's words, an almost consensual relationship of ownership. The novel that is copyrighted, well printed and well bound, appears ready to provide itself as an object to be owned and cherished for generations. In addition to a discourse that employs sentimentality to domesticate the consumption of novels, as Merish describes it, Stowe creates in her novels a model for the possession of novels. Gillian Brown notes, "The love of things that Stowe advocates exceeds and even nullifies consumerist desire by imagining a reciprocity between persons and their possessions, by seeing them as contiguous and congruent. Ownership, which takes things out of the market and keeps them in the home, confers this congruence" (116). As an author, Stowe would have found this distinction between consumption and ownership crucial. While she helped shape the larger rhetoric of sentimentality that was fueling the expanding commercial culture, it did not provide any means of distinguishing between legitimate objects and those that were produced illegally or unfairly. It also did not leave much room for the author as a literary owner. The emphasis on care that appears throughout Stowe's work not only formed an implicit argument for the kinds and qualities of objects, texts included, that one should purchase, but it also offered a rationale for her own much derided defense of her literary property. If seen more as a sentimental owner of property, pouring her heart and soul into her literary objects, rather than as a producer, then Stowe's actions in defense of her property rights have a kind of sentimentalized justification. Who could fault her for striving to protect such an important part of her emotional life?

This is, of course, the importance of the early portrayals of Stowe preparing her novels while simultaneously engaged in raising the children and performing her domestic duties. Like the grandmother's pile of favorite books beside her work-basket, Stowe's works are part of her inner life. To take them unfairly, or to expect that she would not defend them, would be the worst kind of crime. Well-known biographer James Parton employed a similar logic when he used Stowe as his major example in his 1868 article in support of international copyright. Besides her well-known authorship of *Uncle Tom's Cabin*, Parton emphasizes Stowe's activities as a homemaker. First, he offers a catalogue of Stowe's domestic duties, framing them in terms of public service: "She pays her taxes, keeps the peace, and earns her livelihood by honest industry; she has reared children for the service of the Commonwealth" (95). Her writing, like her tax-paying, is a civic duty.

While such a description serves to offer an almost patriotic defense of Stowe's authorial rights, Parton goes further, describing authorship also as a kind of domestic work. In doing so, he suggests that those who have purchased copies of her novels now have a "personal obligation" to its author:

> The person who afforded this great pleasure, and who brought home this fundamental truth ["the great truth that man is not fit to be trusted with arbitrary power over his fellow"] to so many minds, was Harriet Beecher Stowe, of Hartford, in the State of Connecticut, where she keeps house, educates her children, has a book at the grocery, and invites her friends to tea. To that American woman every person on earth who read 'Uncle Tom's Cabin' incurred a personal obligation. Every individual who became possessed of a copy of the book, and every one who saw the story played in a theatre, was bound, in natural justice, to pay money to her for service rendered, unless she expressly and formally relinquished her right,—which she has never done. (97–8)

Here, his description becomes much more intimate. Rather than emphasizing her role as an author, Parton highlights those parts of her personal life that fit the sentimental depiction of domestic womanhood. The obligation of readers, he suggests, is not personal simply because of the individual enjoyment they have taken from Stowe's work; by "humanizing" her, Parton makes the purchasing of her books a personal interaction. Writing books is of a piece with raising children, keeping house, going to the grocery store. It is as much a part of her domestic life as it is that of the reader who keeps the book on his or her bedside table. The creation, consumption, and possession of books carry with them a considerable amount of personal and sentimental weight.

Harriet Beecher Stowe herself never became a very public advocate for changes in the copyright law. Still, her literary success focused America's attention on the problem of literary piracy, and her indefatigable efforts to protect her rights demonstrate just how far authors had to go—both in the world and in their works—to protect their rights. Her failure to provide a liberating alternative to sentimental ownership in *Dred* indicates how her support of property rights conflicted with her strongly held abolitionism. Stowe was far from the only one to fail to recognize the fallacy of equating the struggles over literary possession with slavery, or, at any rate, to offer a sentimental defense of property relations that did not overlap with interpersonal relations. Still, her determination to overcome numerous personal and professional hardships and pursue authorship as a career and her skill in portraying books as an integral part of the domestic scene positioned women writers and sentimental fiction within the discourse of literary property rights. Rather than a rejection of the literary marketplace, Stowe's works attempt to recast the buying and selling of texts in sentimental terms, emphasizing emotional attachment and moral ownership as central components of the trade. One must purchase books with care and with an eye towards the future, preserving texts as prized possessions. For Stowe, ownership always has the potential to become memorialization; both Mary Scudder and Horace inherit their fathers' books. Purchasing cheap, unauthorized reprints of novels, Stowe might have said, would be a truly heartless act.

Chapter Three

'Doing as we would be done by': Walt Whitman, Copyright, and Democratic Exchange

A VEXING CONTRADICTION?

Like Stowe, Walt Whitman's writings and his personal dealings with copyright make the poet vulnerable to accusations of hypocrisy. Critics have largely sidestepped the potentially thorny relationship between the poet's financial transactions and his poetic ideals. Despite careful consideration of Whitman's publishing career, little has been said regarding his views on copyright and the apparent contradiction between the poet's now-famous declaration of 1855, "I celebrate myself, / And what I assume you shall assume, / For every atom belonging to me as good belongs to you" (*Walt Whitman: Poetry and Prose*[1] 27) and his staunch defense of his literary property rights.[2] The omission is most glaring when we consider how Whitman's support of an international copyright law put him in direct opposition to printers, bookbinders, and typesetters—the very artisans Whitman so often aligned himself with in his writing—who argued strenuously against such a law for over fifty years.

Such a contradiction is not simply a matter of artistic beliefs diverging from professional realities. Taking out a copyright would have had serious implications for a poet whose philosophy was built on the notion that the poem belonged as much to the reader as the poet and, furthermore, that the book was more than a book: "Camerado, this is no book, / Who touches this touches a man" (611). Taken at face value, Whitman's careful tending of his copyrights appears not only to contradict his democratic declarations, but also to trouble his bold assertions of artistic independence. By scrupulously protecting his copyrights, Whitman turns to an institutional mechanism to ensure control of his "embodied" text. Copyright would seem literally to guarantee self-possession instead of encouraging the scattering and diffusion of his words on which his poetic identity was based. Yet despite these apparent inconsistencies, a closer examination of Whitman's concerns with copyright—both with the controversy that raged throughout his literary life over international copyright, as well as his own occasionally tangled business dealings—reveals how Whitman viewed copyright not as a necessary evil of publishing or a necessity of self-interest, but as an essential element of the open, democratic exchange he attempted to foster through his poetry.

Whitman was aware of the appearance of contradiction between his feelings about copyright and his poetic ideals. On March 5, 1891, two days after the United States Congress passed what was referred to as the international copyright bill, Horace Traubel recorded Whitman's response:

> We have our international copyright at last—the bill is signed today. The United States, which should have been the first to pass the thing, is the last. Now all civilized nations have it. It is a question of honesty—of morals—of a literature, in fact. I know it will be said by some—Here, now, how is it that you, Walt Whitman, author of 'Leaves of Grass,' are in favor of such a thing? Ought the world not to own the world in common? Well, when others do, we will, too. This copyright bill is the doing as we would be done by. (8: 54–5)

The somewhat grumpy pragmatism evident in Whitman's "do unto others" defense of his views is offset by the revelation that the international copyright law was more than a business matter for Whitman; it was "a question of honesty—of morals—of a literature, in fact." His observation that the United States should have taken the lead in passing the copyright law indicates how he saw the issue tied to broader democratic principles. These remarks echo statements he had written in support of international copyright, both publicly and privately, for nearly fifty years, beginning during his days as a journalist and continuing throughout his years as author of *Leaves of Grass*.[3] While many authors supported such a law, Whitman's view of copyright as a key component of his democratic beliefs and poetic practice is more reminiscent of Cooper and distinguishes the poet from authors like James Russell Lowell who saw it largely as a matter of fair trade.[4] More than a question of self-interest, copyright was truly a "question of a literature" for Whitman, and, as with so many other questions, *Leaves of Grass* represents his best efforts at an answer. The intersection of his artistic and business practices, therefore, reveals how he worked to transform the copyright page of *Leaves of Grass* from simply a legal necessity to an integral part of his poetic project.[5]

Like Cooper and Stowe, Whitman grappled with many of the arguments used by copyright opponents and the implications these arguments
held for his work. Three major lines of argument that persist throughout the
controversy require particular attention when considering Whitman's views
on the matter. While these lines often converge and intersect with one another, they offer a framework from which we can examine the poet's views.
The first, as one might expect, was the issue of fair treatment of authors publishing works in other countries, predominantly in the United States, Great
Britain, and Canada. As we have seen, this component of the debate received
a great deal of publicity, particularly during the antebellum years, and it is
the one that Whitman addressed directly in his writing for the *Evening Tattler* and the *Brooklyn Evening Star* during the 1840s. The second, and the one
that most often caused Congress to strike down international copyright laws,
concerned the oft-stated fears of monopoly power, on the part of both the
author and powerful publishing houses. As Cooper predicted it would in the
1820s, this issue of monopoly power led many trade organizations of printers, type-founders, and bookbinders to oppose passage of these bills. Recon-
ciling the resulting opposition between Whitman as author and Whitman as
defender of the artisan class is an important part of understanding his relation to international copyright. Finally, the third issue that rests at the heart
of the copyright controversy is the question of definition: what is the product being copyrighted? How is the literary work defined in these arguments
about possession, monopoly, and relations between nations? When we consider Whitman's attempts to embody himself in his text, this concern with
the nature of textuality itself becomes important to understanding his feelings regarding the role of copyright.

GIVING DICKENS HIS DUE: WHITMAN'S BUDDING VIEWS

When we consider the question of fair treatment for foreign authors, we
must return to Dickens, who was in his own estimation "the greatest loser by
the existing [American copyright] Law, alive" (qtd. in Moss 3). As a journalist in New York in the 1840s, Whitman was well aware of the author's visit to
the United States in 1842 and the intense criticism Dickens suffered after
speaking publicly about the issue of international copyright (2).[6] Despite
claiming to want nothing more than enough for an "honourable subsistence"
(qtd. in Welsh 31), Dickens was unable to shield himself from accusations of
greed, as is clear in this passage from the *Morning Courier and New York
Enquirer:* "Mr. Dickens . . . has made an appeal to his hosts in behalf of a law
to secure him a certain amount in *dollars and cents* for his writings. We are

. . . mortified and grieved that he should have been guilty of such great indelicacy and gross impropriety" (qtd. in Moss 3).

Similar sentiments were voiced in *The United States Magazine and Democratic Review*[7] a year later: "He [Dickens] has certainly been richly enough paid at home, in pecuniary rewards as well as in public honor, for what he has done, to leave him but slender ground on which to ask a return of mere volunteer generosity on our part for the pleasure his admirable writings have afforded us. How is he injured if we do enjoy that pleasure, free as his home market is left from interference by our republications" ("International" 120). This passage is taken from an article that argues against international copyright, offering a solution other than establishing laws to ensure payment to authors from abroad: "Individuals may, if they choose, volunteer to a great foreign author from whose labors they have derived pleasure and instruction, any tribute of their gratitude they choose" (121). In this way, Dickens' arguments were overturned: he had already received ample rewards for his work at home, and if he were looking for some sort of compensation for his books when published abroad, he would find such compensation more honorable when given voluntarily.

Such responses were appearing in newspapers before Dickens had even left the States (Welsh 32), and, when he returned home, he circulated an angry letter in the London papers criticizing American opponents of international copyright. Shortly afterwards, Whitman, perhaps unknowingly, reproduced a forged "second" letter by Dickens, in an editorial he wrote for the *Evening Tattler* in August of 1842 entitled "Boz's Opinions of Us" (Moss 106).[8] The tone of the letter was such that other editors, even those who reproduced it, quickly denounced it as a "hoax"; one editor (who had published it earlier) wrote that the forger "deserves to be rode on a rail" (qtd. in Moss 109). Dickens, who refused to reply publicly, wrote to a friend, "When I tilt at such wringings-out of the dirtiest morality, I shall be another man indeed—almost the creature they would make me" (qtd. in Moss 109).

Given Dickens' tone and the rush of other editors to reveal the forgery, one would expect that the Whitman editorial first introducing it featured a blistering attack on the English writer. Indeed, at first the article offers a negative assessment of Dickens. Whitman begins by noting, "How sadly we have been disappointed" (*Journalism* 148). However, he seems more than a little ambivalent: it is clear that he disapproves of the tone of what he supposes to be Dickens' critique, but he seems to find other parts of the forged letter admirable.[9] In responding to the letter, Whitman takes the opportunity to state his own position regarding the copyright question, and the introduction of this position seems to shift the direction of the entire piece:

> Let Boz—ungrateful as he has proved himself—let him be treated fairly. He no doubt came over here with the main purpose of effecting an international copyright: we are among those who believe that a law to that effect would be wise and righteous. He did not succeed in this scheme: he sees the American government, having the *power* to take advantage of the labor of foreign authors without remuneration, meanly, (as he thinks) shuffle off from giving those authors their due. Boz, too, cannot look upon the United States with any but English eyes; his likings, habits, uses, and tastes are not as ours. Therefore it is, that we say, let justice be done the man, and let all this go in palliation of his still unpardonable insolence. (148)

His criticism of Dickens is strangely muted here: Dickens' views are largely a result of a different perspective—he has different "tastes." Whitman casts doubt on Dickens' view of the government's abuse of power only in a parenthetical aside, and one that only points out that this is Dickens' opinion—"(as he thinks)"—not that the opinion is incorrect. As for the novelist's call for international copyright, the poet describes such a law as "wise and righteous." It is difficult to determine in this passage what exactly he disapproves of here. He offers no defense of the government in response to Dickens' criticism, and, in light of his stated opinion on the matter of copyright, his silence seems a tacit agreement with Dickens' critique. In fact, by the end of this passage, the accusation of "unpardonable insolence" seems out of place.

This sense of disjunction is heightened by the next line of the article: "One part of his letters, we especially like. It is that wherein he speaks of his having been sought after merely as a subject for curiosity," and then in the next paragraph, "Another thing we cotton to in the letter. It is where he cuts into the flimsiness of our American aristocracy. Reader, look over that part of the epistle twice" (148). When we consider this continual agreement with Dickens in addition to the fact that Whitman reproduces the entire letter, nearly twice as long as his response to it, it becomes clear that he is much more in accord with what he imagines to be "Boz's opinions" than he first seems. His position on the copyright law serves as a way for Whitman to address not only issues of international fairness but also issues of social equality touching closer to home, particularly bearing on the current state of the American elites. He does not develop his argument against the "flimsiness of American aristocracy" in this article. However, as we well know, the poet would lodge his own protest against exclusion a few years later in his all-inclusive *Leaves of Grass*. What is notable here is that for Whitman, the question of copyright was not only about financial equity for authors like Dickens, but it also urged reflection on larger social and economic issues in the United States.

This is not unexpected, for the lack of an international copyright had as great an impact in the U.S. as it did on authors overseas. As the century progressed, those pushing for the law did not simply support it on behalf of authors from other countries. There was an equally strong sense that it would benefit American writers forced to compete with cheap re-prints of popular English novels. It was this unfair competition that prompted Whitman to address the question of international copyright once again in an article entitled "How Literature Is Paid Here" written for the *Brooklyn Evening Star* in 1846: "At this time there is hardly any encouragement at all for the literary profession in the way of book-writing. Most of our authors are frittering away their brains for an occasional five dollar bill from the magazine publishers" (*Journalism* 252). As a writer frequently publishing short stories during this time,[10] he would have found the issue of how magazines paid their writers one of particular personal importance.

Evidence exists that Whitman continued to consider the impact an international copyright law would have on American writers. His name is one of the final signatures on a memorial in favor of international copyright. Although the memorial is undated, the presence of Samuel Clemens' signature (alongside the parenthetical "Mark Twain") indicates that it was possibly written in the 1870s. The text of the memorial that Whitman signed off on is as follows:

> The undersigned American citizens who earn their living in whole or in part by their pen, and who are put at disadvantage in their own country by the publication of foreign books without payment to the author, so that American books are undersold in the American market, to the detriment of American Literature, urge the passage by Congress of an International Copyright Law, which will protect the rights of authors, and will enable American writers to ask from foreign nations the justice we shall then no longer deny on our own part. (*Memorial* n.p.)

While Whitman would have surely enjoyed appearing on a list that included not only Clemens and Louisa May Alcott, but also Henry Ward Beecher, he would also have had no problem with the sentiments of this petition. Throughout his career, he continued to take a realistic view of how an international copyright would benefit American authors, including him.

INTERNATIONAL COPYRIGHT AND DEMOCRACY

Although Whitman continually considered the advantages such a law would have for American authors, his views on international copyright also encompassed larger concerns for the nation and fairness for authors from other nations. Sometime during 1871, Whitman drafted a piece entitled "Washington as a central winter residence" on Department of Justice stationery (*Notebooks*, 2: 912)[11] in which he catalogues the strengths of Washington D.C. as a "first-class winter residence" and argues that "Washington is gradually and we think surely forming a distinctive metropolitan American Character" (912). What is interesting is that in the midst of this celebration of the city and its personages, Whitman takes the time to address international copyright as something that would contribute to the capital's prominence:

> The series of Presidential & Cabinet receptions, forming a continued
> brilliant, exhilarating, democratic spectacle
> Headquarters of the Army
> Diplomatic representatives and their families & staffs
> —The gay spectacle on the avenue of a fine day—the numerous first
> class horses
> in teams or single harness—a peculiar attraction
> The botanical garden and numerous-conservatories
>   International copyright would be a benefit to Washington
> Already many foreign authors visit here—
> Our musical society takes the prize in the New York [*illeg.*] Upon the
> whole, the prospect is that there must gradually grow up here a central
> winter residence, social, literary, political musical & scientific, which
> will view [vie?] with that
>   of any capital in Europe. (915–16)

This passage comes at the end of a long list of notable Washington residents (including Whitman himself) and marks a noticeable shift in the text: the tribute here turns visual, as the repetition of the word "spectacle" suggests. The interjection of international copyright into this spectacle, highlighted by the indentation of the line, suggests that the benefit it would have for the city would be in some way to integrate more equally the foreign authors who are "already" a part of the "democratic" scene. While at the beginning of this piece Whitman lauds the "metropolitan American Character," at the conclusion he seems to suggest that this character, this democratic spectacle, must be at the same time a cosmopolitan one.

To form this character, the poet suggests that foreign authors must be able to thrive just as the "numerous conservatories" and the "musical society" of Washington have thrived, making the capital a winter residence not just for Americans, but also for foreign authors. Thus "international copyright would be a benefit to Washington," because it would allow foreign authors an equal place in the democratic mix of artists, politicians, and scientists that Whitman describes, developing the distinctively cosmopolitan "metropolitan American Character" so important to him. The endorsement of international copyright here seems completely divorced from his personal business interests. Whitman emphasizes the law's importance to his vision of a democratic metropolis that includes equal treatment of foreign authors.[12]

Throughout his time in Washington, Whitman seems to have kept a close eye on the copyright debate. In March of 1872 he wrote to a British correspondent, "It looks just now as though some form of international copyright might be legalized here—If so, this might be worth considering in reference to the reprint of my book in England" (*Correspondence* 6; 10). He attached a *New York Tribune* article referring to a possible law to his letter (10n). Despite the hopes of Whitman and others, the Joint Committee on the Library issued an unfavorable report on the issue of copyright in 1873, citing deep concerns regarding the bill, particularly as it touched on trade issues: "The printers, type-founders, binders, paper-makers, and others engaged in the manufacture of books, in large numbers remonstrate against the measure as calculated to diminish the popular sale and circulation of books, by raising the price thereof, and thus prejudicial to this branch of industry" (Morrill 2). This fear that international copyright would harm American industries had always been and continued to be the primary source of opposition to the law: "Opponents of copyright believed that a law would give to a handful of powerful eastern firms with large resources and European contacts an effective monopoly on the reprinting of foreign books" (Eaton 109). The rise in prices, the feared inaccessibility of texts, and the perceptions of monopoly power all combined to make international copyright an immensely unpopular law for the majority of tradesmen.

Whitman removed his call for international copyright from the 1871 article that emerged from the manuscript, but he persisted in articulating the importance of such a law for American democracy in his description of the interplay of national and international interests in *Democratic Vistas*, written the same year. There Whitman wrote that in addition to the benefits to be found in heroes and great events,

even greater would it be to possess the aggregation of a cluster of
mighty poets, artists, teachers, fit for us, national expressers, compre-
hending and effusing for the men and women of the United States,
what is universal, native, common to all, inland and seaboard, northern and southern. The historians say of ancient Greece, with her ever-
jealous autonomies, cities, and states, that the only positive unity she
ever own'd or receiv'd, was the sad unity of a common subjection, at
the last, to foreign conquerors. (*WW* 959)

Democratic Vistas is in one sense turned inward toward the divisions within
the United States, seeking to reconcile the rift left by the Civil War. However, the text is also quite expansive: Whitman writes that the great American poets would "fuse" "contributions, races, far localities, &c" (959). It is
clear that isolationism had no place in his views of democracy. The har-
mony in which the preferred poets could express "what is universal, native,"
seems similar to the kind of harmonious vision Whitman has of Washington, a distinctly American metropolis that is at the same time cosmopolitan.
The allusion to ancient Greece is particularly powerful here: the danger
from foreign invaders comes not from trafficking with outsiders, but from
"ever-jealous autonomies." If the United States wished to avoid ancient
Greece's eventual subjection, the poet suggests, it must resist privileging and
protecting the "native" at the *expense* of engaging other nations. Although
not addressing the issue in any specific way, his description seems a refutation of the protectionist inclinations commonly held by many who opposed
international copyright.

At the same time, despite his strong belief in open exchange and free
trade, Whitman knew that the lack of international copyright had *created* a
kind of "subjection [. . .] to foreign conquerors" as American authors struggled to compete with cheap republications of foreign works. His frustration
emerges elsewhere in *Democratic Vistas*. In calling for a truly American literature, a "New World literature," Whitman anticipates his readers' questions:

Are we not doing well enough here already? Are not the United States
this day busily using, working, more printer's type, more presses, than
any other country? uttering and absorbing more publications than any
other? Do not our publishers fatten quicker and deeper? (helping
themselves, under shelter of a delusive and sneaking law, or rather
absence of law, to most of their forage, poetical, pictorial, historical,
romantic, even comic, without money and without price—and fiercely
resisting the timidest proposal to pay for it.) (*WW* 995)

This is some of the sharpest language Whitman had employed in published writing on copyright issues since his editorials in the 1840s. Both tradeworkers and authors are absent in this description of the thriving publishing industry: while it is the entire United States "uttering and absorbing" texts, only the publishers "fatten quicker and deeper." Whitman's language suggests not theft so much as deception: the lack of an international copyright law is "delusive and sneaking." This proves to be a constant in his writings about literary piracy: unauthorized reprinting represents the antithesis of democracy, denying honest connection and open competition. Publishers here are not producers—a class that Whitman is happy to celebrate in his work—but rather foragers, refusing to pay fairly for their spoils.

In calling for a "native" literature, Whitman struggles with how to deal with foreign writers. It is clear that he did not seek literary isolationism: his calls for international copyright always allude to fair treatment and open exchange, and he often speaks highly of writers like Sir Walter Scott. Still, in *Democratic Vistas,* he fluctuates between his desire to praise those European writers who had so greatly influenced American writers and markets and his desire to decry them. He writes of Europe's classic texts, "Gather'd by geniuses of city, race or age, and put by them in highest of art's forms, namely, the literary form, the peculiar combinations and the outshows of that city, its particular modes of universal attributes and passions [. . .]— what they supply, indispensable and highest, if taken away, nothing else in all the world's boundless storehouses could make up to us, or ever again return" (997). This sense of European literature offering an indispensable universality is quite different from Whitman's claim elsewhere in his essay that such literature is, in fact, a poison to America's democratic artists and ideals:

> The great poems, Shakspere included, are poisonous to the idea of the pride and dignity of the common people, the life-blood of democracy. The models of our literature, as we get it from other lands, ultramarine, have had their birth in courts, and bask'd and grown in castle sunshine; all smells of princes' favors. Of workers of a certain sort, we have, indeed, plenty, contributing after their kind; many elegant, many learn'd, all complacent. But touch'd by the national test, or tried by the standards of democratic personality, they wither to ashes. (979)

The contradictions that mark Whitman's writing on foreign literature were not unusual in the copyright debate. Samuel Clemens would later fluctuate between hope that the influx of cheap reprints of European classic texts would be a boon for American education and despair in his belief that the literature that was being imported, including works by Scott, was poisoning the minds of American readers. Whitman, who never viewed copyright as a barrier to exclude European writers, nevertheless struggled with the relationship between the heavy influence of pirated texts and the difficulties American writers faced finding publishers and an audience for their works.

The poet offers a striking alternative to embracing or rejecting those influential foreign texts and writers. In an address to a broad range of influential artists and thinkers from other countries, Whitman exclaims,

> Ye powerful and resplendent ones! ye were, in your atmospheres, grown not for America, but rather for her foes, the feudal and the old—while our genius is democratic and modern. Yet could ye, indeed, but breathe your breath of life into our New World's nostrils—not to enslave us, as now, but, for our needs, to breed a spirit like your own—perhaps, (dare we to say it?) to dominate, even destroy, what you yourselves have left! On your plane, and no less, but even higher and wider, must we mete and measure for to-day and here. I demand races of orbic bards, with unconditional and uncompromising sway. Come forth, sweet democratic despots of the west! (998)

What he appears to imagine is something akin to a battle to be waged on an equal footing. Rather than simply calling for the exclusion of foreign texts, he calls for American writers who can incorporate those texts and grow beyond them: "On your plane, and no less, but even higher and wider, must we mete and measure for to-day and here." He has no doubts regarding the outcome of such a contest if only the American artists can incorporate the world literature that has informed and nourished them: the result will be a new generation of writers who can wield even more influence than the European literary giants that preceded them. The irony of the final sentence once again encapsulates Whitman's contradictory stance: the writer who has such force that he or she will be able to consume and overcome the weight of foreign influence must emerge a "sweet democratic despot," forwarding the causes of democracy while simultaneously able to shape opinions and minds with "uncompromising sway."

Such a sweeping charge for American artists does not demand that these authors forego any pecuniary benefits. Whitman asserts that democratic idealism and financial success are not diametrically opposed. Like Cooper, the poet argues that property ownership is one of the fundamental components of a true democracy. In doing so, he concedes that this view may seem "paradoxical":

[. . .] ungracious as it may sound, and a paradox after what we have been saying, democracy looks with suspicious, ill-satisfied eye upon the very poor, the ignorant, and on those out of business. She asks for men and women with occupations, well-off, owners of houses and acres, and with cash in the bank—and with some cravings for literature, too; and must have them, and hastens to make them. (975)

Whitman was always conscious of moments when he was making statements that might strike his readers, particularly those familiar with his work, as contradictory. Such awareness is evident here. His insistence on ownership, work, and wealth, with only "some cravings for literature," appears far afield from his more idealistic calls for a national literature. Still, Whitman insists that, despite the apparent paradox, his poetic message is in no way removed from these more materialistic considerations. In a note to the above passage, he writes,

For fear of mistake, I may as well distinctly specify, as cheerfully included in the model and standard of these Vistas, a practical, stirring, worldly, money-making, even materialistic character. [. . .] My theory includes riches, and the getting of riches, and the amplest products, power, activity, inventions, movements, &c. Upon them, as upon substrata, I raise the edifice design'd in these Vistas. (975)

Whitman always took the side of inclusion, so, on one level, despite his "fear of mistake," his call for including the pursuit of wealth in his "Vistas" is in keeping with his poetic philosophy. It also appears that the poet is deliberately including as a base the "money-making" and "amplest products" that must support American artists, a bold proposition when one recalls the frequent attacks on authors and copyright advocates that depicted them as undemocratic and motivated by greed.[13] The writer who sought to protect his or her copyright and to benefit from it would not be, in Whitman's view, anti-democratic. The capitalist spirit he applauds here is in direct contrast to the "free forage and theft" (996) practiced by the publishers of the day. Those publishers taking a profit that they have not earned are the ones violating the poet's principles, despite their claims to be aiding the education of America's readers. Whitman's theory of democracy has ample room for both competition and financial gain, provided both are marked by openness and honesty.

In later years, the poet was moved by similar logic to oppose proposed tariffs on imported goods in the late 1880s. He remarked to Traubel, "No man is a democrat, a true democrat, who forgets that he is interested in the welfare of the race. [. . .] Is a man a citizen of Camden only? No—no indeed. And if not of Camden, not of New Jersey, nor even of America. No—no—no—no: a man is no democrat if he takes the narrow in preference to the broad view" (2; 55). Traubel reports another evening when the subject came up at a dinner party. The poet said,

> We ought to invite the world through an open door—all men—yes, even the criminals—giving to everyone a chance—a new outlook. My God! are men always to go on clawing each other—always to go on taxing, stealing, warring, having a class to exclude and a class excluded—always to go on having favorite races, favorite castes—a few people with money here and there—all the rest without anything everywhere? That is what the tariff—the spirit of the tariff—means. Chatto and Windus printed Leaves of Grass in England—pirated it— never even sent me a copy of the book until Rossetti suggested they should do so. The book came—the books—and I was taxed for duties. Yes, three dollars and a half. (1; 99)

Whitman's sudden reference to the Hotten piracy, the first unauthorized reprinting of *Leaves of Grass* in Great Britain (he mistakenly refers to Hotten's successors here), indicates the connections he saw between literary piracy and the "spirit of the tariff." More than the duty Whitman had to pay when he was sent the pirated copies, it was the exclusion from the process that angered him; the publishers had "never even sent [him] a copy." The tariff, like the lack of international copyright, gave some groups of people an unfair advantage in the marketplace, sowing hostility. Whitman always took the broader view, insisting that democracy went beyond protecting the national interest from competition and that laws should not be written simply to give American workers an advantage. In his words, everyone should be given "a chance."

His strong feelings regarding the tariff and international copyright put him at odds with large segments of America's working class, this despite the fact that he always sought his truest connection with workers, particularly the printers and those in the trade where he had once served as an apprentice. This seems a bit confusing, but it may in fact be representative of the way Whitman tried to form what M. Wynn Thomas describes as "an ideal" that "was in turn an amalgam of the two worlds Whitman had known—the mutuality which characterized artisan republican and commonwealth ideals being grafted (sometimes easily, sometimes distinctly uneasily) onto the expansive opportunities (but not the opportunism) of the competitive and libertarian free enterprise system" (30). On the one hand, Whitman clearly was in sympathy with the artisans who were such an important part of his development. His close association with the workers, the tradesmen, those who felt dispossessed by the rapid industrial advances,

> flowed quite naturally from the historical experience of that specific social group to which Whitman belonged, both by origin and by conscious allegiance—an experience of being subject to social, economic, and political processes beyond their control, which eventually revolutionized every aspect of their lives, and to which the victims affixed the emotive term 'monopoly.' (27)

On the other hand, Whitman was well aware of the new opportunities and advancements being provided by economic development, and this development included increased trade with international markets. His method of bringing these two worlds together provides us with a means of seeing how, in dealing with international copyright, he does not join those who cry "monopoly" but instead stands against them. As we have already seen, his position is not a result of simple personal interest: we must keep in mind that Whitman's first statement in favor of international copyright came thirteen years before the publication of *Leaves of Grass* and even predates the publication of his temperance novel *Franklin Evans* in November of 1842.[14]

As Thomas has pointed out, the concept of monopoly holds a specific place in Whitman's vision, as suggested by this line from the Preface to the 1855 edition of *Leaves of Grass:* "The American bards shall be marked for generosity and affection and for encouraging competitors . . They shall be kosmos . . without monopoly or secrecy . . glad to pass anything to any one . . hungry for equals night and day" (qtd. in Thomas 73). Here, as in his stated views on copyright, the poet emphasizes the importance of equality, an equality that does not exclude competition, but rather includes competitors who would encourage one another in their hunger "for equals." Such encouragement also figures in Whitman's earlier call for fair treatment not only of underpaid American writers, but also Charles Dickens. The American bard does not thrive by squelching competition, but by meeting it openly and generously. Monopoly, on the other hand, suggests selfishness, and its true evil is that, since it is paired with secrecy, it precludes fair and open participation, even if that participation comes in the form of market competition.

Thomas has also noted this structure: "In a society based on competi-tive individualism there is a distinct advantage in concealing one's assets and one's intentions. Whitman's frankness, in itself an appeal for a reciprocal frankness, is an open challenge to this closed, clam-tight 'system of selfish-ness'" (46). In the unregulated world of literary piracy, authors are clearly excluded from open exchange both with publishers and with readers who are given access to texts not approved by their writers. It seems likely that this exclusion would be a more evil form of monopoly for Whitman, while many of the fears held by tradesmen over international copyright revolved not around exclusion, but the notion of potentially unfair competition. Thomas has argued that such a view of monopoly and competition ultimately pro-duces a "queer mismatch between Whitman's economic and his social theo-ries. Somehow or other a system of untrammeled economic competition is supposed to produce a harmoniously cooperative and egalitarian social order" (77). In light of this contradiction, Thomas has suggested that Whit-man employed his poetry to deal with "unattractive realities" of the expand-ing capitalist culture surrounding him (78). While Thomas offers a compelling reading of Whitman's poetry to support this view, it seems clear that Whitman's publishing practices and his approach to copyright also rep-resent persistent attempts to overcome the contradiction between his social and economic views by emphasizing the connection between tradesmen, authors, and readers in place of the profit-driven self-interest he felt was coming to dominate society.

Whitman always maneuvered to be connected with, if not always in complete control of, his texts, and throughout his career he tended to avoid the larger publishing houses that were frequently at odds with the printers and other tradesmen of the time. Ezra Greenspan provides a good account of what little is known about the original publication of *Leaves of Grass;* without turning to a large firm like Harpers (perhaps, given the material, this would have been impossible), "Whitman was thrown back on his own resources, and with a curious symmetry he returned full circle to the kind of small, local printing office in which he had done his apprenticeship two decades before" (*Walt Whitman* 83). Whitman quite literally aligned himself with the smaller printing establishments that likely were those most opposed to inter-national copyright, or at least to the perceived advantage such a measure would grant to larger firms.

This connection was embodied in the printing process, as Greenspan points out: "He even took an occasional turn at setting his unusually long lines of verse into print" (84). For Whitman, writing and publishing were not clearly demarcated activities. He always worked to be an active participant in the printing of his texts: "Beginning with the 1855 edition and continuing throughout his publishing life, Whitman would write in closer relation to printers and printerly considerations than would virtually any of his more conventionally trained, conventionally published contemporaries" (85). His experience would have offered him a unique double perspective on the copyright question: he clearly advocates the kind of authorial control that the law provides, but for Whitman that control always meant a closer working relationship with printers. The issue was open connection, not secretive monopolies. Just as he felt that American democracy could foster native authors even as it provided fair treatment for foreign authors, his publishing practices collapsed the kind of author/printer/publisher oppositions that remained at the center of the monopoly dispute.

The greatest bond he sought, of course, was with his readers. This was fostered not only by his printing practices, but also by the process of economic exchange itself. Only copyright could guarantee Whitman's place in this exchange between the reader who purchases the book and the writer who produces it. In his discussion of labor and figures of authorship in nineteenth-century America, Michael Newbury uses the image of the market in *The Scarlet Letter* to illustrate the changing nature of the reader/writer relationship. He writes, "we can see in this marketplace not any realization of monetary or exchange relations between the public figure and his audience, but a relationship more fully realized in terms of the public figure's corporal and spiritual sacrifice of self for consumption" (102). Newbury's argument is persuasive, particularly in terms of his discussion of "reluctant" celebrities such as Hawthorne and his various "veiled" literary figures, whose audiences became as interested in the hidden lives of the authors and performers as with the texts and performances themselves. Yet when we consider Whitman, it becomes impossible to separate the process of monetary exchange and corporal offering: as the poet himself repeatedly suggests, it is exactly his body that he is offering for sale to his readers.[15] For Whitman, then, copyright played the additional role of metonymic guarantee: it assured the reader that he or she was getting a "true" manifestation of the writer, as well as guaranteeing that the money that passed from the reader's hand would in some measure arrive in the hand of the writer, linking the two.[16] Piracy corrupts this exchange: the reader purchases a book that is not an authentic product of the writer (quite often the texts underwent unauthorized changes), and the money given in return for the text is not given to the one who writes it. Some measure of equilibrium could be restored with communication and exchange—exactly what copyright laws, as opposed to secretive monopolies, were meant to reinforce.

PIRACY AND POETIC IDEALS:
THE HOTTEN AND WORTHINGTON PRINTINGS

Whitman's experience with the British publisher John Camden Hotten during the late 1860s and early 1870s demonstrated to the poet the necessity of a legal mechanism to ensure metonymic contact with his readers. Hotten was a notorious "pirate" publisher and a nemesis of American authors like Samuel Clemens. He produced two versions of Whitman's poetry: the first, a book of selections from *Leaves of Grass* edited by William Michael Rossetti, and the second, a complete edition of *Leaves* published a few years later and forged to make it seem as if it were published in and exported from the United States. As Morton D. Paley describes in his thorough recounting of the history of Hotten's publication of Whitman, in the beginning the poet entered into negotiations with the publisher under the notion that he could strike a fair deal. In fact, a friend in London wrote to him in October of 1867 that, since he could not effectively stop the publisher from producing an edited text, he would be better off doing business with him:

> Just as I was beginning to consult about [printing a complete edition of *Leaves* in Great Britain] I found that John Camden Hotten had already contracted with W. M. Rossetti to prepare and edit a volume of selections from your Poems. [. . .] On thinking the whole matter over [. . .] I came to think that such an arrangement as that was not without some advantages. In the first place it's a thing which cannot be prevented. Americans have not granted the English any protections for their works or choice about bringing them out, and in the absence of a just law on the subject no one can claim property in his work over here. I may say in passing, however, that in reply to a letter from me to Mr. Hotten he told me that he meant to share with you the pecuniary profits of the venture, and spoke in an honorable tone. (qtd. in Paley 9)

Whitman had long supported international copyright as an aid to American authors. Now he discovered how accurate his earlier views had been. Powerless to stop Hotten, he had no choice but to deal with him.

As the letter indicates, this did not at first seem to be such a dire prospect. In addition to Hotten's "honorable tone," his chosen editor, Rossetti, was a respected literary figure of the time and an admirer of the American poet. Furthermore, Hotten soon wrote to Whitman, sending him a book on William Blake and once again pledging to treat him fairly:

Now, we want the privilege of selling copies of the 'selection' in the United States—if you will allow us: and I have told Mr. Conway that I would give you, or your agent, a royalty of one shilling (or twenty-five cents gold) upon every copy sold in your country. [. . .] On this English edition I will ask your acceptance of a share of our profits—after the original outlay in paper, printing, and binding, has been returned to the publisher. (qtd. in Paley 16)

Given all of this apparent consideration, it is not surprising that Whitman wrote a friend that Hotten had "written [him] very handsomely" (qtd. in Paley 17). The publisher did appear to be offering him a fairly good deal, particularly when it was possible for him to offer nothing at all. Whitman was more than willing to accept Hotten's offer, even the eventual changes to his text suggested by Rossetti, in order to establish a connection with the British reading public.

As with other cases involving Hotten, however, this relationship was to prove decidedly one-sided. British readers received an edited version of Whitman's poems, its racier portions either sanitized or removed, while Whitman received nothing. As Paley points out, in 1871 Whitman wrote to another British publisher seeking an agreement to put out *Leaves of Grass,* "under [his] sanction" (21). Hotten's edition had been, in large part, "under his sanction," but Whitman clearly and rightly felt that, by withholding any payment, Hotten could no longer claim the poet's blessing. Indeed, he wrote another correspondent a few months later, "And while I, the author, am without any recompense at all in America, the English pirate-publisher, Hotten, derives a handsome annual income from a bad & defective London reprint of my Poems" (qtd. in Paley 21). Paley notes that it is only after Hotten withheld payment that Whitman took such a negative view of the edition. He also points out that Hotten's profits were quite small, so any payment would also have been modest (22). Rather than the income lost, what seems to have irritated Whitman the most was the violation of trust.

As the years went by, however, he appeared more ambivalent regarding this affair. There is no doubt that he resented not receiving payment, but he came to regret sanctioning an edited text even more than he did the lost profits. Furthermore, his disappointment seems tempered by his awareness that the Hotten piracies had furthered the circulation of his text. Remarks to Traubel illustrate the poet's feelings:

"Did the Rossetti book ever do me any good? I am not sure of it: Rossetti's kindness did me good—but as for the rest, I am doubtful."

Laughed. "Why, what do you think I personally, selfishly, got out of that edition? Why just three copies on which I had three dollars duty to pay. I don't blame Rossetti for that—that is only one of the humors of the incident." (1; 151)

On another occasion, the poet remarked, "They have sold a good many Whitman books, one kind or another, in England. I never got anything of any account out of it—though I don't know as that matters much: the chief thing is, that the books get about" (450). Whitman could never get over his "selfish" feelings regarding Hotten's acts, but clearly it was not the money that mattered most. His first priority was that "the books get about," and, since he had had such a hand in the publishing of Hotten's volumes, he seems to have been largely content, although he remained troubled that the text had been edited. Traubel records an exchange the two had regarding the volume: "Was he on the whole satisfied with the Hotten book? 'On the whole—yes. Yet any volume of extracts must misrepresent the Leaves—any volume—the best. The whole theory of the book is against gems, abstracts, extracts: the book needs each of its parts to keep its perfect unity'" (282). This statement is a noteworthy example of Whitman's fluctuating feelings regarding the Hotten edition. To state that he was "on the whole satisfied" with the edition is a startling admission from the poet who was so obsessively concerned with controlling his poetry. As he clearly knew, the edition was misrepresentative in more than one regard: it was not only an incomplete text, but it also lacked the formal printed endorsement of its author— a vital component to the poet who sought an open and honest exchange with his readers.

There is no evidence indicating whether or not Whitman knew of the complete *Leaves of Grass* that Hotten published, although given his close contact with his London correspondents it is highly likely that he did. The deception of this edition, prepared to appear as if it were printed in the United States and thus with the poet's permission, would surely have infuriated him. Both Paley and Joel Myerson have outlined the subtle ways that this edition was made to look as though it were printed in the United States. Paley asks a pertinent question: "[. . .] why did Hotten do it? Piracy was legal on both sides of the Atlantic, and had he merely wished to avoid paying Whitman royalties, he need not have put a false imprint on his edition" (31). One possible answer he suggests is that the publisher made the book appear to be an American import so that he "was less likely to attract prosecution" for publishing what might be termed an obscene text (32). Another possibility is that Hotten, having seen the fervor with which the poet was being

greeted by his small but influential number of British fans, hoped to capitalize on readers' desire for an "authentic" *Leaves of Grass*. True connection with
the poet could only come from a book that had been produced under his
watchful eye and that had passed through his hands—Whitman often
emphasized his actual physical contact with his books—and so the reader
seeking the true "experience" would not be satisfied with a pirated British
reprint. It is not surprising, then, that in one of the remaining copies of this
edition, a reader has written, "This edition of 'Leaves of Grass' purporting to
be printed in New York, was in reality printed in London—one of the many
meaningless swindles of the late John Camden Hotten" (qtd. in Paley 30). In
feigning an American publication and proximity with the author, Hotten
went beyond piracy and performed a "swindle."

Whitman's desire for an open exchange with his readers may account
for his actions in the most prominent challenge to this connection, the
pirated edition of the 1860 *Leaves of Grass* published by New York printer
Richard Worthington beginning in 1880.[17] Worthington had purchased the
plates for the edition at auction and resolved to use them to publish copies.
Whitman wrote to his friend Richard Watson Gilder that he had earlier
declined purchasing the plates himself, apparently informing the auctioneer
George A. Leavitt that "said plates were worthless, being superseded by a
larger & different edition—that I could not use them (the 1860 ones)
myself, nor would I allow them to be used by anyone else—I being the sole
owner of the copyright" (*Correspondence* 3: 197). His statement reveals not
only his investment in the most current edition of *Leaves of Grass,* viewing
further copies of an earlier edition "worthless," but it also appears to
demonstrate Whitman's resolve to enforce his copyright. Worthington must
have been aware of the risks involved in publishing a smaller, older edition
without the poet's permission, for, after his purchase, the printer wrote to
him offering a royalty in exchange for poems written since 1860 (and published by Whitman in subsequent editions) to make the book published
with the old plates "complete" (3: 196n). As might be expected, Whitman
rejected the offer.

Yet when he learned later that Worthington had begun publishing
the book anyway, the first action he took was to write this apparent pirate a
letter, addressed "My dear Sir": "Some six months ago, you wrote me (I
was then laid up ill in St Louis) that you had purchased the electrotype
plates of the 1861 [sic] Boston ed'n of my *Leaves of Grass*—& making me
some proposals about them—To which I made an answer at the time, as
you probably bear in mind. Are you still the owner of those plates? Do you
still hold to the offer then made by you? Please write me here" (186). This

is not the response one would expect from an author who has learned that pirated copies of his book are being published. It is possible that Whitman only sought to ascertain if it was Worthington producing the copies, but his allusion to the previous offer seems to indicate that Whitman was in fact seeking to restore his financial connection with the distribution of *Leaves of Grass.*

Whitman himself appears aware how unusual this might seem: when he wrote to Gilder[18] telling him what had occurred and seeking legal help, someone "that could take the thing in hand," he writes, "But I have to add that about September 1880 (I was in London Canada at the time) I wrote to Worthington referring to his previous offer, then declined by me, and asking whether he still had the plates & was disposed to make the same offer: to which I rec'd no answer. I wrote a second time; and again no answer" (197). That Whitman felt that he "*had* to add" a reference to his earlier letters to Worthington reveals that he was aware of how that correspondence might appear: not so much as a rebuke but as an attempt to establish a working relationship. This early conciliatory response is at odds with his declaration to Gilder: "I am the sole owner of the copyright—& I think my copyright papers are all complete—I publish & sell the book myself—it is my sole means of living" (198). Although Whitman declared his rights several places in his letters, it was only when Worthington refused to respond to his inquiries about his earlier offer that he sought action against him. While there is no reason to believe that Whitman would have accepted any offer made by the publisher, it is revealing that his initial correspondence with the publisher makes no mention of stopping publication.

In writing of this affair, the poet emphasizes the "secretive" nature of Worthington's act: "I had supposed the whole thing dropt, & nothing done, but within a week past, I learn that Worthington has been *slyly* printing and selling the Volume of *Leaves of Grass* from these plates" (emphasis added, 197). The use of the adverb "slyly" is significant here: as already noted, "monopoly or secrecy" has no place in Whitman's conception of an American democracy, and even more than the unauthorized publication of *Leaves of Grass,* it is the "secrecy" that seems to bother Whitman the most. This is again made clear in a letter Whitman wrote to his friend Harry Stafford a few days later: "A rascally publisher in New York named Worthington has been printing and selling a cheaper edition of my own books for his own profit, no benefit to me at all—& it has been going on privately for a year— I only found it out for certain about ten days ago" (199). As much as the fact that Worthington had been reaping all of the financial rewards, what disturbs Whitman is that the whole affair had been conducted "privately" for so long. Even a year later, after Whitman had received a first payment from Worthington for the copies sold, he still could not forget the secrecy of the crime, as is emphasized in a letter written to Osgood & Co. in 1881 informing them that Worthington had sold "languid *surreptitious* copies" (emphasis added 196n).

Despite his complaints and his protestations that he owned the copyright, he never did stop the printing of these copies. Instead, he began accepting compensation from Worthington. These payments were remarkably small: $40.50 in 1880 and a total of $69.50 for the years 1881 and 1882 (Miller xxvii-iii). The contradictory nature of his response to Worthington continued in later years. Traubel records Whitman's response to the incident in 1888:

> Sometimes W. seems indignant. Sometimes he only laughs the affair away. "Worthington is a humbug—pays me nothing; yet I am averse to going to law about it; going to law is like going to hell: it's too much like trouble even if we win. Worthington no doubt has a theory justifying it which puts me out of his court. In a case so obvious it would seem as though things might very easily be brought to a head in my behalf. But who knows? The law's a tricksy thing to fool with, even for righteousness' sake." W. laughed: "It's a really long story. Worthington is known in the trade as 'holy Dick': he combines piety with his other virtues. [. . .] Dave rails at me for not pushing Worthington—and Tom, too, says: 'You should drive him to the wall.' I say yes, yes, yes: but when it comes to doing anything I rather decide for no. Holy Dick! He's a sour mess to me: I don't feel much like having any sort of encounter with him, good or bad." (195–6)

From the beginning, Whitman had cited the "trouble" of going to court as a reason for his bearing the unauthorized printings. The poet's remarks undermine this excuse by suggesting that, even upon reflection, he had a difficult time understanding his behavior in relation to Worthington: "I say yes, yes, yes: but when it comes to doing anything I rather decide for no." His ability to laugh about the matter, his unwillingness to engage with the "tricksy" law "even for righteousness' sake," might suggest that his ambivalence is simply a lack of concern. Indeed, one wonders what else kept him from concurring with the recommendations of his friends to take legal action.

As Traubel mentions, Worthington's action could still raise Whitman's ire, however, his inaction notwithstanding. The poet returned to the subject with Traubel a few days later:

I would like to rehearse the whole story—it has elements all its own. It is a long story, too. Worthington—'Holy Dick' they call him—bought the plates—has done as he pleased with them ever since—never consulting me. To hell with Walt Whitman! Walt Whitman be damned! [. . .] Jim Scovel once went to New York and frightened him into making a payment of fifty dollars, that fifty dollars being turned over to me. I think there was another twenty-five dollars paid at another time—I don't know when. I acknowledged both, on account, as royalty. Worthington wrote to me, at St. Louis, while I was with Jeff, years ago, proposing that I should make a five years' contract with him—he wanted a new edition, containing new matter (I should say this was about 1877)[19]—which proposal I turned down quick and sharp, telling him that three later editions or more had made the old plates worthless—except, I might have added, for trouble. I again prohibited his printing and selling of the old book but he went on, no doubt thinking me a 'soft,' as I have in fact been. Kennedy does not know about the royalty I accepted. There may be some construction of the law which would interpret my acceptance of any royalty as a consideration—I do not know. (250)

Whitman's first remarks here are more in line with what we might expect of the poet; he was evidently angered by the publisher's unwillingness to take his wishes into account. He now views his refusal to take the publisher to court as marking him as "soft," and he appears embarrassed by his decision to accept royalty payments, just as he seemed embarrassed by his attempts to strike a deal with Worthington years earlier. His reluctance to tell his close friend about the royalties may suggest a sense of culpability, a feeling that he had somehow sanctioned what he and others viewed as an offense against him.

This sense of responsibility helps explain why Whitman refused to take Worthington to court when he first began publishing copies. Perhaps he feared that losing a public court battle would morally vindicate "holy Dick" and that the publicity of a court case could lead to ridicule of the poet who "scattered himself freely." It is also possible he did not feel the financial need to push for larger payments or some legal settlement. Although he had just come through some lean years in the late 1870s, the first three years of the 1880s saw him doing remarkably well.[20] Still, Whitman cited the "trouble" and economic hardship brought by legal action each time he refused to move against Worthington, as he did in his letter to Stafford: "—will lead to a law suit, as I shall have to sue him, & I hate getting into law—it is almost as bad to me to sue, as to be sued—then it cost[s] money" (*Correspondence* 3: 199). This concern regarding the cost of going to court seems puzzling; given his relative financial security in 1880, when the whole affair came to light, why not fight for exclusive control of the book that was his "sole means of living" (198)?

One interpretation of these tangled events and of the poet's later ambivalence is that once he was no longer excluded, once the printing was no longer "secret" and he had been returned to the system of exchange, even in a mostly symbolic way (the payments from Worthington being remarkably small compared to Whitman's total income during these years), Whitman's primary objections were lifted. *Leaves of Grass* was being spread throughout the marketplace, if not at first with his permission, then at least ultimately with his awareness and tacit approval, and a token portion of the money that readers spent on the work was making its way to the author. In addition, the book was published from plates for an edition that Whitman had personally overseen. This incident reveals that, despite his justly celebrated control over his text, his management did not resemble the type of monopoly power feared by printers who opposed the international copyright law. Whitman did not seek to exclude all printers and publishers save the most powerful houses on the east coast and abroad; what he detested was being excluded himself.

Whitman's desire for contact may account in part for his enthusiastic response to a letter sent to him in 1881 by Dr. John Fitzgerald Lee, seeking permission to do a Russian translation of *Leaves of Grass:* "Your letter asking definite endorsement to a translation of my *Leaves of Grass* into Russian is just received, and I hasten to answer it. Most warmly and willingly I consent to the translation, and waft a prayerful *God speed* to the enterprise" (*Correspondence* 3: 259). After elaborating on the links between Russians and Americans, Whitman proceeds:

> And as my dearest dream is for an internationality of poems and poets binding the lands of the earth closer than all treaties or diplomacy—As the purpose beneath the rest in my book is such hearty comradeship for individuals to begin with, and for all the Nations of the earth as a result—how happy indeed I shall be to get the hearing and emotional contact of the great Russian peoples!
>
> To whom, now and here, (addressing you for Russia, and empowering you, should you see fit, to put the present letter in your book, as a preface to it,) I waft affectionate salutations from these shores, in America's name. (3: 259)

Although nothing came of the translation project, Whitman's letter is won-derfully indicative of his attitudes regarding foreign publication and gives us insight into why international copyright was so important to him. There is no mention of finances in this ebullient letter "most warmly and willingly" consenting to the project. The source of his excitement is clear: the prospect of an "internationality of poems and poets" and the opportunity for him "to get the hearing and emotional contact of the great Russian peoples!" In his eagerness, Whitman transforms his permission into an epistle to the Russian citizenry, transforming Lee into all of Russia and his letter into a preface for the proposed edition.

As we have seen, Whitman's book served as a metonymic extension of himself, one that could bring him into contact with a multitude of readers. This is the kind of connection that international copyright could guarantee: with the law, Whitman would have to be informed of each foreign publica-tion, giving him opportunity to include "personal" messages to his new audi-ence abroad.[21] Even without such a law, Whitman seemed thrilled by the prospect that he might make "emotional contact" with people from other nations. Such contact could only take place through open exchange and cor-respondence, completely different from the "secret" theft of literary piracy. Whitman emphasizes this openness in a letter to his Danish friend Rudolf Schmidt: "I have heard that my book is to be translated into German, by some friends in Dresden—also into Russian by some Russian exiles & a Mr Lee a Russ-English scholar—*I have been written to about both propositions* & of course have expressed warmest assent" (emphasis added 258). The kind of inclusion that seems to please Whitman so much here would have become the rule under international copyright and indicates why the law held such importance for him.

POETIC EMBODIMENT: *LEAVES* AS PROPERTY AND POET

The poet's belief that international copyright could enable more open and fair correspondence between writers and readers is tied to his fervent belief that his poetry served as a medium for that connection. Ezra Greenspan has explored this question thoroughly, arguing "Whitman's need for 'contact' with his readers—to use a term which habitually gets his poetic accentua-tion—was an obsession" (*Walt Whitman* 109). In pursuit of this obsession, as Greenspan convincingly argues, Whitman struggles desperately to construct a poetic language that will allow him to move beyond the text. In the first edition of *Leaves of Grass*, Whitman writes, "I was chilled with the cold types and cylinders and wet paper between us. / I pass so poorly with paper and types. . . . I must pass with the contact of bodies and souls" (*WW* 89). Whitman literally tries to move through his text to connect with his readers. In the first piece of the 1855 *Leaves of Grass* (the poem eventually titled "Song of Myself"), he goes so far as to merge with his reader: "It is you talking just as much as myself. . . . I act as the tongue of you, / It was tied in your mouth. . . . in mine it begins to be loosened" (*WW* 84). It is difficult to untangle the tongues and mouths of reader and writer in this phrase, as Whitman tried throughout his writing to make separation a difficult matter. In "So Long," Whitman writes, "It is I you hold and who holds you, / I spring from the pages into your arms" (611). Whitman plays on the literal reading process—the reader holding the text and the author "holding" the reader's attention—in an attempt to pass from the text into immediate physical contact with the reader, to "spring from the pages" and literalize the embrace.

Needless to say, this is a conception of textuality fundamentally different from those frequently cited throughout the course of the debates over the international copyright law. From its inception, copyright law in the United States had closely associated authors with inventors, in accordance with the mandate of the Constitution "securing for limited Times to authors and inventors the exclusive right to their respective writings and discoveries." Not surprisingly, then, copyright was always closely aligned with patents, conflating texts and prototypes into property owned by the inventor/author. This language was taken up in 1837 in the earliest proposed legislation for international copyright: "That authors and Inventors have, according to the practice of civilized nations, a property in the respective productions of their genius, is incontestable" (qtd. in Rawley 203). Of course, the nature of the "property" and the author's rights to it certainly were contestable. *The United States Magazine and Democratic Review* demanded, "when one individual has created a good which is susceptible of multiplied reproduction, to the benefit of others or of the whole human race, without diminution of his special enjoyment of his own [. . .] is the principle of Property so exclusive in its monopoly, as to forbid the unlimited diffusion of a blessing which God has chosen one man to be the minister of to the race?" ("International" 120). The fear of monopoly always accompanied the notion that texts and inventions were more or less than mere property: if seen as "blessings" sent from God, then how could any one man or woman claim to have exclusive rights to the "multiplied reproductions" which in no way detract from the creator's enjoyment?

The Joint Committee on the Library, in its unfavorable report on international copyright in 1873, employed the argument that authors deserved only partial credit for their work. Relying heavily on the connection made between science and authorship in the Constitution, Senator Morrill writes, "If it [authorship] be conceded to be the soul of science, it is essential that its productions should be embodied in books, and these involve the varied skills, industries, and cunning workmanship of many hands, and at last, and not the least important agency, the enterprise, capital, and address of the publisher through whom these books are to be introduced to the reading public" (4). The report is indicative of the development of the publishing trade and the multi-faceted business it had become during the nineteenth century. In light of these advances, the notion that foreign authors could have sole control over the "product" of the labor of so many individuals, particularly since those authors had already presumably reaped their rewards in their native countries, was seen as an injustice, yet another reason to strike down the proposed law.

Years later, in an apparent attempt to address this argument, Senator Chace wrote in his Report from the Committee on Patents in 1886:

> the Constitution provides for securing the rights of both inventors and authors and recognizes a property right both in ideas clothed in the form of a mechanical contrivance and those clothed in words. An invention for which a patent is granted is but an idea put in a mechanical form, but the subject of the patent is the idea or mechanical principle, and that the Government protects; whereas copyright does not secure any monopoly to the idea or thought but only to the form of words or language with which the idea is clothed. (I)

Senator Chace attempts to defend copyright from the charge of unfair monopoly by suggesting that authorship is not simply "the soul of science" and that the protections offered by copyrights and patents are fundamentally different: patents protect the idea while copyright protects the "form of words or language with which the idea is clothed."[22] Senator Morrill had concentrated on the form in terms of the manufactured product, arguing that since the book was the product of many kinds of labor, it could not be subject to authorial control. Senator Chace asserts that copyright serves to protect the form of the words that the author produces—not the book as a product, but the specific pattern of language that the author creates. Two fundamental subjects of ownership are at issue: the idea and the form it "wears." The question of how one would define this division, as well as the notion of form itself, would continue to be a source of contention in the battle for international copyright. Testifying before the House Committee on the Judiciary in 1890, George Haven Putnam attempted to alleviate fears of authorial monopoly by arguing that "A copyright gives him [the author of a biography] the control simply of the forms of words in which he presents those facts" (United States 34). The split between ideas and the words used to express them was a fundamental line of argument, with copyright supporters like Putnam attempting to separate the "form" of words from the material "form" of the published book, while opponents sought to collapse both notions.

Whitman too was trying to eliminate any split between idea and form in his own writing. Words were not simply the "clothes" for his ideas; he attempts to refute this sort of platonic dichotomy of form and ideas throughout his poetry: "I send no agent or medium," he writes in "A Song for Occupations," "offer no representative of value, but offer the value itself" (*WW* 357). Words do not function as mere representatives for Whitman. They are the "value itself," the value that is inherent in human connection. Whitman writes in "A Song of the Rolling Earth": "Human bodies are words, myriads of words, / (In the best poems re-appears the body, man's or woman's, well-shaped, natural, gay, / Every part able, active, receptive, without shame or the need of shame.)" (363). This embodiment in words is fundamental to Whitman's poetic project, his attempt to connect physically with his readers.

As Whitman proceeded to publish editions of *Leaves of Grass,* he continued his attempts to "authenticate" this embodiment not only through his close participation in the publication process, not only through his poetic language, but also by "imprinting" his presence on the text with his signature. This connection between his embodiment in the text and the authentication of his signature is made explicit in Whitman's epigraphic introduction to the 1889 printing of *Leaves of Grass.* He writes, "Doubtless, anyhow, the volume is more A PERSON than a book. And for testimony to all, (and good measure,) I here with pen and ink append my name: [Whitman's signature]" (qtd. in Myerson 131). Whitman's signature is the guarantee of, a "testimony" to, the embodiment that he proclaims. A similar epigraph appears at the front of the 1876 edition: "Ever with pleas'd smile I may keep on, / Ever and ever yet the verses owning—as, first, I here and now, / Signing for Soul and Body, set them to my name, [Whitman's signature]" (*WW* 147). Here, the term "owning" is quite ambiguous. Although Whitman signs for "Soul and Body," the ownership of that body remains in play. Even as the reader purchases the book once owned by Whitman, the verses continue to "own" Whitman. Rather than fixing possession or certifying a transaction, his signature attests to an ownership "Ever and ever" fluctuating.

Whitman had begun signing his name to the texts in 1876 with the publication of the "Author's Edition." Every copy of this edition bears his actual signature on the title page (Myerson 65), heightening the sense of literal correspondence with his readers: an advertisement found inside one of the copies of the 1882 edition invites readers to write to him at his Camden address to obtain a copy (97). Readers sent signed letters and payments, and in return Whitman sent signed texts. He continually experimented with methods of establishing this personal connection with his texts and readers. The title page of the 1888 printing, for example, announced that the text was an "Authenticated & Personal Book (handled by W. W.)," assuring readers that the book they held in their hands had once been in the hands of its author (qtd. in Myerson 121). Of course, announcements like these and signatures were in fact a kind of "supplementary" guarantee. Copyright is itself an institutional means of guaranteeing this precise exchange between reader and writer.

Whitman himself seems aware of the supplementary nature of his signature, for in the 1881 edition of *Leaves of Grass* he provides a facsimile copy of his signature on the front page. In Whitman's editions, there has always been an interesting play between the name of the author and the copyright page, beginning with the "anonymous" publication of the 1855 text, copyrighted by "Walter Whitman." It is this early copyright page that certifies his connection to the text, a connection that is apparently "reinforced" by his signature and then a "copy of his writing" in 1881. There is a precedent for this in the existing copies of the 1855 *Leaves of Grass*. Joel Myerson has located two copies of this edition in which the copyright notice is not printed, but handwritten by Whitman himself (13). In writing about American copyright law, McGill has noted that "Rather than a simple sign of ownership, the copyright notice bears witness to a multistep process by which the public, which authenticates the book and consents to restrict its distribution, is acknowledged" ("Matter" 45). The care with which he transcribed the legal statement into two copies of the book speaks to the importance Whitman gave to this recognition of his book's public nature. More importantly this "copy-writing" collapses the institutional statement of ownership with the personal statement of the signature. It becomes difficult to assign one primacy over the other.

Although *Leaves of Grass* was initially "anonymous," save for the modest "Walter Whitman" on the copyright page, in the copyright notices that followed in subsequent editions, Whitman's name would become more and more prominent, sometimes appearing in all capital letters, sometimes occupying its own line of text.[23] While the 1831 amendment to the copyright law stated that the author "shall give information of copyright being secured, by causing it to be inserted [. . .] on the title page, or the page immediately following it" (*An act,* United States 437), no other specific guidelines were given. The copyright statement became yet another way Whitman's identity was fused with the text; he exploited all means available, including the legal means offered through copyright, to make each copy of the book embody the personal exchange he called for in his poetry.

If Whitman embodied himself in *Leaves of Grass,* then each edition was a unique expression in need of preservation. Traubel records that in one of the many discussions he had with the poet regarding the different editions of *Leaves of Grass,* Whitman said, "They all count—I like all—I don't know that I like one better than any other" (qtd. in Traubel 1: 280). His close attention to the most current edition did not mean that he ceased to value previous editions: as he made clear to Traubel, each "counted." We know that Whitman always valued the most current expression, the most recent volume, yet this quotation shows precisely that he did not see a new edition as *replacing* those former editions.[24] Each has its own identity, and Whitman was prepared to embrace them all.

Whitman's concern for all of his editions and the need to protect them provides the necessary backdrop for reading the copyright page of the 1891 issue of *Leaves of Grass* (fig. 1). A catalog of previous editions and copyrights dominates the top half of the page. By presenting the year and place of publication for each edition, the page preserves each as a distinct entity despite the fact that the book retained the same title. The only exceptions are the copyright notices that recognize the inclusion of material previously published separately: for example, the copyright notice for the 1876 edition, which included *Two Rivulets.* Whitman thus presents a copyright page that symbolically fulfills his desire for a volume that would include and recognize all of his individual expressions. He seems to be trying to use this last copyright page to stretch the covers of his final volume to embrace all of the former editions. Indeed, had Whitman succeeded in publishing a volume that included all of the separate editions in one, the copyright page for that edition would not have looked much different from the one that confronts the reader of the final version of *Leaves of Grass.*

The cataloguing of editions is only the first of many noticeable differences in this final copyright page. Unlike those from other editions, this one nearly submerges Whitman's name: it appears only in small print in the middle of a page crowded with type (fig. 1). Whereas the copyright page of the first edition is notable primarily for providing a clue to authorship and for the last appearance of "Walter" Whitman in the text, this one is notable for the fact that one must read carefully to find Whitman's name at all. Unlike the various earlier permutations of the copyright notice which put Whitman's entire name in capital letters or on its own line of print, here the name is simply made part of the Librarian of Congress' sentence; it is even split apart, "Walt" and "Whitman" appearing on separate lines at opposite margins. Unlike those earlier copyright pages which highlight Whitman's identity as author of the text, here it is as though the citation of previous editions itself conveys Whitman's identity and does the work of authentication and possession once accomplished through his name alone.

The government sanction protecting these different expressions, the strong sub-text that underlies this list of copyrights and their renewals, is reinforced by the lengthy note from A. R. Spofford, Librarian of Congress, registering the inclusion for copyright of "Good-bye My Fancy" in *Leaves of Grass* (fig. 1). The formal wording provided here is the same wording that the 1831 amendment to the copyright law mandated should appear "in a book to be kept" by the clerk of the district court for record-keeping; this wording was not required for texts that were circulated (United States 437). While the copyright page in Whitman's texts was always a complex space in which the institutional statement of ownership co-mingled with the personal statement of the signature, here even the copyright notice itself becomes more complex. It takes on the tone of a formal address; rather than merely a neutral statement from the office of the Library of Congress regarding ownership, it almost seems to sanctify Whitman's final copyright: "Be it remembered . . . That on the 10th day of May, *anno Domini,* 1891, Walt Whitman, of Camden, N.J., has deposited in this office the title of a Book." Spofford's governmental statement is the only voice other than Whitman's to appear outside of quotation marks in the entirety of *Leaves of Grass,* and the solemn tone of his message, particularly the command "Be it remembered" and the statement of "*anno Domini,*" makes this final copyright notice seem like more than simply a legal confirmation of Whitman's property rights: the statement takes on almost ritualistic overtones.[25]

Spofford's language does more than sanctify the occasion of Whitman's final copyright: it thrusts the text into the future. The bracketed comment following the copyright notice gives the exact date, following the 14-year renewal, when the copyright will expire. Whitman himself was always thinking of his future readers, as in "Crossing Brooklyn Ferry": "Closer yet I approach you, / What thought you have of me now, I had as much of you— / I laid in my stores in advance, / I consider'd long and seriously of you before you were born" (*WW* 311). However, although his poetry often makes reference to the future, nowhere does he explicitly refer to the twentieth century. Thus, the specificity of those dates on the copyright page—1919 and

May 19, 1933—is startling, seeming to fix a particular moment in the future in a way Whitman's poetry never did. More importantly, while his poetry serves to effect a rendezvous, either in the moment of reading or in that future where he has assured us he will be "somewhere waiting" for us to find him (*WW* 247), these dates truly signify the ultimate dispersion of Whitman's text, the date when the institutional apparatus of copyright that had supplemented and served Whitman's authorial control would finally serve to dissolve that control and release his book into the public domain.

It seems that Whitman foresaw this future dissolution and attempted one last time to use this site of institutional and personal authority to exert an influence over the publication of his text. As had been the case with each previous edition, Whitman once again most valued the newest expression, and thus the final message of the copyright page comes from the poet himself: "As there are now several editions of L. of G., different texts and dates, I wish to say that I prefer and recommend this present one, complete, for future printing, if there should be any" (fig. 1). This is, of course, the only time that he included a message on the copyright page. The inclusion not only personalizes the "public" copyright page in a new way, but it also allows Whitman to reinforce the institutional recognition of his individual works. Each edition, he stresses, is a "different text," and his recommendation of this last edition, following as it does an exhaustive list of previous editions, highlights the unique identity of those preceding texts, each a separate embodiment of Walt Whitman. Where once his name had been the focal point of a modest two- and three-line copyright page, seen only as part of a governmentally required formality, here instead is a final catalog of Whitman's editions. His voice shares space with the public voice of the Librarian of Congress, and the name Walt Whitman seems lost in the procession of dates and places representing the publication history of *Leaves of Grass*. As Whitman sought to do throughout his career, here he collapses both public and private space and author and text.

At the same time, his final statement of preference for this last edition "complete, for future printing, if there should be any" adds a sense of poignancy to that "expiration" of Whitman's copyright in 1933, marking with keen accuracy the limit of the authorial connection and control Whitman had worked so hard to keep for almost half a century. In 1888, Whitman remarked to Traubel, "[David McKay] tells me he is to produce an Emerson—an early Emerson on which the copyright has expired. What a cute—devilishly cute—lot the publishing wolves are. There they are, the whole hungry herd—a dozen set of eyes straining for a chance to pounce on these things the first minute of freedom" (Traubel 2: 176). Whitman seems to have

COPYRIGHTS, &c.

1st ed'n 1855, Brooklyn (N. Y., South District)—renew'd (1883) 14 yrs.
2d ed'n 1856, Brooklyn—renew'd (1884) 14 yrs.
3d ed'n 1860, Boston, Thayer & Eldridge Pub'rs.
4th ed'n 1867, N. Y., So. Dist.: Pub'd New York.
5th ed'n 1871, Washington, D. C.
6th ed'n 1876—Centennial issue—inc'd'g Two RIVULETS: two vols.
7th ed'n 1881, Boston, Mass.: Osgood Pub.: [This includes in the present vol. pages 1 to 382.]
8th ed'n 1882, Philadelphia: McKay Pub'r.
Sands at Seventy: Annex, 1888—November Boughs—Philadelphia.
A Backward Glance, &c.: November Boughs, 1888—Philadelphia.
Good-Bye my Fancy: 2d Annex, 1891—Philadelphia.

Library of Congress . . . . . . Copyright Office, Washington.
No. 18382 W.
To wit: Be it remembered . . . That on the 19th day of May, *anno Domini*, 1891, Walt Whitman, of Camden, N. J., has deposited in this office the title of a Book, the title or description of which is in the following words, to wit:
GOOD-BYE MY FANCY,
2d Annex to Leaves of Grass.
Philadelphia . . . David McKay . . . 1891.
The right whereof he claims as author, in conformity with the laws of the United States respecting copyrights.
A. R. SPOFFORD,
Librarian of Congress.

[Which last-named copyright (holding good to 1919—then, on application, continued 14 years further) expires May 19, 1933.]

☞ As there are now several editions of L. of G., different texts and dates, I wish to say that I prefer and recommend this present one, complete, for future printing, if there should be any; a copy and fac-simile, indeed, of the text of these 438 pages. The subsequent adjusting interval which is so important to form'd and launch'd work, books especially, has pass'd; and waiting till fully after that, I have given (pages 423-438) my concluding words.   W. W.

Figure 1. Copyright Page of the 1891 Edition of *Leaves of Grass*

Source: Special Collections Department, Main Library, University of Iowa, Iowa City, IA.

heard the wolves howling as he prepared this message for his final copyright page. Confronting his inability to keep them at bay once his copyright expired, the poet simply asked for consideration from a publishing profession that had given him little reason to hope for it.

The careful cataloguing on the final copyright page reminds us that Whitman's ability to preserve the distinctiveness of each of his editions depended upon copyright law. In its absence, texts were regularly printed, changed, and adapted without the author's knowledge or permission. Whitman sought to prevent such piracy throughout his career, and when he could not, as in the case of Worthington, he sought to re-establish a connection with his text, no matter how tenuous or financially unrewarding. This connection was essential to him, for *Leaves of Grass* was his way of reaching out to readers throughout the world. In his vision of an open democratic exchange, he and the public would knowingly engage in a transaction in which each purchased copy moved from the author's hand to the reader's. As we have already seen, Whitman viewed the reading process in physical terms, an embrace that enfolded both parties. In Whitman's view, copyright law guaranteed that he was always a willing participant in the embrace and that his readers were receiving his work, his "body," in exactly the form he intended. Again, this gesture of affection is a crucial component of his vision of democracy marked by "adhesiveness or love, that fuses, ties and aggregates" (*WW* 973). His support for the passage of an international copyright law in the United States, therefore, was more than a matter of simply protecting his business interests: it was inextricably linked to his idea of an equal, open, and connected democracy.

Chapter Four

Protecting and Promoting Mark Twain:
Samuel Clemens and the Uses of Copyright

THE LITERARY PROSPECTOR

On the front cover of the original edition of *Roughing It*, there is an illustration of a prospector driving a wagon. The wagon is loaded with sacks of ore, one of them bearing the initials "M. T." (fig. 2). The image, like the book itself, serves as a fitting introduction to Clemens' views on his literary property, views that diverged sharply from those of contemporaries like Whitman. While the work represents the kind of prospecting Clemens would practice throughout his career, mining not only his personal experiences but his former writing for material, the drawing fairly represents Clemens' greatest find: the name and persona of Mark Twain. Critics have noted the connection between Clemens' experiences as a miner and his authorial practice. Alan Gribben writes, "His biographical experiences were viewed the same way he had seen men in Nevada and California approach those inert, lucrative mountains: he intended to work them like a paying ore mine; his life was a lode, vein, grubstake, payload, tracer, unpanned claim, bonanza" (46). If Clemens' life was his gold mine, then the persona that emerged from that mine was far more valuable than even the books that his experience yielded.

Like the prospector forever carrying his loot—"M.T."—Clemens would find protecting his rights to that name and the works on which it was built to be an unceasing pursuit. This effort was necessary not only because of repeated attempts to pirate his work, but also because of his personal views on property rights; for much of his career, he saw these rights as matters of individual responsibility, rather than as divine or natural rights. He felt that one had to defend these rights actively to keep them. Property that was not carefully managed and maintained—be it a promising silver "ledge" or a short story—was fair game, like abandoned diggings in Nevada. Clemens

Figure 2. Front Cover Illustration of 1872 Edition of *Roughing It*.
Source: Special Collections Department, Main Library, University of Iowa, Iowa City, IA.

had to keep a close watch over his persona and his works or accept their dispersal into the marketplace. He saw copyright as uniquely within his purview, and so he could alternate between favoring close protectionism or unrestricted circulation when the mood and occasion suited him.

Understanding the changes in Clemens' feelings about copyright during his career, particularly those moments when he seems to disavow his belief in what Siva Vaidhyanathan has described as a "divine" right to literary property, reveals a great deal about how the discourse of copyright had been transformed by the latter half of the nineteenth century. It also reveals how Clemens' early career shaped his ideas about literary property rights and how the link between his authorship and his public performances went beyond the content and style of his work. As Richard Lowry has convincingly demonstrated, authorship for Clemens was not simply the act of writing and publishing his works:

> What he did was both less and more than an art form; what he did, in fact, to borrow Huck Finn's verb for writing, was to 'make' books—not only to write them but to typeset and print them, to publish them, to market them, and finally maybe even to live them. Thus, the distinction between 'writing,' on the one hand, and 'building,' 'scribbling,' and 'making,' on the other, stemmed from Twain's understanding of how profoundly social an endeavor was authorship. (4)

In addition to being a "social" endeavor, one can easily insert the word "public." Clemens deliberately positioned himself before his readers in almost every step in the writing process. As a result, each of these steps, ranging from the writing to the publication to the marketing, was, for Clemens, part of asserting his particular identity as author. His business practices were, therefore, another way for him to perform authorship; thus, like the prospector staking his claim—simultaneously declaring his property and his identity as prospector—Clemens' copyrights demonstrated his profession as well as his possessions.

His early success as an author was closely linked with his success as a public speaker, and vice versa. His letters from Hawaii (the Sandwich Islands) were immensely popular, and they helped to drive the success of his early lecture appearances (Hoffman 112–13). At the same time, those early lectures increased his fame and helped propel his move to the East Coast. Yet there was more at work than the synergy between Clemens' writings and performances as Mark Twain. The third element contributing to the early success of the Western platform performer and journalist was the unregulated reproduction of his early writing. His short story, "The Celebrated Jumping Frog of Calaveras County," was reproduced by numerous newspapers, which helped lead to the publication of his first book in 1867, a small volume entitled *The Celebrated Jumping Frog of Calaveras County and Other Sketches*. Like the title story, this book was subjected to a great deal of unauthorized reprinting, particularly abroad.

Later in life, Clemens recognized the important role literary piracy played in his early accomplishments. Writing in his notebook in 1888, Clemens mused, "It may be a good thing sometimes for an author to have *one* book pirated & a scramble made—I think it true. Look at my first book" (*Notebooks* 3: 364). As we shall see, Clemens wrote this note at a time when his views regarding copyright and literary piracy were a great deal different from those of many other authors. He had not only recently given testimony in Congress against the International Copyright bill being supported by James Russell Lowell and the American Copyright League, an association of which he was an active member, but he was also involved in a public dispute with his friend Brander Matthews regarding copyright and the necessity for changing the current situation between the United States and Great Britain.

This consideration of the possible benefits of piracy was not simply the result of mature reflection on his early years. In 1870, as he completed *The Innocents Abroad*, Clemens wrote to his American publisher, Elisha Bliss, "I don't copyright the 'Round the World' letters because it don't hurt anything to be well advertised—and these are getting pretty well advertised—but you see out of 50 letters not more than 6 or 10 will be copied into any *one* newspaper—and *that* don't hurt" (*Letters to His Publishers* 29). He had anticipated that his latest project would imitate the popularity of his Sandwich Island letters and lectures, re-prints and word-of-mouth driving up his sales.

In this case, however, Clemens learned that his hopes for piracy-driven advertisement for his book had been thwarted by the industry of the publishers of the *Alta*, the newspaper to which he had been sending his travel letters. Upon returning from his first trip abroad, he undertook a lecture tour, hoping to capitalize on his experiences and the letters he had been sending to the California paper and to build an appetite for the book he planned to write. However, unlike his successful Sandwich Islands performances, the author was dismayed to find his new work seemed to draw much smaller audiences. He placed the blame for this considerable turn of fortune on the *Alta*'s decision to copyright his letters.[1] Years later, he commented in his autobiography, "I inquired into this curious condition of things and found that the thrifty owners of that prodigiously rich Alta newspaper had *copyrighted* all those poor little twenty-dollar letters and had threatened with prosecution any journal which should venture to copy a paragraph from them" (*Autobiography* 243–4). His dismissive criticism of the owners of the *Alta* for their "thriftiness" in exercising a right he would later frequently champion is surprising, as is his further comment on the negotiations with the *Alta*: "I said that if they had acted fairly and honorably, and had allowed the country press to use the letters or portions of them, my lecture skirmish on the coast would have paid me ten thousand dollars, whereas the *Alta* had lost me that amount" (244). Clearly he had been relying on his letters being reprinted, and he seems to have felt wronged by the fact that the *Alta* had prevented this piracy. Considering Clemens' own later threats to prosecute anyone publishing any of his material without permission and compensation, his views of this early situation indicate that he had a much greater degree of flexibility regarding his literary property than has hitherto been suggested by literary scholars.

There is further evidence that he could be sanguine about the pirating of his texts when it appeared to forward his career. Despite an angry feud with the British publisher John Camden Hotten—Whitman's nemesis, as well—the author seems to recognize how Hotten's industry had increased his fame. Dennis Welland notes:

> In or about 1873 Clemens, at the request of Charles Dudley Warner, wrote a brief account of his own life and work. It contains this statement: 'In England the Routledges and Hotten have gathered together and published all my sketches; a great many that have not appeared in book form here. There are four volumes of these sketches.' The total absence of rancour against Hotten in this passage which is the more reliable for not being written for effect, and the candid recognition of his important role in introducing Mark Twain to the English reader represents, I believe, Clemens's true and considered attitude to this remarkable and dynamic publisher [. . .]. (29)

While Welland might be making too much of this statement—he himself acknowledges that Clemens would have been unlikely to say a kind word regarding Hotten—it is true that the passage demonstrates Clemens' keen awareness of the importance of his introduction to his English audience, and in this statement, at any rate, he does not seem overly concerned with how this introduction was accomplished. For many of his most productive years, he seems to have been torn between two contradictory necessities: the need to secure his rights to his literary property in order to profit from them, and the need to make sure that the public was exposed to his work in order to heighten his popularity and increase subscription sales. His attempts to negotiate these demands, not to mention his awareness of his audience's feelings regarding his persona, combined to make his opinions regarding copyright law much more mutable for far longer than those of many of his peers.

This flexibility is evident in Clemens' recollections of the early years of his career. An amusing anecdote regarding the publishing history of one of his early short stories reveals much regarding his shifting views on the practice of literary piracy and on the nature of literary property. The story was "Jim Wolf and the Cats," first published in 1867. He writes of the story,

> A year or two later 'Jim Wolf and the Cats' appeared in a Tennessee paper in a new dress—as to spelling; it was masquerading in a Southern dialect. The appropriator of the tale had a wide reputation in the West and was exceedingly popular. Deservedly so, I think. He wrote some of the breeziest and funniest things I have ever read, and did his work with distinguished ease and fluency. His name has passed out of my memory.
>
> A couple of years went by; then the original story cropped up again and went floating around in the original spelling, and with my name to it. Soon, first one paper and then another fell upon me vigorously for 'stealing' 'Jim Wolf and the Cats' from the Tennessee man. I got a merciless basting, but I did not mind it. It's all in the game. Besides, I had learned, a good while before that, that it is not wise to keep the fires going under a slander unless you can get some advantage out of keeping it alive. (*Autobiography* 138–9)

This was not the end of the journey of this particular story. Several years later, while Clemens was in England in 1873, he met an aspiring writer in dire straits who hoped to gain the famous author's assistance in publishing one of his short stories in a London magazine. Clemens kindly complied: "The thing he sold to Tom Hood's *Annual* for three guineas was 'Jim Wolf and the Cats.' And he did not put my name to it. So that small tale was sold three times. I am selling it again now. It is one of the best properties I have come across" (143).

There are three important observations to be made regarding his recollection. The first is the amiable nature Clemens shows in telling the story. When one considers how he would frequently lash out at literary pirates, he seems almost exceedingly generous in his description of the Tennessee pirate.

Rather than an unforgivable sin, the crime of piracy and the accusations that inevitably follow are to be expected as "all in the game." If, by "game," we assume Clemens is referring to the profession of authorship, then clearly his views of the profession in 1898 are in stark contrast to statements more frequently cited by scholars regarding his view of the importance of copyright protection to the success of an author.

The second significant element of this anecdote is his depiction of his short story not as a product of his own creation, but as a piece of property distinct from his authorship of it: "So that small tale was sold three times. I am selling it again now. It is one of the best properties I have come across." The value of the story is not, Clemens seems to suggest, a result of his identity as author; it is a valuable product regardless of his connection to it, as its repeated sale by different authors demonstrates. Clemens might be attempting to express a kind of modesty by disavowing the importance of his authorship of the tale, or, conversely, he might be keeping a close watch on his literary reputation by making the case that his works can sell regardless of the famous name attached to them. Of course, he casts himself in a favorable light by implying that he must have done an excellent job of telling the story in the first place to motivate others to wish to claim it as their own; however, at the same time he distances himself from authorship of the story.

Finally, the story of "Jim Wolf and the Cats" is not created so much as it is found, a "lucky strike" for the literary prospector, whether that prospector be the Tennessee humorist, the English confidence man, or Clemens himself. It appears that whoever "comes across" the story can take advantage of it, provided a rightful owner does not take steps to intercede. As a result, the ownership of the story is not static, resting solely with the creator; it must continually be re-asserted. If one fails consistently to demonstrate possession, the work can pass into the hands of another.

It is because of the importance of the performance of ownership as a condition of his identity as author that critics have been attracted to the image of Mark Twain as an unconditional champion of copyright. There is no denying that Clemens often took very public steps to defend his copyrights, not only launching a variety of lawsuits to stop pirates, but also making frequent public appearances and lobbying congressmen to increase protection of author's rights. However, by focusing on these performances without analyzing the author's logic in pursuing them, and, by failing to pay equal attention to those statements that appear to contradict this more public and familiar stance, critics have missed the more complex negotiations Clemens was undertaking with the public over copyright and the nuances of his views regarding property. In his otherwise excellent analysis of Clemens' views on copyright and the relation between those views and *The Adventures of Huckleberry Finn*, Victor Doyno downplays the apparent contradictions in his actions and statements. While he does point out that "at one early point" Clemens opposed international copyright (175), he argues, "Twain's attitude toward the issue of international copyright changed radically between 1880 and 1886" (175), suggesting that, at this point, Clemens became the champion of literary property rights we have come to know. Doyno bases the bulk of his analysis of *Huck Finn* on this "later" version of Clemens, not on the author's "early point" of 1880. As a result, he misses much of the consistency that marks Clemens' position throughout this period of his career.

Similarly, in his book decrying recent copyright decisions and the radically extended rights granted authors and intellectual property holders, Vaidhyanathan lays the responsibility for the much broader rights granted twentieth-century literary property holders at Clemens' feet:

> By the end of the nineteenth century, publishers and authors had taken great strides in fighting the republican principles that had informed early American copyright laws and cases. And as the United States stepped forward to assert itself as an imperial power in the world, Mark Twain prepared to assume the position once held by Noah Webster, the champion of private publishing interests cloaked in the rhetoric of noble public service. (55)

There is no denying that Clemens could be a very vocal advocate for copyright law, particularly in the 1890s; however, as Vaidhyanathan himself acknowledges, for much of his career, he was much more ambivalent, even shrewd, regarding issues of literary property. As frustrating as it may be for those critics wishing to see the author as either the hero or the villain in the battle for the extension of copyright, Clemens' attitudes toward his own copyrights could in fact shift according to occasion. The protection of his literary property could become dependent upon expediency rather than principal depending on the circumstance.

It seems likely that his personal fortunes played a role in his eventually unconditional support for copyright. The failure of his publishing company, Charles L. Webster & Co., in 1894 and his financial losses likely influenced his emergence as an almost radical defender of literary property. Similarly, his investment in the Paige Compositor and his subsequent reluctance to alienate printers and to attract the ire of the typesetter unions may account for some of his reluctance to endorse the international copyright bill up for consideration in 1886. In a notebook entry of that year, Clemens drafted a notice "To Printers" regarding the Paige Compositor, stating,

> You will make as much as you did before. You can sit at your work. Perfectly cleanly. Your work can be done in a drawing room. There will be more & bigger papers, & more men required. Printers are peculiarly well instructed men. They all know the history of the great labor saving & speed-enhancing inventions, & they know that no hostility in the world can stop such a machine from coming into use, or even notably delay it. (*Notebooks* 3: 191–2)

Given his concern for the opinion of typesetters, or, if the editors of the notebooks are correct, his concern for the well-being of the typesetters who might be replaced by his machine (400n), Clemens might have determined that it was in his long-term best interests, and in the interests of the beloved machine, to part ways with the American Copyright League in 1886. By focusing on his ambivalence regarding copyright and his views during his career up to and throughout the early 1880s, one can see that his sometimes contradictory views were motivated by more than self-interest. What has been described as a "radical change" is, in fact, part of an evolution of Clemens' vision of authorship as public performance and of his acute awareness of his readers as audience. Perhaps no other author of the nineteenth century engaged in such public negotiations of his copyright, and, if one considers the value of his copyrights and the universal recognition of his public persona, perhaps no other author risked so much.

HOLDING HIS CLAIM:
ROUGHING IT AND THE RESPONSIBILITY OF OWNERSHIP

In one of his most memorable sketches touching on the issue of property rights, Clemens writes in *Roughing It* of an elaborate prank played upon a government officer sent to Nevada to assume the title of U. S. Attorney. The local residents, determined to put the newcomer in his place, draw the attorney, General Buncombe, into a false property dispute. The lawyer's supposed client seeks his aid after claiming a landslide has moved his neighbor's ranch down the hillside and completely on top of his own ranch. The rancher "on top" now claims the property as his own, insomuch as he never left his cabin while the client failed to stay on his own property during the landslide and "hold possession." The General tries the case and is astonished when the "judge" rules against his client, proclaiming, "[I]f Heaven, dissatisfied with the position of the Morgan ranch upon the mountain side, has chosen to remove it to a position more eligible and more advantageous for its owner, it ill becomes us, insects as we are, to question the legality of the act or to inquire into the reasons that prompted it" (225). The General, stunned by this decision and by the judge's later offer of a compromise (the judge admits that it would be possible for the aggrieved rancher to dig under the Morgan ranch to regain possession of his property), leaves Nevada and only manages to realize that he has been the victim of a prank two months later.

Vaidhyanathan employs this tale to describe Clemens' eventual attitudes regarding copyright. He argues that although the author appears to mock the appeal to divinity in defense of Morgan's property rights, he would later come to support such absolute notions of property rights. Entitling this section of his book "Mining and Writing," Vaidhyanathan employs the sketch as a means of introducing important questions about copyright and Clemens' feelings about the law:

> Is ownership a matter of location or substance? Does Dick Hyde own the land because he owned the area within those lines on a map, or does Morgan own it because he owns the actual dirt and house that make up the property? Similarly, does an author forever 'own' the string of words he or she produces, or does it enter the public domain as 'commons'— to use political science terminology—once it reaches the eyes, minds, and bookshelves of the reading public? Copyright, like land in Nevada, is slippery. Property rights in America are traditionally a matter of convention and agreement, and not, as the judge in the landslide case asserted, a matter of divine decree or "natural" law. While Twain employed an appeal to divinity as a target of ridicule in the landslide case, he actually grew to hold by the end of his life opinions about copyright law that were remarkably similar to the judge's 'natural law' ruling about real property. (59)

There is no denying the questions this sketch raises, but, by failing to consider it in relation to the rest of the book, and even more fundamentally, by failing to examine it in terms of the lengthy description of *mining* that surrounds it, Vaidhyanathan misreads its significance as an indication of Clemens' views on property rights. He in fact places the emphasis on the wrong argument. If writing is in some way connected to mining—and we have already seen that, for Clemens, this was the case—then we must also ask how the "laws" of the mining camps and Clemens' experiences there inform his writing. For, while there is no denying the ridiculous nature of the "divine edict" argument given by the judge to support his decision, there are other laws of the miners that are also at play in this story. There is another argument offered in the case, and, while equally ridiculous when considering the "facts" of this prank, it does not seem subject to the same scorn that comes into play elsewhere in *Roughing It.* It is the argument of the second rancher who rides his ranch down the hill that gives us the best insight into Clemens' feelings.

When the supposedly aggrieved Dick Hyde rides to the General in search of aid, he quickly describes the exchange he had with his neighbor and the argument Morgan used to justify his continued occupancy of the ranch:

> "And when I reminded him [. . .] that it [the second man's cabin and ranch] was on top of my ranch and that he was trespassing, he had the infernal meanness to ask me why didn't I *stay* on my ranch and hold possession when I see him a coming! Why didn't I *stay* on it, the blathering lunatic—by George, when I heard that racket and looked up the hill it was just like the whole world was a ripping and a tearing down that mountain side—[. . .] and in the midst of all that wrack and destruction sot that cussed Morgan on his gate-post, a wondering why I didn't *stay and hold possession!*" (222–3)

As the repetition and the italics make clear, Morgan offers but one defense of his claim; he never left his ranch during the landslide, thereby "holding possession," while Hyde's unfortunate penchant for self-preservation led him to abandon his property and yield possession in the face of the landslide. Understandably, General Buncombe is dismissive of Morgan's logic and refuses to believe that anyone would take such a claim seriously. Hyde informs him that "[E]verybody in town sustained Morgan; Hal Brayton, a very smart lawyer, had taken his case" (223).

Buncombe's position as an outsider to the community is now doubly manifest. Everyone in the town is "in" on the joke, and, in order to goad the newcomer to participate, they all must be seen as upholding Morgan's claim. At the same time, however, this supposedly unanimous support must be based on some kind of logic to be at all believable, and it is Morgan's logic that provides this foundation. The rancher is simply employing the rule that governs the miners around him; property can only be held if one visibly exercises his ownership of it. Property abandoned is property up for grabs. Buncombe dismisses the people of the Territory as "fools," but his own foolishness is a direct result of his inability to understand the ways of the community, including the common exercising of property laws and their logical limits. In fact, he learns as much when the townspeople are actually called as witnesses. Although "[t]hree-fourths of them were called by the defendant Morgan, [. . .] their testimony invariably went in favor of the plaintiff Hyde" (224). If he had been paying attention, Buncombe might have wondered what had become of the unanimous support for Morgan that Hyde had claimed when he first told the general of the incident. One can surmise that if the general had not been so cocky about his own legal expertise and so eager to demonstrate it, and, if he had taken the time to understand his community, he would not so easily have fallen prey to this prank. Even after he is able to win from the judge the concession that the "divine decree" argument is insufficient, he is still unable to reverse the declaration that Morgan must be responsible for maintaining his property: he must "dig it out from under there" if he wishes to continue owning it.

This sketch is not, as Vaidhyanathan suggests, a meditation on the question of whether or not "ownership [is] a matter of location or substance" (59). This issue is never presented as subject to debate. Rather, the sketch turns on the issue of "holding possession." What must one do to maintain control of property? The prank exposes the limits of what can be required of an owner: clearly one cannot be expected to weather a landslide in order to maintain ownership of his or her land. Buncombe, eager to show his Eastern expertise, approaches the question in the manner Vaidhyanathan appears to, considering it as a question of the definition of property. Vaidhyanathan asks, "Does Dick Hyde own the land because he owned the area within those lines on a map, or does Morgan own it because he owns the actual dirt and house that make up the property?" (59). But this is the wrong question: if General Buncombe wanted to avoid falling victim to the prank, then he would have to recognize that the fictional case presented him is a distortion of the property law all of the people in his new home live by and practice every day.

The landslide case is not, however, as great a distortion of the necessity to protect property rights as one might think. Clemens describes the extremes this notion of "holding possession" could be taken to in the mad pursuit of mining wealth:

> To show what a wild spirit possessed the mining brain of the community, I will remark that 'claims' were actually 'located' in excavations for cellars, where the pick had exposed what seemed to be quartz veins— and not cellars in the suburbs, either, but in the very heart of the city; and forthwith stock would be issued and thrown on the market. It was small matter who the cellar belonged to—the 'ledge' belonged to the

finder, and unless the U.S. government interfered (inasmuch as the government holds the primary right to mines of the noble metals in Nevada—or at least did then), it was considered to be his privilege to work it. Imagine a stranger staking out a mining claim among the costly shrubbery in your front yard and calmly proceeding to lay waste the ground with pick and shovel and blasting powder! (*Roughing It* 289)

One can easily imagine that Buncombe would have been just as skeptical regarding a miner's claim of a right to dig in someone else's basement as he was of Morgan's claim to Hyde's property. In this former case, however, Buncombe would have found himself truly on the losing side. As Clemens makes clear, the only alternative a property holder had in those heady times was to carefully lay claim to every square inch of his property, advertising his stake in any possible "ledge" on his land. This was a matter of posting a notice at the site and of registering a copy of the notice in the mining recorder's office, as well as making sure that no more than ten days elapsed without providing evidence of "working" the claim. For the homeowner of the Territory, this gave an entirely new meaning to the words "housework" and "housekeeping"!

Upon his arrival in Nevada and his commencement of his career as a miner, Twain accepts these rules and immediately puts them to use:

We took up various claims, and *commenced* shafts and tunnels on them, but never finished any of them. We had to do a certain amount of work on each to "hold" it, else other parties could seize our property after the expiration of ten days. We were always hunting up new claims and doing a little work on them and then waiting for a buyer— who never came. [. . .] We lived in a little cabin and cooked for ourselves; and altogether it was a hard life, though a hopeful one—for we never ceased to expect fortune and a customer to burst upon us some day. (230–1)

In the highly speculative, largely unregulated mining community of Nevada, ownership is never absolute and property can only be secured through constant vigilance. The money to be made in mining, Twain learns, comes not from gold or silver, but from the staking of claims and the subsequent sale of those claims. Property is not presented as something one simply owns; it is what one "holds" through labor, and only for the length of time necessary to secure a purchaser. The value of the property becomes manifest only upon its sale.

Forgetting these principles could be disastrous, as Twain discovers first-hand when he and a colleague come upon a "blind lead," a ledge below ground thought to be "worth a million" (258). He and his partner carefully take possession in the fashion that has already been established—"The notice was put up that night, and duly spread upon the recorder's books before ten o'clock" (260)—and promptly begin planning how to spend their fortunes. Because of its importance, Clemens once again reminds his readers of the laws that govern property possession in the territory: "By the laws of the district, the 'locators' or claimants of a ledge were obliged to do a fair and reasonable amount of work on their new property within ten days after the date of the location, or the property was forfeited, and anybody could go and seize it that chose. So we determined to go to work the next day" (262–63). Unfortunately for Twain, he learns that same day that a friend has grown gravely ill, and, leaving a note for his partner telling him to do the required work, he leaves town immediately. The outcome is not hard to predict. His partner leaves him a note, as well, and they both neglect to do the work necessary: "At midnight of this woful [sic] tenth day, the ledge would be 'relocatable,' and by eleven o'clock the hill was black with men prepared to do the relocating" (268). Property could be "relocated"—whether that property were Hyde or Morgan's ranch or Twain's ledge—if an owner failed to demonstrate his possession. To make certain the moral is not missed, Clemens repeats it once again, "We would have been millionaires if we had only worked with pick and spade one little day on our property and so secured our ownership!" (269).

There are several clear parallels between these descriptions of Twain's dealing in ledges and Clemens' dealing in copyrights: the limited duration of the initial claim, the constant industry required to maintain possession, and the value of the property depending upon its sale. All of these ideas seem to have informed Clemens' views on literary property. "Jim Wolfe and the Cats" is only his story so long as he exercises his possession of it; once he has failed to do so, some other literary prospector can "come upon the property" and employ his right to make money off of it if he can. Given these similarities, it is not surprising that Clemens hearkened back to these principles of his mining days when he was composing arguments to use against Brander Matthews in their dispute over copyright law. He writes in his notebook in early 1888:

> In the mines, if you neglected for a certain time to work your claim,
> it was held to be abandoned, & anybody could take it. It did not hurt
> the character of the taker. He was not a thief. The 'pirate' who takes an

American's abandoned book is not a thief. You have no reasonable complaint against him.

If you had leveled your complaint agst the Am. author & publisher
you'd have *had* a complaint. (*Notebooks* 3: 366)

This last statement seems to be a remarkable exercise in blaming the victim,
but it also provides a good idea of the emphasis Clemens put on the author
and publisher's responsibility for maintaining a copyright.

As excessive as this language might appear, he makes an even harsher
statement in "Mr. Matthews's Second Article," a draft of a reply to Matthews:

When you speak of the 'misdeeds' of certain British publishers, the
word has no meaning. The blame belongs with the American author; it
is he that deserves the lash. *The American author is the father, the creator,
of the so-called British 'pirate.'* He begot him, he is his own child; he feeds
him, nurses him, coddles him, shelters him, protects him; & if he did
his plain simple duty & withdrew this support, the 'pirate' would in
that instant cease to exist in *fact* as he has already & long ago ceased to
exist in *law.* (emphasis in original 366n)

This is an unmistakable extension of earlier statements in his notebook: not
only is the author responsible for the piracy of his work, but also it is his failure to do "his plain simple duty" that creates piracy in the first place.
Because he had the resources to conform to both British and American law,
Clemens' felt that the laws as they stood were quite adequate to protect
American authors, hence his claim that pirates had "ceased to exist in law."
The "pirate" emerges only as a result of the sloth and irresponsibility of the
writer. The picture he draws of the relationship between authors and pirates
and the status of literary property makes the Nevada mining camps seem
quite tame. All of publishing seems to be made up of literary "claim
jumpers": no restraint is to be expected of them, for they are products of an
author's own carelessness.

Clemens was a canny literary prospector, and he would hold, sell, and
"abandon" his claims with care. There is a great deal of correspondence
addressing the maintenance of his copyrights from the early years of his
career, coinciding with the publication of his books *The Innocents Abroad*
and *Roughing It. Jumping Frog* had served to verify the value of the "Mark
Twain ledge," and he dealt with his subsequent works accordingly, guarding
his claim while at the same time allowing just enough of the "ore"—whether
that be travel letters later revised into books or an occasional short story—to

circulate and continue whetting the public's interest in "Twain" products. As he was making arrangements for the publication of *Roughing It,* he gave a great deal more thought to overseas sale of the work than he had his previous works. He wrote his publisher, Elisha Bliss, in 1871,

> Have you heard anything from Routledge? Considering the large English sale he made of one of my other books (Jumping Frog,) I thought may be we might make something if I could give him a secure copyright.—There seems to be no convenient way to beat those Canadian re-publishers anyway—though I *can* go over the line and get out a copyright if you wish it and think it would hold water. (*Letters to His Publishers* 67)

This letter gives a good insight into Clemens' views on copyright and his literary property during this time period. Rather than nursing a grudge against Routledge for his (pirated) success with *Jumping Frog,* Clemens seems to accept the work's popularity in an unauthorized re-print as almost a calling card, an opening for further business arrangements. He also seems remarkably sanguine regarding the Canadian piracy of his novels, an attitude that may seem surprising to those familiar only with Clemens' much more publicized battles with the Canadians. He was looking to make deals, to sell stock in "Twain," and an important component of this was making deals with those already convinced of the worth in the claim. Those investors, as Clemens' arrangement with Routledge indicates, were often exactly the same people who had so aggressively moved in on the "Twain" stake in the first place. Their success could interest them in later owning a share of it legally.

Clemens' acknowledgment of the importance of gaining name recognition during these early years of his career is a good example of his early publishing acumen. As Richard Lowry notes, "By the 1870s, not only was a name essential for economic success, a work had virtually no *literary* value unless it was known by its author" (32). This was particularly true in the case of subscription publishing, where book agents traveled the countryside attempting to woo potential buyers with attractive "mock-ups" of books, containing compelling excerpts and the promise of many pictures. The assured track record of a favorite author was also an attractive incentive to buy a book on a subscription basis.

Subscription publishing, as Bliss approached it, was not entirely removed from Clemens' experiences in the mining territories of Nevada. In *Roughing It,* Twain learns that the real money in mining rests not in what is dug from the earth but from the buying and selling of claims, and he reflects on the importance of names in pursuing this lucrative form of "mining":

> We prospected and took up new claims, put "notices" on them and gave them grandiloquent names. We traded some of our "feet" for "feet" in other people's claims. In a little while we owned largely in the "Gray Eagle," the "Columbiana," the "Branch Mint," the "Maria Jane," the "Universe," the "Root-Hog-or-Die," the "Samson and Delilah," the "Treasure Trove," the "Golconda," the "Sultana," the "Boomerang," the "Great Republic," the "Grand Mogul," and fifty other "mines" that had never been molested by a shovel or scratched with a pick. (193)

The prevalence of this practice is emphasized by Twain's reiteration of it as he switches careers, becoming a reporter for a territorial newspaper: "You could go up on the mountain side, scratch around and find a ledge (there was no lack of them), put up a 'notice' with a grandiloquent name in it, start a shaft, get your stock printed, and with nothing whatever to prove your mine was worth a straw, you could put your stock on the market and sell out for hundreds and even thousand of dollars" (285–86). Such speculation, Twain notes, depended upon name recognition, and a newspaper reporter could do valuable service in increasing the credibility of these mines. Twain writes that a visit to the newspaper office would often immediately follow the taking up of a claim, the claimholder seeking some kind of written notice of the claim to publicize it: "They did not care a fig what you said about the property so you said something" (287). This same approach to publicity often served Clemens well as an author and publisher.

THE DEBATE CONTINUES: INTERNATIONAL COPYRIGHT LEGISLATION IN THE 1870s

As we have already noted, the debate over copyright law largely abated during the Civil War, and first re-emerged in the most public fashion with the second edition of Henry Carey's *Letters on International Copyright* in 1868.[2] In addition to the allusions to slavery Carey included in his new preface (noted in Chapter Two), Carey repeated his description of the debate over copyright as pitting the selfish interests of authors against those of readers:

> On the one side, there will be found a few thousand persons interested in maintaining the monopolies that had been granted to authors and publishers, foreign and domestic. On the other, sixty or eighty millions,

tired of taxation and determined that books shall be more cheaply fur-
nished. War will then come, and the domestic author, sharing in the
'disgrace and danger' attendant upon his alliance with foreign authors
and domestic publishers, may perhaps find reason to rejoice if the people fail to arrive at the conclusion that the last extension of *his own privileges* had been inexpedient and should be at once recalled. (14)

Once again, forty years later, here is the cry of monopoly that Cooper had
predicted would be a major component of the debate over international
copyright. Carey uses extreme language, vaguely suggesting that the resist-
ance to new legislation is akin to America's revolutionary struggle—the people will rise up, "tired of taxation"—and making the argument one of the
public versus authors and publishers. The coming "war," a war that carries
overtones of further civil strife, will also resemble its revolutionary model in
the unholy alliance between authors who invite "disgrace" and their foreign
counterparts. Not only is the debate between the privileged few and the
many, the oligarchy and the democrats, but it is also between true Americans
and those who have international ties.

Given the nature of this rhetoric, it is not surprising that Carey's *Letters*
continued to be a touchstone of the debate over international copyright. As
Congress once again took up the issue in 1872, one congressman, Stevenson
Archer of Maryland, gave a speech refuting Carey. If we recall that his arguments had originally been made in 1854, we realize how prevalent his objections had become. In his defense of international copyright, Archer accepts
Carey's author vs. reader dichotomy and the suggestion of conflict, but this
time the conflict imagined is not domestic. The congressman declares,

The truth is, the responsibility rests with every individual who reads
these pirated books, especially unless he uses all due means, by protest
and otherwise, to put a stop to such robbery. And since the large mass of
our people do read such books, and that, too, without so much as a
protest, it is the people themselves who are to blame. And although
there is no shadow of doubt that a vast majority of them are in favor of
the law proposed, yet as it is next to impossible for them to act in con-
cert in the matter, so as to express their will, the responsibility really
rests on their Representatives, who, knowing as they do, that not only
justice, but the sovereign people as well, are on the side of international
copyright, should unhesitatingly act in the matter, and that speedily, for,
as I just said, if long postponed, our English friends may turn the tables
on us with a vengeance. (Archer 14)

Rather than a civil war, Archer seems to imagine an erupting conflict with Great Britain, which might decide to end its patient suffering and strike back at the U.S. Once again, the nature of the confrontation is left deliberately vague, although it is likely a trade war.

An even more interesting element of this passage is his reference to the readers. If American authors suffer, which he insists they do, it is because of the readers' support for the practice of piracy. This is not because readers have bad intentions; they simply lack the will to resist the lure of cheap books. They are both powerful in their support of piracy and powerless to stop it. On the one hand, he suggests that it is the readers who instigate the widespread piracy of texts because of their continued purchasing of them; on the other, he argues that the majority favors an international copyright bill and would take action against piracy if it could. Because they do not have the ability to do the right thing, Archer urges their representatives to act for them for the higher good. While stopping short of condemning readers for their part in the encouragement of unauthorized publications, Archer is one of the first supporters of international copyright to place the blame not at the feet of the U.S. government or the publishers, but of the readers themselves.

If copyright equals conflict, then the primary question came to be which side the public supported. Throughout the debate, opponents of international copyright suggested that they were on the side of American citizens, enlisting their support to stop any measure that they claimed would hinder the education of the American public and endanger democracy. George Haven Putnam recalled in a speech given to the New York Free-Trade Club that when the international copyright bill was considered in 1872, "Messrs. Harper, in a letter presented by their counsel, objected to any measure of international copyright on the broad ground that it would 'add to the price of books and interfere with the education of the people'" (30–1). William Cullen Bryant, editor of the New York newspaper *The Evening Post,* provided a forum for both sides of the debate, although his own views in favor of the bill were well known. One writer, advocating a flat fee of five percent of profits rather than an actual copyright for foreign authors, suggested

> The interests of the public and the publishers in this matter of International Copyright are bound up together. If we give up the right of republication, we thereby place ourselves entirely at the mercy of the English authors and publishers, and we will have to accept their wares in any form and at whatever price they may choose to make.

> That this would result in a large advance on the cost of all new
> books, and thereby in a great limitation in the sale of the most
> important works of science and education, no one acquainted with
> the English system of publishing and the English character will for a
> moment doubt. (Elderkin 1)

The writer employs three arguments here that are relevant to the present discussion. He includes the by-now familiar invocation of the unscrupulous
nature of the English, an accusation of greed that seems to have persisted
since the days that Dickens spoke out regarding the law. Once again citing
the anticipated rise in prices, the writer also argues that international copyright would hinder American education and advancement; while no one
might lament higher prices for romances, critics hoped they might speak up
in opposition to an increase in the price of "the most important works of science and education." The most interesting tactic this writer employs, however, is to suggest that readers and publishers are on the same side, each
fighting against English domination.

Was the public, then, aligned with the "pirates"? This was a claim that
most supporters of international copyright were understandably reluctant to
accept, although as the cause gained momentum throughout the remainder
of the century, they became more and more inclined to confront their readers on moral grounds. During the debate over the law in 1872, most advocates were more inclined to suggest that readers were simply uninformed. An
editorial of this time, presumably written by Bryant, provides a good example of how copyright advocates dealt with the difficult question of public
approval of their cause. Bryant provides a concise and useful breakdown of
how several different factions interested in the issue felt. He honestly states
the opposition of the publishing trade to the new bill—"it would be idle to
deny that the publishing interests of the country as a whole, are arrayed
against an International Copyright"—as well as that of the tradeworkers:
"They consider it as it affects their own business, and, so far as we can learn,
are almost unanimously opposed to any and every form of International
Copyright" ("International Copyright Plans" n.p.). Not surprisingly, he
states the almost universal support of authors for the bill, who are primarily
motivated not by greed, he suggests, but "by professional spirit and sympathy, and by a sense of justice."

Bryant finds himself in a much more difficult position when it comes
to describing the feeling of readers on the subject. This is, presumably, the
audience he is attempting to reach in his editorial. His description of their
views is revealing:

The Consumers of Books

> The reading public in general remain to be heard from. At present
> there seems to be less popular interest in the question than there has
> occasionally been at former times. The people do not seem to be
> uneasy lest books are going to be made dear, as the opponents of
> copyright assume. Their sympathy with authors is strong, and assum-
> ing, as Congress seems ready to assume, that foreign authors must in
> some way have a copyright here, it seems most likely that the book-
> reading public at large would much rather have the law drawn in the
> interests of the authors than of the publishers. (n.p.)

When one considers how actively *The Evening Post* was advocating for
international copyright, it is admirable that Bryant was so candid in his
assessment of the opposition to the bill. His description here is much more
vague. Readers are uninterested in the matter, but Bryant suggests that this
is positive in that it speaks against the oft-cited public anxiety over the
increase in prices of books. In place of any definite position on the issue,
Bryant apparently can only offer the assertion that readers are in "sympathy" with authors and that this bond makes it "most likely" that readers
would side with authors rather than publishers. On the whole, Bryant does
little better than Archer in his effort to demonstrate the public's endorsement of international copyright, and, at this stage in the debate, opponents
seemed to offer more compelling claims of popular support.

With only authors, publishers, and tradespeople speaking out on the
matter in 1873, Congress was reluctant to act. In February, the Joint
Committee on the Library, which had been asked to prepare a report on
the "practicability" of international copyright, weighed in against any such
legislation. The report's author, a senator from Maine, commented upon
the silence of the public: "we are not aware of any popular representation
or demand, by memorial or remonstrance, or otherwise, on behalf of
either book buyers or readers or the mass of the people" (Morrill 2). Referring to the Constitutional language mandating copyright only for the purpose of promoting science and the useful arts, the report continued, "A
demand for copyright, national or international, as a measure of protection to a property right simply, necessarily tends to sink the question of
science to the level of a commercial transaction, and subjects it to the
odium of an indefensible monopoly" (3). The committee further argued
that, given copyright's original purpose, the needs of publishers and printers had to be addressed:

Authorship, standing by itself, although the essential element, still, it is not all the world of letters, and cannot in any measure, having at heart the interests of literature, be considered as standing independent and by itself. If it be conceded to be the soul of science, it is essential that its productions should be embodied in books, and these involve the varied skill, industries, and cunning workmanship of many hands, and at last, and not the least important agency, the enterprise, capital, and address of the publisher through whom these books are to be introduced to the reading public.

These interests press upon the legislator at the very threshold of any measure of international copyright, demanding consideration and protection. (4)

In addition to alleging possible harm to those industries so vital to the progress of science, the report once again repeated the claim that international copyright would be "a hinderance to the diffusion of knowledge among the people and to the cause of universal education" (8). Bryant could only throw up his hands, noting, "The impression is that nothing will be done this year, and that the only value of the investigation will be in calling the public attention to the demands and rights of literary men in this matter" (Editorial n.p.). While it is difficult to gauge public opinion, it is clear that as far as Congress was concerned, the opponents of international copyright were winning the battle, their arguments being repeated again and again in the legislature.

This was the public atmosphere in which Clemens first seriously looked to protect his literary property. Throughout his career he often appeared to take the prospector's approach to publicity that he had described in *Roughing It*, viewing any notice as positive—one thinks of his response to the banning of *Huck Finn* by the Committee of the Public Library of Concord, Massachusetts (Hoffman 322)—but he was, in truth, very concerned with how his audiences perceived him. Indeed, some of Clemens' most high-profile attempts to protect his copyrights are marked by a degree of humor that would often persist in his statements on the subject even while his legal activities were in extreme earnest. He wrote the following preface to a pamphlet he considered publishing in 1873:

It is not my desire to republish these New York Herald letters in this form; I only do it to forestall some small pirate or other in the book trade.

If I do not publish some such person may, and I then become tacitly accessory to a theft. I have had a recent unpleasant experience of this kind. I have copyrighted the letters here in London simply to prevent their republication in Great Britain in pamphlet form. My objection to such republication, either in America or England, is, that I think everybody has already had enough of the Shah of Persia.[3] I am sure I have. To the letters I have added certain sketches of mine which are little known or not known at all in America, to the end that the purchaser of the pamphlet may get back a portion of his money and skip the chapters that refer to the Shah altogether. (*Letters to His Publishers* 79–80).

Although he did not publish the planned pamphlet or the preface, his words here give us a good example of how the author attempted to present himself to his audience while defending his copyright. His desire to protect his literary property is not, he assures the reader, a matter of self-interest. He is, rather, helping us to avoid too much of a subject that he is sure will already have bored his audience.[4] It is not about him and his profits; it is about "everybody." Beyond the self-deprecation of this tactic, it is interesting how Clemens seems to take the widespread piracy of his work for granted; he assumes his readers will have encountered his work already.[5]

Despite this acknowledged participation of his readers in robbing him of his profits, Clemens does not risk alienating them through moralizing. The readers are not complicit in the theft of his work, he assures them, although clearly he recognized that they are the chief beneficiaries; instead, he states that, if he were to fail to protect his copyright, *he* would be the "tacit accessory" to the theft.[6] Again, the responsibility for stopping such piracies rests largely with the author. Finally, he converts this self-effacing justification of publication as defense of copyright into an advertisement: the reader is promised something new in addition to those already pirated letters. The publication of the pamphlet is not a mere exercise in throwing borders around his already trampled-upon literary property; it is, he tells his readers, an opportunity for them to read something besides the all-too-familiar pirated piece on the Shah.

Clemens clearly viewed the protection of his literary property as his responsibility, but, at the same time, he seemed wary in these early days of addressing the issue of copyright law very publicly. As his popularity increased, however, it became difficult for him to keep silent on the issue. It is not surprising that in 1875 William Dean Howells wrote him, asking, "don't you want to air your notions of copyright in the Atlantic?" (Smith, *Howells-Twain* 1: 98). The normally outspoken author appeared suddenly reluctant to take a public stand on the issue. He replied to Howells,

> I did think of writing upon copyright (without signature), but con-
> cluded that the most effectual method of carrying out my views will be
> to get all authors signatures to my petition & then go to Washington &
> besiege Congress myself, (appearing simply as agent for bigger men.)
> This is of course the best way—& to make it effectual, no literature
> must let the cat out of the bag beforehand. (98)

Clemens' parenthetical admission that he would only write upon the subject
without affixing his name to the piece is a clear indication of his lack of
enthusiasm for becoming publicly involved, as is his strange plan to "besiege
Congress" and—once again in parenthesis—"simply as agent." Each bold
declaration of intent is followed by a parenthetical disclaimer refusing to
appear in his capacity as author. His hesitation to be seen as a proponent of
the law explains his rather weak argument that any press attention given to
the circulating petition and his championing of it would limit its effective-
ness when one expects the exact opposite to be more likely. Despite his
strong feelings on the subject and his desire to protect his literary property,
Clemens does not appear to have wanted to risk his blossoming popularity
by being seen as opposing his readers.

This becomes even more evident when Howells appears willing to
accept his plan and begins to move on it. Clemens writes with even more
detail regarding how it is to be carried out:

> My plan is this—You are to get Mr. Lowell & Mr. Longfellow to be the
> first signers of my copyright petition; you must sign it yourself & get
> Mr. Whittier to do likewise. Then Holmes will sign—he said he would
> if he didn't have to stand at the head. Then I'm fixed. I will then put a
> gentlemanly chap under wages & send him personally to every author
> of distinction in the country & corral the rest of the signatures. Then
> I'll have the whole thing lithographed (about a thousand copies) &
> move upon the President & Congress *in person,* but in the subordinate
> capacity of a party who is merely the agent of better & wiser men—men
> whom the country cannot venture to laugh at. (99)

There is the familiar expression of humility here that marks so much of
Clemens' correspondence; he is one that the country presumably would "venture to laugh at," so, if the cause is to get the serious attention it deserves, he
must appear as only a "subordinate" party. He once again seems to qualify his
strong statement of intent—he will "move upon the President & Congress *in
person*"—but only in a secondary capacity. It is an odd statement; his choice

of emphasis seems to suggest that he understood or felt that a personal appeal would be the most effective form of lobbying, but he then seems immediately to undermine this self-confident statement. There is also the peculiar structure of his plan: it appears that every other prominent author living must sign the petition first before Clemens will sign his name. Once again, this could be an example of his deference to the Boston literati; however, one cannot ignore the fact that his plan also serves to distance him from his own petition. In his letter he includes a draft of his proposed petition, but he notes that it should only be regarded for its "substance," not its language, stating, "I want Mr. Lowell to furnish the words (& the ideas too,) if he will do it" (100). While critics have noted this petition drive as evidence of Clemens' convictions regarding copyright, none has commented on his apparent uneasiness.[7]

Even his target for the petition, the Congress, seems carefully chosen. He notes in his letter, "You see, what I want to drive into the <public> Congressional mind is the simple fact that the moral law is, '*Thou* shalt not steal'—no matter what Europe may do" (100). Clemens' decision to strike out the word "public" again denotes a hesitation to confront his readers regarding the practice of literary piracy. Surely the message regarding stealing should be directed to them, as well. He would have to be aware of the fact that one way of pressuring Congress would be to garner public support for his cause. As a popular author and speaker, he was a natural candidate for undertaking such a job. His reluctance to consider it, even in private correspondence with Howells, is telling.

In place of heading up a serious petition drive intended to influence his readers as well as Congress, Clemens once again offered a humorous piece of prose, this time a satirical petition. In "Petition Concerning Copyright," he satirizes the logic governing copyright law, taking aim at the distinction between literary property and other property. The petition states, "*Whereas,* Forty-two years seems an exceedingly just and righteous term, and a sufficiently long one for the retention of property; *Therefore,* Your petitioner, having the good of his country solely at heart, humbly prays that 'equal rights' and fair and equal treatment may be meted out to all citizens, by the restriction of rights in *all* property, real estate included, to the beneficent term of forty-two years" (*Sketches New and Old* 209). Clemens included the name Mark Twain at the bottom of this petition, an apparent sign that, when couched in humor, he was willing to make a public statement regarding copyright law. It is worth mentioning, however, that once again his target seems carefully chosen. The petition is explicitly aimed at Congress and the folly of its laws. He emphasizes this point in "A Paragraph Not Added to the Petition":

The charming absurdity of restricting property-rights in books to forty-
two years sticks prominently out in the fact that hardly any man's
books ever *live* forty-two years, or even the half of it; and so, for the
sake of getting a shabby advantage of the heirs of about one Scott or
Burns or Milton in a hundred years, the lawmakers of the "Great"
Republic are content to leave that poor little pilfering edict on the
statute-books. (209)

In this paragraph, as in his petition, Clemens directs his attention exclusively
at Congress rather than addressing the more thorny issue of reader responsibility. While reluctant to attack the public, he was never slow to criticize the
government. The issue he chose for his critique is one that had attracted less
controversy; although copyright extension has been one of the primary issues
of intellectual property in recent years, it was not equally prominent for
much of the nineteenth century following the amendment extending copyrights in 1831. By publishing this petition in his collection of humorous
sketches, Clemens intended to enlist public support for change to the copyright law, yet his choice of topic is removed from the most pressing issue of
the day, international copyright, and it does not seem calculated to inspire
self-reflection on the part of readers except, perhaps, to encourage them to
think more carefully about the nature of literary property. On the whole, the
petition represents a rather timid public intervention in the controversy.

Howells, on the other hand, shows a much greater willingness to
engage the issue directly, as he demonstrates in the review of *Sketches, New
and Old* that he wrote for the *Atlantic Monthly.* There he pays inordinate
attention to the two-page story, appearing to magnify its importance within
the lengthy collection. He praises the "ironical prayer" for the force of its
argument, then immediately goes further than Clemens himself appeared
willing to go: "If property in houses or lands—which a man may get by dishonest trickery, or usury, or hard rapacity—were in danger of ceasing after
forty-two years, the whole virtuous community would rouse itself to perpetuate the author's right to the product of his brain, and no griping bidder at
tax-sales but would demand the protection of literature by indefinite copyright" (qtd. in Budd 151). While Clemens had pitched his satire in such a
way as to indict the legislature, Howells reinterprets it as an attack on a
hypocrisy that conceivably everyone shares in, suggesting that the self-interest of owners of real estate would prompt them to act where "virtue" has not.
Even more than that, Howells suggests that authors have a clearer and more
moral right to their property because it has not been gained through any
potential "dishonesty." Clemens could have pitched his satire much more in

this direction if he had chosen; that Howells sharpens its message tells us much about the differences in the views of the two authors and how they chose to broach the subject with their readers.

COPYRIGHTS AND TRADEMARKS

Clemens may have chosen to act cautiously in defending his copyrights, but he could ill-afford to show the same caution in defending the primary source of his wealth: Mark Twain. In the 1870s, as Clemens was solidifying the reputation of Mark Twain, he worked hard to protect the name of while approaching the issue of copyright with a degree of self-effacement that would fall away later in his career. The need for protection was making itself well known. As Andrew Hoffman writes, "To some, Mark Twain was a detachable persona, a stock figure invented by one man but playable by many, like Hamlet or Oedipus. Mark Twain had become a public possession and Sam had lost absolute control over him" (230). This was not a loss that Clemens was ready to accept, and in 1873 he took action. Hoffman writes,

> Then, in a brash defense of his Mark Twain persona, he initiated a $20,000 lawsuit against a publisher who had promoted a miscellany containing some early Twain material by using his pseudonym. Sam sued not for infringement of copyright, because the published material had none, but for trademark infringement. The idea that a nom de plume might be a trademark had never been tested and this case proved a swift success. Sam had demonstrated he had a proprietary interest in his invented persona to the satisfaction of the judge, who granted an injunction. (211)

Clemens himself does not seem to have had such a clear idea of what he was undertaking or the repercussions it might have for future artists who would use this case to stake a claim in their artistic persona. He wrote Warner, "Yesterday I sued a New York fraud for $20,000 damages for violating my copyright" (*Letters to His Publishers* 76). His statement seems to indicate a misunderstanding of either his own suit or of copyright law for, as Hoffman points out, he did not have a case against the publisher regarding copyright infringement.

Still, he seems to have felt that the case had won him broad protections. When another publisher contacted him two years later regarding publishing some of his older writings in an anthology, the author's response shows a vehemence not previously seen in his copyright dealings:

It was hardly right of you to *announce* me and THEN propose to ask my permission. But I gather from your letter that your justification for this was that you felt free to take possession of any uncopyrighted matter of mine which might be lying around, and you meant to ask permission only in the case of copyrighted matter. There was another publisher who allowed that queer sort of morality to fool him. He discovered, in a United States Court, to his serious pecuniary cost, that my sole ownership of my matter is perfect and impregnable—I mean *all* of my matter—every single page I ever wrote. (88–9)

His diction indicates a belief that he had staked total and complete possession of his property, that his trademark suit had won him perpetual ownership. There appears to be a degree of bluster, however, not only because the decision clearly did not grant him such sweeping protection, but also because he reveals in a letter written a short time later to his then-publisher Charles Osgood that he recognized that he did not possess the protection he claims:

If Gill uses my matter without printing my name anywhere in his book he will do himself no good and me no serious harm—and neither will he be violating trademark, I suppose.

But what he is really up to, I imagine, is to use my name inside the book but not on the cover.

Say—the man is a natural deceiver. The title of his series shows it: Treasure *Trove* means treasure *found*, I think—whereas his is more properly Treasure *Stolen* and ought to be so styled. (89)

Despite his fervent hope that his trademark victory would protect all of his writing, Clemens realized that he had in fact gained only very specific protections.

Regardless of his apparent powerlessness, Clemens was not mollified; he continued to send Osgood complaints about Gill and various plans for either stopping or ridiculing the publisher, including a statement that he intended to publish, with or without Gill's signature, proclaiming, "Being under the impression that unwatched (that is to say, uncopyrighted) literary property was without protection in law, and could therefore be seized under the black flag and used with impunity, we recently laid hands upon a quantity of such goods" (91). The statement included a postscript to be signed by any author or publisher Gill had "pirated." Clemens wrote, "Then you must have every aggrieved author and publisher sign it (I would rather a greater name than mine should come first in the list—seems to me it would be better but I am not strenuous)" (90). The parenthetical reluctance to serve as the primary agent, couched in terms of self-deprecation, is by now familiar.

It does not seem that Osgood went along with this scheme, but, once again, Clemens' language is instructive: he portrays Gill as believing works that have not been copyrighted are "unwatched." This recalls the link between literary property and mining claims; if they haven't been actively protected, they are fair game. In this case, however, Clemens mistakenly assumes that his trademark victory has effectively granted him perpetual copyright, an on-going claim on his property. Once again, this appears to be more of an attempt to dissuade pirates than an accurate representation of his understanding, for when it came time to take Gill to court, Clemens wrote Osgood that he wished the publisher tried "Simply for *violating my trademark*—copyright not to be mentioned" (93). This was essentially the only case that Clemens had, a fact he acknowledged when he learned that his lawyer had settled with Gill on the condition that the publisher remove the author's name, even though he kept the article: "Of course this destroys the possibility of my suing him for violating trade-mark, and I don't wish to sue him for anything else" (94–5).

Even after he had been repeatedly vexed by unauthorized reprintings, including the damaging Canadian piracy of *The Adventures of Tom Sawyer*, he showed a remarkable degree of amicability to a California publisher who wrote to him regarding publishing his work. The publisher employed the mining language that seems to have defined much of Clemens' early thinking regarding literary property, writing, "We have worked over your old diggins somewhat, filching anything of yours that we can find: but would prefer to be honest and deal with you direct" (qtd. in Smith 1: 219n). Smith has noted the mining language, remarking, "The *Argonaut*'s prospecting seems already to have extended beyond Mark Twain's 'old diggins,'" noting that the magazine was copying Clemens' most recent works (219n). Rather than blasting the publisher as he had Gill only a couple of years before, Clemens wrote Howells regarding the request: "Have written Frank Pixley that I would speak to you [. . .] & if you were willing to simultane with the Argonaut, I would write him so. [. . .] I didn't tell him you *wouldn't*, because I'm not authorized to speak for you—but told him to write you himself if he preferred. He is a good fellow, but Dam the Argonaut" (219). It is not surprising that Howells rejected the request to share Clemens' *Atlantic* articles with another American editor. What is surprising is Clemens' magnanimity here; no doubt his feelings were somewhat mollified by his apparent fondness for the editor, but this does not negate his surprising willingness to abide a confessed pirate, even as he condemns the magazine.

CLEMENS AND THE CANADIANS

Perhaps one of the most famous nineteenth-century struggles over copyright involved Clemens and Canadian publishers, most notably Belford Brothers. The piracy of *The Adventures of Tom Sawyer* caused him particular vexation, for he had believed that, in making careful arrangements with his publishers in England, he provided adequate protection for the novel. He exchanged anxious correspondence with his British agent, proclaiming, "We cannot issue for 6 weeks yet, and by that time Belford will have sold 100,000 over the frontier and killed my book dead. This piracy will cost me $10,000, and I will spend as much more to choke off those pirates, if the thing can be done" (*Letters to His Publishers* 106).[8] Clemens learned to his dismay that nothing could be done regarding Belford's publication of *Tom Sawyer*. He wrote a month later,

> We find our copyright law here to be nearly worthless, and if I can make a living out of plays, I shall never write another book. For the present I have placed the three books in mind, in the waste basket [. . .].
>
> The Canadian "Tom Sawyer" has actually taken the market away from us in every village in the Union. We cannot accomplish anything against the newsdealers because the newsdealer is privileged to sell a pirated book until we give him personal and distinct notice, that the book is copyrighted.[9] The Publishers say that as near as their lawyers can make it out, English copyright is not worth anything in Canada, unless it be recorded in Canada, within sixty days after publication in England. . . . (106–7).

Having dealt with literary piracy to various degrees prior to the publication of *Tom Sawyer*, he was already familiar with the various weaknesses of copyright law. Two things unique to this case seem to have given him pause: the first was the severity and proximity of the loss: thousands of pirated copies of his novels were directly competing with his copyrighted edition. This was far more serious than the pilfering of stories for an anthology or the publication of an edition overseas that did not bite into his subscription publication. The other unique aspect of this case is that Clemens truly believed he had done what was necessary to protect his copyright, to guarantee his claim. The Belford piracy was an attack on his understanding of property rights; he had "held" possession, so how could he now find himself with no recourse?

Given the tone of his response to the apparently unstoppable piracy of his novel, it is not surprising that critics have focused on his battles with Belford as an indication of his passionate belief in literary property rights. If we accept the author's claim that he is ready to throw over his novel writing because of the flawed nature of copyright protection, then it would certainly seem that Clemens had a strong conviction regarding the matter. Indeed, he was disheartened by his inability to stop the Canadians. In reply to a request from Howells to write a piece for the *Atlantic,* he wrote, "Ah, don't I wish I could venture to write for the Atlantic! The only thing in the way is Canada. If Mr. Houghton can copyright my stuff in Canada & hold it *himself,* & will prosecute & stop any infringement, I shall be glad enough to write; but I cannot trust any more Canadians after my late experience. I suppose they are all born pirates" (Smith 1: 236). This rhetorical "throwing up of hands" is a fair indication of the author's feeling of powerlessness. His wish that Houghton would take responsibility not only for copyrighting his work but also for punishing those who infringed upon it suggest a radical retreat on his part.

His response to Canadian piracy, as fervent as it was, does not indicate a burgeoning belief in an abstract notion of literary property rights as matters of divine or natural law, however. This was still not a part of his views on the matter. Belford's piracy showed Clemens that copyright law, in fact, did not support his Western notions of the law. When he lost his big stake in Nevada through neglecting to work the mine within the first ten days, he did not challenge the injustice of it; he knew that he had failed to do what was required to hold the property. With Belford's successful printing of *Tom Sawyer,* Clemens learned for the first time that he could do everything that he believed was necessary to maintain his property and still lose his rights.

Despite his apparent despair, he did not stop writing. So strong was his drive to complete *A Tramp Abroad* that it appears even the problem of Belford was something of a minor distraction:

> That most infernally troublesome book [The Tramp Abroad] is at last hidden from my sight & mind in the jaws of three steam presses. Orders received for 25,000 copies—not a very satisfactory start, but the diligent Canadian has warned everybody that he will glut the market at half-a-dollar within ten days after we issue; proclaims that he has bought advance-sheets right along from pressmen & understrappers in the three printing-offices, attending to the matter in person here under

an assumed name. Such is Belford! However, these things discomfort
me not in the slightest degree. My joy in getting the book out of my
hands fills me up & leaves no room for trivial griefs. (290)

Such expressions more likely demonstrate the satisfaction he felt finishing his
novel than his willingness to submit to Belford's piracy, for, while he continued writing, he frequently bent his mind to the problem of international
copyright, seeking a way to circumvent the apparently intractable problem of
Canadian piracy.

Once again, he focused his efforts on pushing for legislative action
while continuing to pursue legal address in the courts, rather than attempting to influence his readers directly. He believed that the trademark decision
he had won in 1873 would provide him the legal remedy he needed to move
against Belford. He pursued a trademark violation case against the publisher
for printing a collection entitled *Sketches of Mark Twain* in 1880 even as he
contemplated other solutions. [10] In 1883, a judge ruled that his trademark
of "Mark Twain" could not grant him more copyright protection than the
law had granted "Samuel Clemens" (Doyno 189). As his case worked its
way through the judicial branch, he attempted to move the legislative and
executive to action. He wrote to Howells in March of 1880, "I have just
written Congress asking for a law making the selling of <Cana> pirated
books a penal offense, punishable by fine & imprisonment, like dealing in
any other kind of stolen goods. Wish we could have had something of the
sort recommended in the President's message" (Smith 1: 295). When it
came to working behind the scenes, Clemens had by now become an active
copyright advocate.

He learned a couple of months later that such legal action would be
impossible, and he wrote to Howells, "So I have changed my mind & my
course; I go north, to kill a pirate. I must procure repose *some* way, else I cannot get down to work again" (307). Fortunately, he did not take such drastic
measures. Instead, when it came time to secure the copyright of his next
novel, *The Prince and the Pauper,* he did his best to fulfill the requirements of
Canadian law to guarantee copyright protection. He wrote to his new publisher, James R. Osgood,

How would it do, to set up the first and last signatures in Boston, and
do the rest in Canada? You see, what I'm after is a *preventive;* it is
preferable to even the best of cures. Those sons of up there will steal
anything they can get their hands on—possible suits for damages and
felony would be no more restraint upon them, I think, than would the

> presence of a young lady be upon a stud-horse who had just found a
> mare unprotected by international copyright. In the one case, theft and
> piracy is the fateful doom; in the other, copulation and adultery. (*Let-*
> *ters to his Publishers* 144)

This is a unique naturalistic description of literary piracy. While it clearly
shows Clemens' contempt for Belford, it is also strictly in keeping with his
ideas regarding authorial responsibility. Piracy seems a sexual, instinctive
compulsion; the pirate cannot be expected to restrain himself from following
his basest instinct by any sort of respect for morality and decency. The odd
image of the powerless "young lady" upon the determined stud-horse would
appear to demonstrate the strength of the pirate's compulsion. International
copyright is here not a right as much as it is a prophylactic. One does not
expect the stud to change its behavior; in Clemens' example, the onus is
upon the mare to somehow prevent the "adultery" of piracy. The image suggests the author's pessimism finally in the government's ability to be proactive
in stopping the publishers. His commentary on the state of legal remedies for
piracy is biting: no current law provides any effective restraint, the threat of
lawsuits after the fact is as ineffective as timid snaps of a whip. Absent a law
strong enough to drive the behavior of publishers, one must be produced
that would protect the author. After believing he had found a legal remedy in
trademark law only to find that he was mistaken, after finding that harsh
threats of prosecution were useless without legal backing, he can be forgiven
for considering the current legal measures little more than useless. It would
be natural to expect that Clemens, himself a victim of unbridled theft, would
become a tireless defender of copyright as a protective measure. In truth,
however, his position on the issue went through some marked changes.

CONFRONTING CONTRADICTIONS

Only by acknowledging Clemens' belief in an author's responsibility to protect his or her copyright, and his awareness of how piracy could aid as well as
harm an author, can we understand the letters that Clemens wrote to Howells
a few months after he failed to move Congress to act. The letters cause problems for critics who wish to see the author as a consistent champion of literary
property rights. In August of 1880, Clemens wrote to his good friend:

> I have been thinking things over, & have changed my mind to this com-
> plexion: I would rather the N.Y. Times & all the other journals *would*
> copy my stuff—it keeps a body more alive & known to the broad &

general public, for the Atlantic <only> <only> goes to only [. . .] the
select high few. Yes, I would rather write for the modester wage of one
whose articles increase not the subscription list, & then be copied in the
general press; for I should find my vast reward in the augmented sales of
my books. (Smith 1: 319–20).

His attitude seems in part a response to the pending release of *A Tramp
Abroad.* His willingness to accept a degree of piracy is limited to articles, in
the expectation that such republication will increase the public appetite for
the complete book. The logic he employs here—that widespread publication of his articles would increase sales—suggests that he remembered the
failure of his lecture tour in support of *The Innocents Abroad.* Clemens also
seems to argue that the protection of his copyrights by the *Atlantic* limited
his readership to a cultural elite rather than allowing him to reach the
"broad & general public" he sought. His views on republication seem both
populist and pragmatic: Clemens wanted to be a "man of the people,"
appreciated by the rich and educated and enjoyed by the farmer and the fac-
tory worker; such a varied readership, of course, could only improve his
bottom line.[11] His views seem particularly self-interested when one considers that he is, in effect, telling Howells that he would rather not help his
friend increase the circulation of his magazine. The only subscriptions he
cared for were for his books.

Although his generosity seems more than a little qualified here,
Clemens made an even stronger statement regarding piracy and its possible
benefits to the public only a couple of months later. Because the letter is
striking in its apparent departure from the widely accepted idea of Clemens
as a defender of literary property rights, it is worth examining in its entirety:

Will the proposed treaty protect us (*& effectually*) against Canadian
piracy? Because if it doesn't, there is not a single argument in favor of
international copyright which a rational American Senate could
entertain for a moment. My notions have mightily changed, lately.
Under this recent & brand-new system of piracy in New York, this
country is being flooded with the best of English literature at prices
which make a package of water closet paper seem an 'edition de luxe'
in comparison. I can buy Macauley's History, 3 vols., bound, for
$1.25. Chambers's Cyclopedia, 15 vols., cloth, for $7.25. (we paid
$60), & other English copyrights in proportion; I can buy a lot of the
great copyright classics, in paper, at from 3 cents to 30 cents apiece.
These things must find their way into the very kitchens & hovels of

the country. A generation of this sort of thing ought to make this the most intelligent & the best-read nation in the world. International copyright must becloud this sun & bring on the former darkness and dime-novel reading.

Morally, this is all wrong—governmentally it is all right; for it is the *duty* of governments—& families—to be selfish, & look out simply for their own. International copyright would benefit a few English authors, & a lot of American publishers, & be a profound detriment to 20,000,000 Americans; it would benefit a dozen American authors a few dollars a year, & there an end. The *real* advantages all go to English authors & American publishers.

And even if the treaty *will* kill Canadian piracy, & thus save me an average of $5,000 a year, I'm down on it anyway—& I'd like cussed well to write an article opposing the treaty. Dern England! Such is *my* sentiments. (Smith 1: 334, 336)

Clemens seems to have suddenly adopted almost completely the arguments of Carey and other copyright opponents. His belief in the educational benefits to be gained from the sale of cheap pirated books seems to grow as he writes, until he doesn't appear to be concerned even with the protection of his own books. When he begins discussing the possible benefits of a new copyright treaty, he still seems intent on securing protection for American works from Canadian piracy. Considering the numerous arguments offered in support of international copyright, Clemens' suggestion that protection from Canadians offered the only rationale that could be mustered in support of the treaty seems almost radical.

He seems aware of this, noting that his views have "mightily changed, lately." Now he is not only interested in his own works reaching the general public, but he is also convinced that the lack of international copyright will lead to an upsurge in the American intellect. Once again, his argument employs naturalistic metaphors: the widespread piracy and sale of texts is a "sun" which can only be darkened by the "cloud" of international copyright. This is in line with his consistent portrayal of piracy as a natural, if contemptible, practice; however, in other ways his arguments are in no way unique. Opponents of copyright had argued for years that the law would hurt the educational opportunities of Americans. Other authors had always argued that such possible benefits did not justify the immoral means of gaining them. Clemens concedes that "morally, this is all wrong," but he places greater emphasis on the possibility of intellectual improvement that the current copyright situation offers.

This is perhaps the most obvious distinction between Clemens' view here and those of other authors: his assertion that the government, in denying international copyright, was doing its duty even as it was violating moral principles. He seems to accept the "us against them" logic employed by copyright opponents, agreeing with the assertion that the law would benefit British authors at the expense of American readers. Even though he acknowledges that he would also benefit from the law, he appears willing to give up this benefit for the good of the "family" that must "look after its own."[12] His exclamation, "Dern England!" appears to be a somewhat half-hearted attempt to portray his opposition to international copyright as part of an opposition to England.

Critics who have written about Clemens' persistent support for literary property rights have had a difficult time addressing these letters. Doyno offers two possible explanations: the first involves taking the letter at its face value. Doyno writes in reference to Clemens' letter to Howells, "Even though he had been victimized by the lack of U.S. participation in an International copyright treaty, Twain considered national literacy as a higher priority. [. . .] This altruistic attitude would, however, ultimately change" (187). The second explanation Doyno offers would seem to contradict any reading of authentic altruism in Clemens' remarks: "When he wrote this letter, however, Twain had thought that he had discovered his own private protection against the Canadian pirates. As of April 12, 1879, Sam Clemens believed that his use of the nom de plum 'Mark Twain' protected even his uncopyrighted work as a trademark would" (188). These explanations would appear to be mutually exclusive. If Clemens thought that he had private protection against piracy, then his stated willingness to absorb continued losses from Canadian re-prints ostensibly "for the good of the nation" is entirely disingenuous. Why he would make such a claim in correspondence with his good friend if he did not mean it is difficult to imagine.

Yet the idea that Clemens has suddenly elected to accept personal loss in order to promote national literacy is also somewhat unsatisfactory. What would have caused such a conversion? Vaidhyanathan also acknowledges the author's apparent emphasis on the benefits to readers, an emphasis he suggests was aided by the expressed recognition that "[e]ven Twain benefited from this system as a reader," causing the "mixed feelings" evident in his letter (60). Vaidhyanathan argues that Clemens abandoned his altruism when he learned that readers weren't making the same educational choices that he had made: "[. . .] Twain grew to realize that Americans were not buying the works of Lord Macauley in anything approaching the numbers in which they were consuming the sugary novels of Sir Walter Scott. [. . .] As he founded his publishing house and studied the intricacies of the law further, Twain pushed himself to the forefront of the movement for international copyright during the 1880s" (60–61).

A couple of difficulties emerge when we consider Vaidhyanathan's account. The first stems from the idea that Clemens, an experienced participant in subscription sales by 1880, would have been unaware of American reading preferences; it is hard to imagine the savvy writer and entertainer only slowly discovering at such a late date that many Americans would rather read Sir Walter Scott than Lord Macauley. The second is Vaidhyanathan's presentation of the evolution of Clemens' views. Because of his investment in the idea of Clemens as a tireless champion of authorial rights, Vaidhyanathan is too ready to view the sentiments of this letter as anomalous, a temporary ambivalence that is cleared up by Clemens' growing investment in the publishing trade and his increasing disappointment in American readers. As we have already seen, Clemens' views regarding copyright had always been quite fluid, his primary guiding principle being authorial responsibility. This would not change during the 1880s: only after the passage of the amendment allowing international copyright in 1891 and the author's unrelated bankruptcy would Clemens' views harden in the manner Vaidhyanathan suggests.

Although the degree to which Clemens seems to advocate the advantages of literary piracy in 1880 is unusual, when we consider his sentiments in the context of his publishing at this period, a kind of expediency becomes evident. As he had written to Howells, he believed that a certain amount of piracy actually boosted sales. Piracy certainly benefited readers who could purchase cheaper texts, but Clemens also felt that it was not without long-term benefits for authors, as well. At the same time, he was dealing with a matter of perception. In October 1880, he was well into the process of completing *The Prince and the Pauper,* a novel that takes a hard look at class distinctions in England. One can imagine the author was reluctant to advocate a treaty that "would benefit a few English authors, & a lot of American publishers, & be a profound detriment to 20,000,000 Americans." His work on the novel may account for the somewhat awkward cursing of England— "Dern England"—and his odd choice of words in stating his hope that pirated books would eventually find their way into "the very kitchens and hovels of America." The language, "hovels," and the sentiment both suggest the opposition to hierarchies that infuses *The Prince and the Pauper.* Clemens' altruism might then be seen both as preserving the integrity of the Mark Twain persona and championing the lower classes in the United States. Samuel Clemens could potentially damage Mark Twain if the latter were perceived as advocating a bill that opponents had long argued would primarily hurt the under-privileged. This is not simply a matter of indicting Clemens or accusing him of selfishness or hypocrisy; rather, it is to suggest that he was always aware of how his public actions intersected with his publishing interests.

He negotiated this difficult balancing act by continuing to work aggressively to protect his own rights within the limits of the law without strongly criticizing the reading public for its participation in and tacit support for a system that deprived him of profits. In 1881, Clemens traveled to Canada in an attempt to secure a Canadian copyright for *The Prince and the Pauper.* While in Montreal, he gave a speech in which he touched on the subject of his errand. As one might expect, he used his sense of humor to temper his remarks and, once again, emphasized his own agency in preventing piracy rather than taking his readers to task for supporting it:

> [. . .] I did not come to Canada to commit crime—this time—but to prevent it. I came here to place myself under the protection of the Canadian law and secure a copyright. I have complied with the requirements of the law; I have followed the instructions of some of the best legal minds in the city, including my own, and so my errand is accomplished, at least so far as any exertions of mine can aid that accomplishment. This is rather a cumbersome way to fence and fortify one's property against the literary buccaneer, it is true; still, if it is effective, it is a great advance upon past conditions, and one to be correspondingly welcomed.
>
> It makes one hope and believe that a day will come when, in the eye of the law, literary property will be as sacred as whiskey, or any other of the necessaries of life. In this age of ours, if you steal another man's label to advertise your own brand of whiskey with, you will be heavily fined and otherwise punished for violating that trademark; if you steal the whiskey without the trademark, you go to jail; but if you could prove that the whiskey was literature, you can steal them both, and the law wouldn't say a word. It grieves me to think how far more profound and reverent a respect the law would have for literature if a body could only get drunk on it. Still the world moves; the interests of literature upon our continent are improving; let us be content and wait. (*Mark Twain Speaking* 158)

By spelling out the steps he has taken and emphasizing his compliance with the law, Clemens seems to be almost wishfully proclaiming his copyright. Rather than a denunciation of the state of things that led him to make the trip in the first place, his speech represents more a tone of resignation. It also reflects his ongoing preoccupation with trademark. As Doyno notes, the author was convinced at this point that his trademark protection of his name would grant his literary works protection (188). Rather than taking aim at copyright violation in this speech, therefore, he seems more interested in humorously lamenting the degree of protection granted literature in comparison to more mundane items. This strategy makes copyright and literary piracy a legal question more than a moral question; it once again allows Clemens to shift responsibility away from readers and even publishers: "if you could prove that whiskey was literature, you can steal them both, and the law wouldn't say a word." The analogy does not hold up under scrutiny, but it doesn't seem to be meant to: it appears to be primarily a means of targeting the law governing copyrights rather than those publishers perpetrating literary piracy.

As was the case in the early 1870s, the author's views seem to be somewhat out of step with those of his contemporaries in search of stronger copyrights. In his address to the New York Free Trade Club in 1879, George Haven Putnam declared,

> It is true that there have been in the history of our country governments which seemed impatient of the claims of any 'literary fellers;' but the majority of our administrations have shown a fair respect for such 'fellers,' and even a readiness to make use of their services.
>
> The difficulty has really been, however, not with the administrations, but with the people at large, who have failed to fairly educate themselves on the subject, or to recognize that an international copyright was called for not merely on principles of general equity, but as a matter of simple justice to American authors. (16)

While advocates for copyright law continued to argue that the public had a role to play in the debates over the law, Clemens continued to portray the question as only tangentially dealing with readers. Whenever he spoke or wrote publicly about copyright or literary piracy, he was careful to make it more a matter of the behavior of authors and the status of the law itself.

ADDRESSING HIS READERS:
HUCKLEBERRY FINN AND INTERNATIONAL COPYRIGHT

The early 1880s saw little progress in the securing of authors' rights. During this same time, however, Clemens' ideas regarding the subject became more complicated. As his books grew in popularity, he became more and more involved in their publication and sale. Hoping to secure a greater share of the profits, he had left the American Publishing Company and signed a deal with James Osgood to sell his books by subscription. When this method also failed to meet his expectations, Clemens began his own publishing company with his niece's husband, Charles Webster. Thus, during the years immediately preceding publication of his masterpiece, *The Adventures of Huckleberry Finn,* Clemens was both publisher and author. At the same time, his growing interest in the Paige Typesetter meant that he was intimately concerned with the opinions of tradespeople, as well. His views on copyright broadened in tandem with his interest in the production and sale of his books.

Doyno has done an excellent job of analyzing the ways in which *Huckleberry Finn* reflects Clemens' concerns regarding the lack of international copyright. Doyno's most intriguing claim is that the oft-maligned return of Tom Sawyer near the conclusion of the novel represents Clemens' critique of the popularity of pirated European fiction. He writes, "Tom represents an average American boy who has become a Europeanized victim of the cheap fiction. Unlike Jim, a physical slave of his color, Tom's enslavement is mental, literary" (204). Doyno believes that the representation of Tom Sawyer in the novel is an indictment of the lack of international copyright law and reflects the author's disappointment in American readers who failed to seize the educational opportunities presented them by the availability of inexpensive British texts. Tom's preference for sensational fiction is directly linked to his abusive treatment of Jim. Doyno writes,

> Clearly both Tom and the reprinters imposed foreign values, while stealing both time and labor. Consequently, because of a generally unquestioned higher status attributed by Tom and the reprinters—and by too many American buyers—to European values, one free adult, Jim, could be reimprisoned—relegated to an entirely unjust inferior status—while the youthful Huck could be controlled or enslaved by Tom's reading. (204)

Tom's behavior transforms him into a kind of cautionary tale regarding the obsession with European literature.

As we have seen, Clemens was cautious in challenging his readers regarding their purchasing habits, preferring to blame legislators for the widespread practice of piracy rather than consumers. Embedding a warning to his readers within his novel in the form of an illustrative example would allow him to confront them in a way he had refrained from doing elsewhere.

Further evidence for this reading can be found in his depiction of the wrecked steamboat *Walter Scott.* As Doyno points out, the author often lamented the influence of Scott's novels on American readers (201–2; 204–5). On the *Walter Scott,* Huck and Jim encounter truly murderous bandits, not the heroic ones from the books that Tom idolizes. Further illustrating the contrast, the books that are taken from the ship all tell of foreign lands, of "kings and dukes and earls" (*Adventures* 84), a literary foreshadowing of the appearance of the evil Duke and Dauphin. Clemens is apparently offering a dose of reality in answer to the popular European fictions so fashionable at the time.

Doyno's argument does tend to downplay Clemens' conflicting ideas and feelings regarding copyright law during this period, however, and it overlooks the careful nuance he employed when addressing his readers on the subject. If the novel decries the literature flooding the American marketplace as a result of the lack of adequate copyright protections, it also seems to provide some criticism of the law itself, suggesting that an unreflective or totalizing right to property is excessive and perhaps ridiculous.

The first example of this counter-argument comes near the beginning of the novel and involves Tom Sawyer, hardly coincidental since he is presented as the most literary of the characters. Tom has persuaded the boys to join him in pretending to be a gang of robbers. Membership in the gang requires taking an oath:

> So Tom got out a sheet of paper that he had wrote the oath on, and read it. It swore every boy to stick to the band, and never tell any of the secrets; and if anybody done anything to any boy in the band, whichever boy was ordered to kill that person and his family must do it, and he mustn't eat and he mustn't sleep till he had killed them and hacked a cross in their breasts, which was the sign of the band. And nobody that didn't belong to the band could use that mark, and if he did he must be sued; and if he done it again he must be killed. (8)

The humor of this passage works primarily through the odd juxtaposition of consequence: if someone outside of the gang uses the mark, they are sued upon a first offense and murdered upon the second. Such punishment is of course made more likely by the banal nature of the gang's sign.

When the boys praise the oath and ask Tom if he had come up with it on his own, he acknowledges creation of "some of it, but the rest was out of pirate books, and robber books, and every gang that was high-toned had it" (8). Tom may have acquired some of the oath from "pirate books," but he'd be more likely to come across the rather unromantic idea of suing for trademark infringement from reading about *pirated* books. This innovation puts one in mind of Clemens' preoccupation with such infringement as the most nefarious treachery and his declaration to Howells that he was going north to Canada "to kill a pirate" (Smith 1: 307). The humorous suggestion of self-mockery is a constant in Clemens' public comments on copyright during these years, and, in this case, possibly undermines his own litigious defense of his trademark. Without question, his "Mark" is more unique than the gang's mark of a cross, but by representing the crime as inevitable and the methods of redress as absurdly disproportionate, Clemens casts some doubt on his own legal activities.

This strategy echoes the one Clemens employs in the "Notice" at the beginning of the text. There, the author appropriates the institutional power of the copyright page for his own humorous ends by fabricating his own prefatory page and authority figure. Rather than the Librarian of Congress, Clemens presents us with "G.G., Chief of Ordnance." While punishment for infringing the copyright is not spelled out—the simple existence of the copyright notice itself meant to dissuade wrongdoers—the punishment for refusing to follow the rules of the Chief of Ordnance is made explicit: "Persons attempting to find a motive in this narrative will be prosecuted; persons attempting to find a moral in it will be banished; persons attempting to find a plot in it will be shot." Doyno has written of the notice: "The book is posted, so to speak, as a section of land might be; a part of the American literary landscape is reserved, absolved from the burden of meaning" (259). This is most certainly true, and Clemens surely recognized that readers—down to the present day—would read the text in precisely the manner he attempts to disallow. In that case, what is the effect of this warning that will almost certainly be ignored?

As with Tom's ridiculously excessive response to an almost unavoidable trademark infringement, the imaginary overseer of reading practice threatens harsh discipline for those who attempt to read the novel in a most common fashion. One will certainly fall afoul of this restriction. The joke works not only because the promised punishment appears both extreme and inevitable, but also because it plays upon the readers' knowledge of the prefatory page as a site of power and the presence of a government figure suggesting some form of enforcement. The copyright page itself thus seems doubly lampooned: the notice serves to demonstrate just how weak and toothless the copyright statement is, and it seems to ridicule the very presence of a government figure at the beginning of the novel. Why are we to take A.R. Spofford, Librarian of Congress, any more seriously than G.G.,

Chief of Ordnance? The legal authority of Spofford is at the very least put into question by Clemens' spoof.

Of course, such authority is questioned throughout the novel. Huck and Jim are much more likely to examine myriad justifications for the unlawful appropriation of property than they are the legal and moral rationales for protecting and keeping it:

> Mornings, before daylight, I slipped into corn fields and borrowed a watermelon, or a mushmelon, or a punkin, or some new corn, or things of that kind. Pap always said it warn't no harm to borrow things, if you was meaning to pay them back, sometime; but the widow said it warn't anything but a soft name for stealing, and no decent body would do it. Jim said he reckoned the widow was partly right and pap was partly right; so the best way would be for us to pick out two or three things from the list and say we wouldn't borrow them any more—then he reckoned it wouldn't be no harm to borrow the others. (72)

Here and elsewhere, motive and circumstance are the primary concerns when considering how much respect is to be granted property rights. The plan that emerges from their discussion is immediately put into practice, first with their resolution not to steal crabapples and persimmons—an easy resolution as "crabapples ain't ever good, and the p'simmons wouldn't be ripe for two or three months yet" (73)—and then again when they come across a wrecked steamboat. Huck is determined to board the vessel, and he says to Jim, "we might borrow something worth having, out of the captain's stateroom. Seegars, *I* bet you—and cost five cents apiece, solid cash. Steamboat captains is always rich, and get sixty dollars a month, and *they* don't care a cent what a thing costs, you know, long as they want it" (73–4). While much of what Huck and Jim engage in might be seen as indiscriminate theft, it is, in fact, quite regulated and moderate. The introduction of the Duke and the Dauphin, willing to rob orphans and sell Jim down the river, emphasizes this difference in degree.

Clemens never fails to specify that theft is still theft; however, he ably demonstrates that no right of property is absolute. There are always those crimes that are mitigated by circumstance. The most prominent of these is, of course, the "theft" of Jim. What makes Huck's resolution to "go to hell" so powerful is his conviction that he is committing a crime and a sin (235). He does not consider the injustice of rendering a man a thing, nor does he question the Widow's right to "own" Jim. He accepts both and still follows his conscience rather than the law. Clemens does not allow this act of moral courage to change Huck's character or his view of what he is doing; indeed, one gets the distinct impression that this act may likely lead Huck to further acts of lawlessness:

> I studied a minute, sort of holding my breath, and then says to myself: 'All right, then, I'll *go* to hell'—and tore it up [the note he had written to the widow telling her where to find Jim]. It was awful thoughts, and awful words, but they was said. And I let them stay said; and never thought no more about reforming. I shoved the whole thing out of my head; and said I would take up wickedness again, which was in my line, being brung up to it, and the other warn't. (235)

Huck is doing the right thing, but his choice is remarkable precisely because he believes he is doing the wrong thing. Clemens presents Huck's action as a theft made both necessary and morally acceptable because of circumstance and intent, but it is still a crime.

This is an important point when one compares Huck's decision to free Jim with Tom's decision to help Huck achieve his goal. From the beginning, Tom realizes that he is not breaking any laws at all, although his behavior regarding Jim is far more morally repugnant given his knowledge of the former slave's freedom. For all of his shenanigans, Tom sticks by the law in this novel, an aspect of his character that Huck acknowledges when he learns Tom's secret regarding Jim: "and so, sure enough, Tom Sawyer had gone and took all that trouble and bother to set a free nigger free! and I couldn't ever understand, before, until that minute and that talk, how he *could* help a body set a nigger free, with his bringing-up" (318). What Huck understands is that Tom always follows the letter of the law: his obedience to the authorities does not stop at romance books and the way adventures must unfold. Tom's preeminent concern with his own self-interest, as it is presented in this novel, does not suggest a willingness to act against "his bringing up." When one considers the world Tom represents, a world of law and order that opposes Huck's contingent morality and that is deliciously satirized by Tom's resolve to first sue and then murder those who infringe upon trademarks, it is not surprising that Huck "lights out for the Territory" (321).

Doyno is correct to see in Tom Sawyer a radical example of what Clemens may have feared was the result of Americans' unhealthy preoccupation with foreign novels. Yet this depiction is part of a larger representation of the dangers of extremism. The character of Tom lampoons more than the books he loves to read; his lack of Huck Finn's subtle moral compass lends him an absolutism in this novel that brings to mind some on both sides of the battle over literary property. Tom may act out, but in the end he has internalized Widow Douglas's precepts regarding stealing more than he may realize. The result is a character far less likable than his ragamuffin comrade. When weighing Tom's sins as a reader of pirated fiction versus his tortured adherence to "the rules," his lawfulness does not come out well in the balance.

A CHARACTERISTIC PERFORMANCE

Clemens' allies in the struggle for an international copyright law must have been disappointed by his often relativistic, self-interestedly pragmatic views on the subject. While *Adventures of Huckleberry Finn* is hardly the paean to theft and illegality that its conservative critics believed it to be, neither is it an unequivocal defense of property rights. When Clemens came to speak and write on the subject of copyright shortly after the publication of his novel, he took a similarly moderate position, far different from that of his authorial colleagues. This led to some surprising Congressional testimony (at least surprising to the American Copyright League, of which he was a member and at whose invitation he appeared before Congress) and a very public disagreement with good friend and fellow copyright advocate Brander Matthews. His statements trouble notions of any hardening of his stance at the zenith of his career.

Clemens appeared before the Senate Committee on Patents of the United States on January 28, 1886, along with a number of other authors and publishers, to testify regarding two competing bills touching on international copyright. The bill preferred by the American Copyright League was the Hawley bill, which gave foreign authors the same copyright protections granted American citizens, providing their own nations guaranteed American authors the same. The first speaker spelled out very clearly the purpose of the League's testimony: "The American Copyright League has sent the executive committee of its council to appear before you to-day to advocate the bill, No. 191, known as Senator Hawley's bill, and to that alone we shall confine ourselves" (3). The League made this statement specifically to avoid clouding the issue with discussion of a "manufacturing clause" that would mandate foreign works be entirely manufactured in the United States. It wanted a statute aimed at protecting authors rather than tradeworkers. As one speaker for the League put it, "If you want to use this as a machine for protecting industry here, why not protect the industry of the pirate as well as the interest of everybody else? He is a great public benefactor.

[. . .] We say that there is an attempt to confuse the two things, and that they have nothing to do with one another" (7). The American Copyright League was convinced that if the bill were drafted in such a way as to prioritize the protection of manufacture, then it would fail to protect the rights of authors adequately.

Clemens does not seem to have been a party to this strategy. When called upon to speak, he demurred, claiming,

> I seem to come here in the interest of the Copyright League, and the Copyright League's interest, as you have heard, is centered upon the first bill mentioned here, called the Hawley bill, and I do not wish to make any speech at all or any remarks, lest I wander from the just path marked out for me by these gentlemen.
>
> [. . .] I am in the position of one who would violate a hospitality, rather, if I should speak my mind. I did speak my mind yesterday to the most intelligent member of the committee, besides myself [laughter], and it fired him, it grieved him, and I almost promised that I would not divulge what my right feeling was; but I did not promise that I would not take the contrary course. (8)

Although it is plain that he does not support the American Copyright League's position, he claims that he agreed to appear on their behalf anyway, endeavoring to keep his true feelings silent. This is an odd stance. Since he was one of the most prominent speakers present, it is difficult to imagine anyone, including the members of the American Copyright League, believed that the committee would not question him. Indeed, this opening statement fairly begs for elaboration. He managed to put off "taking the contrary course" for a short time, but it was not long before he went separate ways from the clear agenda set forth by the opening speaker on behalf of the copyright bill.

Urged by the Secretary of the Copyright League to "speak right out like a little man" (15), Clemens replied, "I consider [. . .] that absolves me from all obligation to be dishonest, or furtive, or clandestine, or whatsoever term you may choose to apply to the attitude I have held here before— rather an attitude of silence, in order that I should not commit or in any way jeapard [sic] the interest of this bill" (15). His remarks before the committee did more than undermine the efforts of the American Copyright League on behalf of the Hawley bill; they reinforced arguments made by copyright opponents throughout the nineteenth century. Clemens first stated,

> I do consider that those persons who are called 'pirates,' [. . .] were
> made pirates by the collusion of the United States Government, which
> made them pirates and thieves. [. . .] Congress, if anybody, is to blame
> for their action. It is not dishonesty. They have that right, they have
> been working under that right a long time, publishing what is called
> 'pirated books.' They have invested their money in that way, and they
> did it in the confidence that they would be supported and no injustice
> done them. (15)

In the past, Clemens had made remarks somewhat similar to these, blaming
the government rather than the pirates for their actions. One recalls his
metaphor of the young lady on the stud horse. Rather than suggesting the
government has been weak holding the reins, the author here suggests that
the legislature has "made" the publishers pirate texts through their inaction.
Still, given his own stated frustrations with pirates such as Hotten and
Belford, this is a surprisingly generous statement on behalf of a class of publishers who had been robbing foreign authors for years. He had certainly
never questioned the use of the term "pirate" before, even when he placed
the majority of the blame on authors for a lack of responsible stewardship of
their property.

But Clemens went further than clearing pirates of wrongdoing. In
arguing for the inclusion of the "manufacture clause" that the American
Copyright League was striving to keep out of the bill, he significantly
reduced the authorial stake in the publishing process. His statements may be
magnanimous, but for proponents of copyright who had been arguing for
years on behalf of the central role of the author as creator/producer of literature, they must have also been nearly treasonous. Clemens stated,

> I should like to see a copyright bill passed here which shall do no harm
> to anybody concerned in this matter, and a great many more people are
> concerned in it than merely the authors. In fact I suppose, if the truth is
> confessed, the authors are rather less concerned pecuniarily in any copy-
> right measure than many other people—publishers, printers, binders,
> and so on. The authors have one part in this matter, but theirs is the
> larger part. [. . .] I simply consider that there are other rights involved
> aside from those of the author, and they are vested rights, too, and
> nobody has a moral right to disturb that relation. (15–16)

Since the early nineteenth century, authors had argued that their rights in
their literary property should be the same as those of any owner, that they

should have exclusive and perpetual control over the products of their creative energy. Now Clemens, one of the America's most popular authors, states before Congress that authors "are rather less concerned" in copyright than binders? It is possible that his testimony was influenced by the recent success of the publication of Grant's *Memoirs;* perhaps he had begun to view himself more as a publisher than an author. At the same time, his ever-growing investment in the Paige Typesetter may have made him reluctant to appear as advocating for a bill damaging to the interests of tradeworkers. Whatever the motivation for his testimony, it cannot be denied that it was not what the American Copyright League had in mind and that it ran counter to arguments made by the vast majority of authors, including some of Clemens' close friends.

His testimony makes it difficult to sustain a view of the author as a tireless advocate of authorial rights during the 1880s. Vaidhyanathan and Doyno, even while at times acknowledging some ambivalence on Clemens' part, have nevertheless downplayed his remarks. Doyno acknowledges the fact that Clemens appeared before Congress but includes no direct quotations from his testimony. In the absence of such citation, Doyno gives the impression that Clemens was a much stronger supporter of the proposed bill than he was. Doyno writes, "In the full transcript of the hearings one finds repeated images of 'piracy,' of America as 'the Barbary coast of literature,' and of 'stolen fruit' underselling legitimate native products" (193). While this is certainly true, Doyno fails to mention that Clemens spoke out against the use of the word "pirate" and, as we have seen, defended pirates' rights by suggesting the publishers had greater reason to be concerned regarding copyright laws than authors did.

Vaidhyanathan, for his part, does mention Clemens' opposition to the Hawley bill because of the lack of a "manufacture clause," but, like Doyno, he does not include any direct citation of Clemens' remarks. His summary of the statements is somewhat problematic. He writes:

> When Twain testified before a Senate committee later in 1886, he balked at endorsing the particular international copyright bill in question because he thought it harshly treated British publishers, many of whom had treated him well, and unjustly absolved the American system. By this time, he had grown tired of political finger-pointing between the two nations, when both were responsible for the massive price differences. In addition, Twain had grown somewhat pleased with British copyright law because it afforded longer protection for works and allowed Americans to gain protection by traveling to

England during the publication. Twain's biggest problem with the 1886 copyright proposal, known as the Hawley Bill, was that it would punish publishers who had been reprinting British works cheaply, and probably close them down, laying off many printers. He urged a protectionist amendment that would require a foreign work to be printed in an American plant to receive American copyright. His objections were complex and technical, but he did not waver in his call for reciprocal protection among England, Canada and the United States. (61)

It is unclear where Vaidhyanathan sees signs of Clemens' "fatigue" with the wrangling over copyright, but it is true that by this time he had no significant problem with English copyright law. His stature and circumstances allowed him to comply with the law relatively easily, coordinating simultaneous publication with his British publishers and traveling to Canada when necessary. As we have seen, it is also true that Clemens worried about the effect the Hawley bill would have on printers. What is potentially misleading about Vaidhyanathan's summary is his dismissal of Clemens' objections as "complex and technical." As the statements quoted above indicate, his objections to the bill were all too plain: the author's stake in any discussion of copyright was smaller than that of others involved in the publishing process, and thus the concerns of these others should take precedence.[13]

Clemens' testimony in relation to this matter was damaging to the cause of international copyright not only because it reiterated the arguments of copyright opponents, granting them greater credibility, but also because it relied too heavily on his own experience—the experience of a successful author and publisher, not of an unknown writer first going into print. In this regard, his statements regarding copyright suffered from a distinct lack of technicality. He stated that when an American author copyrights his or her book in England, "He gets just as perfect a copyright as it is possible for a Government to give. No English author is stronger in his copyright than an American author who has a book copyrighted there" (16). Author and publisher George Ticknor Curtis, who had also attended to testify on behalf of international copyrighted, attempted to draw Clemens out, apparently to make the point that matters were not so simple. When he asked the author how one went about getting one of these strong English copyrights, Clemens replied, "I have been through so many processes that I hardly know how to explain it. But the matter has always been simple with regard to England. Whatever complication there has been has occurred with Canada. You merely have to go and remain on British soil, under the British flag, while your book is publishing in England" (16). Such a trip might have been easy for Clemens, but it was hardly an option for every new author, particularly with no guarantee of successful sales.

Not content to rest at this somewhat vague explanation of the supposed ease with which one could obtain an English copyright, Clemens later interjected,

> I have for years received a larger royalty in England than I was receiving in America [. . .]. [. . .] I might also mention that in the case of General Grant's book the royalty paid in England on that book is the largest that was ever paid on a book in any country in any age of the world, and that the royalties paid in Germany and in France are exceedingly large, and of course the German and French copyrights on that book result through conventions with England. (17)

The possible damage caused by Clemens' testimony can be seen if one recalls the course of debate over international copyright. When the question first emerged, it was framed largely in terms of doing right by foreign authors; Henry Clay's first action on the subject in the 1830s was instigated and supported by a petition signed by such authors. Little progress was made on this front as opponents argued that writers like Dickens were rewarded enough in their own country. As the debate continued, American advocates began framing the question more and more as a matter of justice for native authors, as well. The success of Stowe's works made this argument stronger, as here at last was an American author who was suffering large losses due to the lack of an international copyright law. Clemens' statements appear to undermine this line of reasoning: here he was, one of the most popular and recognizable authors in America, testifying that the only ones who truly suffered from the lack of international copyright were foreign authors. American authors, if they did their duty and guarded their property carefully, could do quite well overseas. This was nothing new from Clemens: he had always maintained that it was an author's responsibility to protect his or her property by whatever means, however convoluted or complicated, were provided.

His position on this subject, however, was not shared by his colleagues, and his statements left them in an awkward predicament as they made their case. Curtis, following up on Clemens' testimony, was forced to try and modify his statements:

> I agree to a certain extent with Mr. Clemens, but then his own personal experience is an exceptional one, and the case of which he speaks, the

publication of General Grant's book, is still more exceptional. [. . .] I have had the unfortunate experience in the course of my life to be the author of several books which have had sales in England. I never derived anything from those sales, neither did my American publisher derive anything from them. (17; 18)

Clemens said from the beginning that he was speaking from his own experience, but, given his own background and his frequent dealings with other authors, he certainly could have provided more information regarding how unusual his profits were. While it is impossible to gauge the impact of Clemens' testimony in the eventual defeat of the Hawley bill, it is clear that it did far more to support arguments used against international copyright than to uphold the cause.

While they downplay this testimony significantly, both Vaidhyanathan and Doyno make prominent use of a piece that Clemens published in *The Century* magazine less than a month later. The magazine had solicited opinions on the question of international copyright from a number of prominent authors, and Clemens' statement once again appears to indicate at least an ambiguity in his views. In it, he reverses the position he had taken in 1880 regarding the benefits of cheap access to European books. As both critics point out, he now adopts the same line of argument that Cooper had advanced so many years before: it is a danger to American democracy and morality to have people reading so many European works. Considering the proliferation of inexpensive books, Clemens writes,

> Is this an advantage to us? It certainly is, if poison is an advantage to a person; or if to teach one thing at the hearthstone, the political hustings, and in a nation's press, and teach the opposite in the books the nation reads is profitable; or, in other words, if to hold up a national standard for admiration and emulation half of each day, and a foreign standard the other half, is profitable. (qtd. in Doyno 197)

Gone is Clemens' earlier notion that affordable access to foreign literature will make America the most educated nation on the globe. Instead, it will lead to the poisoning of young minds, the same corruption that Doyno insightfully argues is demonstrated in the behavior of Tom Sawyer in *Adventures of Huckleberry Finn*.

In making this argument, Clemens joined a host of his colleagues who were now decrying the insidious influence of foreign books. Similar statements appeared alongside Clemens' in *The Century*. Even Brander Matthews, with whom Clemens was soon to have a very public disagreement regarding international copyright, employed a similar tactic in a pamphlet published by the American Copyright League titled "Cheap Books and Good Books," writing of inexpensive English novels, "These are the books which the women of America, allured by the premium of cheapness, are now reading almost exclusively, to the neglect of native writers. There is a resulting deterioration of the public taste for good literature; and there is a resulting tendency to the adoption of English social standards" (5–6). In many of these statements, more space was given to the idea that international copyright would protect American readers than to the notion that it was intended to protect the author.

But does Clemens' *Century* article demonstrate "how much his opinion had changed since 1880" (196–7), as Doyno suggests? It certainly indicates that Clemens had lost his belief in the positive influence of cheap foreign literature. In other respects, however, he employs the same rhetoric that he had used in all of his public statements regarding copyright. While arguing that "The statistics of any public library will show that of every hundred books read by our people, about seventy are novels—and nine-tenths of them foreign ones" (197), he once again refrains from criticizing American readers for their habits. Instead, he infantilizes them, employing a racialist metaphor to criticize the legislature: "Thus we have this curious spectacle: American statesmen glorifying American nationality, teaching it, preaching it, urging it, building it up—with their mouths; and undermining it and pulling it down with their acts. This is to employ an Indian nurse to suckle your child, and expect it not to drink in the Indian nature with the milk" (197–8). This is, as Doyno mentions, putting the matter "pungently and sarcastically" (197), but it is still absolving both readers and publishers of responsibility. How can the American reader, a "suckling child," be expected to make educated or moral decisions regarding what he or she reads? The primary shift is from Clemens portraying the reader as innocent in the exchange of pirated texts, or, at the very most, acting "naturally," just as he had argued the pirate does, to now portraying the American reader as helpless and unable to choose what he or she consumes. More than a shift in viewpoint, his statement suggests a growing bitterness that sours but does not alter his opinion.

The consistency of the author's view of the matter is evident in the letter he published in response to his friend Brander Matthews' 1887 article "American Authors and British Pirates." In the article, Matthews goes to great lengths to point out the numerous ways that American authors suffered from British piracy because of the lack of international copyright. Although he does acknowledge that "At bottom, the publishers, good or bad, are not to blame; it is the condition of the law which is at fault" (212), he spends the majority of the article detailing the crimes committed by unscrupulous British publishers: "The English publishers have not only taken the liberty of reprinting these books, they have also allowed themselves the license of renaming them at will. [. . .] there are three volumes credited to 'Mark Twain' under titles which he never gave them, *Eye Openers, Practical Jokes,* and *Screamers*" (206). In citing popular authors like Clemens who had suffered piracy overseas, Matthews clearly intended to evoke public sympathy and support for these authors in the search for international copyright.

How great must his surprise have been then when Clemens responded a few months later with "American Authors and British Pirates: A Private Letter and a Public Postscript." Presenting himself as an "apparent sufferer" coming forward to "say a fair word for the other side" (47), Clemens proceeds in his article to defend English publishing, placing any blame for piracy on the authors themselves:

> [. . .] your complaint is, that American authors are pirated in England. Well, whose fault is that? It is nobody's but the author's. England furnishes him a perfect remedy; if he does not choose to take advantage of it, let him have self-respect enough to retire to the privacy of his cradle, not sit out on the public curbstone and cry. To-day the American author can go to Canada, spend three days there, and come home with an English and Canadian copyright which is as strong as if it had been built out of railroad iron. If he does not make this trip and do this thing, it is a confession that he does not think his foreign market valuable enough to justify the expense of securing it by the above process. Now it may turn out that that book is presently pirated in London. What then? Why, simply this: the pirate has paid that man a compliment; he has thought more of the book than the man thought of it himself. (47)

There is nothing new in his claim that the responsibility of protecting copyright rests with the author. What is striking in this article is the energy with which he defends English publishers and criticizes his friend and fellow member of the American Copyright League. In stalwartly supporting his view, he undermines the argument that American authors, like their foreign counterparts, stood to gain from a change in the law. While in *The Century* magazine he had infantilized readers, here he infantilizes authors who complain of British piracy of their work. It would seem clear that Matthews must be included in this list, as he is the one making the complaints public. Perhaps most incredible is Clemens' claim that an author who is pirated has not been robbed, but only "complimented." This seems to go beyond his most extreme earlier statements of authorial responsibility and property. In speaking of his experience in the mines, he never described his loss of his million-dollar stake in Nevada to the other miners as a "compliment" to his mining skills!

Despite his earlier problems with England, Clemens now seems to feel differently about his business relations there:

> I think we are not in a good position to throw bricks at the English pirate. We haven't any to spare. We need them to throw at the American Congress; and at the American author, who neglects his great privileges and then tries to hunt up some way to throw the blame upon the only nation in the world that is magnanimous enough to say to him: 'While you are the guest of our laws and our flag, you shall not be robbed.' (48)

Clemens, of course, never suggests saving a brick or two for the readers who purchase the works. He offers a number of supposed refutations to Matthews' article, but they all amount to the above. The English are blameless, as are the publishers. He does not seem to consider how this will affect the cause of international copyright, a cause he still claims to support; his interest lies solely in redirecting Matthews' criticism.

Matthews was, understandably, taken aback by Clemens' reply, which he "read and re-read with growing astonishment" ("American Authors [. . .]: An Open Letter" 54). In responding to the author's criticism, he cited numerous other writers who had suffered from English piracy, including Charles Dudley Warner, to "testify only to that Complimentary Piracy which you seem to think a young author must needs find most gratifying" (56). As stunned as he was by Clemens' suggestion that unauthorized reprinting was a form of flattery, Matthews is even more amazed by the idea that the author is the only one at fault:

> You seem to say that the American author alone is guilty, and that the British pirate is not even *particeps criminis* [a partner-in-crime]. After studying this passage of your Postscript, I can now better appreciate the force you lent to the arguments of Tom Sawyer, when you made him plead with Joe Harper not to be a hermit; after listening to Tom, Joe "conceded that there were some conspicuous advantages about a life of crime, and so consented to be a pirate." (59)

While Clemens had always directed attention away from publishers in his public writing, Matthews makes it clear that such a stance was not shared by many of his fellows in the copyright movement who had suffered losses as a result of problems with the law.

Matthews offers a number of rebuttals to Clemens, but his larger point echoes George Ticknor Curtis's reply to Clemens' Congressional testimony noting that the author's experience was "an extraordinary one." Matthews writes, "you have judged others by yourself. Because the law suits you well enough, you think that it is equally satisfactory to all. A trip to Canada is an easy thing for you, who live in Hartford, and who are rich enough to 'Endow a college or a cat.' It is not as easy for a poor author who may chance to live in Florida or in Texas" (62). Matthews was not the only one to notice that Clemens extrapolated from his own experience in defending English copyright law. A writer for *The Nation* summarized the exchange of articles in 1888, and even put Clemens' recent article within the context of his earlier congressional testimony:

> Two years ago Mr. Clemens stated before the Senate Committee on Patents that the American author could get in England 'as perfect a copyright as it was possible for a Government to give' [. . .]. But when asked by what process the American author could secure such copyright, his answer was: 'I have been through so many processes that I hardly know how to explain it.' He has now published a veritable 'Mark Twain' explanation of the process, after reading which no one will twit Mr. Clemens—as he does his opponent—with being a lawyer. ("English Copyright for American Authors" 110)

Clemens had always claimed a fear that no one would take his arguments on copyright seriously if they knew they came from a humorist. The illogic of his refutation now brought upon him the criticism he had sought to avoid. Throughout his career, he always modified his public remarks carefully, taking pains not to accuse his readers or publishers of wrongdoing. This was as much a result of his business interests as an author, publisher, and investor in the Paige Typesetter as it was of his days in the mining camps of Nevada. Clemens viewed the protection of literary property as a personal responsibility. By going so far as to place blame almost solely on the wronged author and absolving the publisher, by championing as perfectly just a law that required authors to travel to another country to secure their rights, Clemens actually placed himself in opposition to the friends and colleagues with whom he had worked on copyright issues throughout his career.

Perhaps because of the criticism in *The Nation,* Clemens did not respond gracefully to his friend's rebuttal, although he did manage to refrain from responding publicly. He wrote three replies to Matthews that were never published: "Mr Mathews's Second Article," "Concerning the British 'Pirate,'" and "P.P.S. A Recapitulation" (*Notebooks* 3: 362n). As we have already noted, Clemens amplified his rhetoric in these texts, still maintaining that when a book was pirated, the author was the one to blame. Although Matthews had refrained from the kind of *ad hominem* attacks that Clemens employed—Clemens had jokingly suggested that Matthews might be institutionalized ("American Authors" 54)—Clemens nursed a grudge regarding this dispute for some time. Matthews writes, "[. . .] Mark took offense and for a year or two he seemed to avoid me. Like most humorists, he was inclined to take himself seriously and to be more or less deficient in the negative sense-of-humor which often fails to accompany the more positive humor" (*These Many Years* 231). If Matthews had been given the opportunity to read the replies that Clemens was drafting, he would have been further convinced of the author's ill humor.

What Clemens' testimony and his public response to Matthews demonstrate is that his views on copyright were substantially different from those held by many in the international copyright movement. They also reveal a remarkable consistency in his beliefs on the subject: while he lost the faith in the benefits of cheap books that he expressed so enthusiastically in 1880, he still maintained the position that copyright was primarily an author's responsibility. He also stuck to the position that authors and Congress were chiefly to blame for literary piracy. If unrestrained by the law and the careful eye of the author, publishers are naturally disposed to pirate works and readers to buy them. It has been the tendency of critics to laud Clemens as a defender of literary property rights without carefully analyzing his arguments and noting how distinct they are from those of his colleagues. Both Doyno and Vaidhyanathan avoid specific examination of his testimony, and only Vaidhyanathan addresses Clemens' "Private Letter and Public Postscript" at all. He notes only that it is "an article about international copyright" (63) and "a response" to Brander Matthews (204), without pointing out that it is also a stinging rebuttal of a good friend and prominent member of the American Copyright League. Only later in his career, in the 1890s, would Clemens shift away from his long-standing position and become an unqualified leader of the copyright movement.

FROM MINER TO PROPERTY HOLDER

Clemens held fast to his unique set of principles of ownership for the bulk of his career. As we have seen, he often viewed circulation of his texts as ultimately more important than strict control, believing that publicity would help his sales. While he had always seen protection of literary property as a responsibility of authors, he never seemed to argue that an author had a divine or natural right to his property. His or her works were, in many respects, mines: once a novel had been mined for all it was worth, the author moved on, just like the prospector on the cover of *Roughing It*. After his bankruptcy, this philosophy endangered his livelihood, and Clemens would later thank Standard Oil businessman and friend Henry Rogers for helping him to avoid making a terrible mistake:

> The long, long head that Mr. Rogers carried on his shoulders! When he was so strenuous about my copyrights, and so determined to keep them in the family, I was not able to understand why he should think the matter so important. He insisted that they were a great asset. I said they were not an asset at all; I couldn't even *give* them away. He said, wait—let the panic subside and business revive, and I would see; they would be worth more than they had ever been worth before.
>
> That was his idea—the idea of a financier, familiar with finance; of a capitalist, deep in railroads, oil, banks, iron, copper, telegraphs, and so on, and familiar with those things, but what could he know about books? What was his opinion about copyright values worth, if it clashed with the opinion of experienced old publishers? Which it did. The Webster failure threw seven of my books on my hands. I had offered them to three first-class publishers; they didn't want them. If Mr. Rogers had let Mrs. Clemens and me have our way, the copyrights would have been handed over to the publishers.
>
> I am grateful to his memory for many a kindness and many a good service he did me, but gratefulest of all for the saving of my copyrights—a service which saved me and my family from want and assured us permanent comfort and prosperity. (*Autobiography* 261–2)

As Clemens worked his way out of debt and looked toward the future security of his family, his feelings regarding copyright changed. His remarks regarding Rogers suggest that it was only through the persuasion of his friend that he came to see the benefit of simply holding fast to his copyrights. As Vaidhyanathan has ably demonstrated, he became a champion of perpetual copyright, arguing that, as novels were essentially property, they should be granted the same protections any form of property is offered. An author's profession should not make his rights subjugated to the public good: "For Twain, copyright was for the benefit of the author, his ideal of a cultural entrepreneur [. . .]" (78). Where copyright had once been the responsibility of the author, in the 1890s it became for Clemens a potential boon for the author, a legal mechanism that could declare novels to be the equivalent of real estate, capable of being passed on and held indefinitely.

Copyright was always an important subject for Clemens. While his opinions sometimes appear to be contradictory, they indicate his unique approach to the subject of literary property and his conscious communication of his beliefs to his readers. A performer and writer with one eye carefully regarding his audience, Clemens often modified his statements to assign blame without alienating the source of his livelihood. While he has been commonly portrayed as a leader in the copyright movement, he was unafraid to oppose friends and prominent figures in the American Copyright League to protect his own interests. His well-known battles with Canadian pirates have left the impression that he was staunchly opposed to all piracy, but as his notebooks of the 1880s indicate, he considered his own career as having benefited significantly from the widespread piracy of *The Jumping Frog*. His views on property rights, for much of his career, are strikingly similar to those shared by his character Huck Finn: motive and circumstance are at least as important as moral precepts. While Huck is able to move west to avoid the strictures of society, his creator, unable to flee bankruptcy and an uncertain future, was forced to embrace the right to property as a moral absolute. In the mines, Clemens had learned that the value of property came from its exchange, staking claims and then selling them. This idea of property informed his views for much of his career. If Samuel Clemens is to be viewed as a champion of authorial rights, he must be seen as a conflicted one, forced to abandon the free-wielding prospecting days of his youth for a more sober hoarding of resources near the end of his career. The prospector who adorns the cover of *Roughing It* seems finally to have returned to society, stopping his wagon and soundly investing his treasure in a savings account, content to support his family on the interest.

Conclusion

Copyright and "The Auction of the Mind"

Even as critics have paid increasing attention to the debates over copyright law, they have often replicated the binary positions set forth by many nineteenth-century participants in those debates. Thus, the act of taking out a copyright emerges as a concession to institutional power or as a mechanism of transformation, rendering an artwork a piece of property and an artist a businessperson or "owner." Copyright pages themselves have long been virtually ignored in literary criticism, not only because of their ubiquity, but also because they seem to be entirely divorced from the pages that follow them. With language written and endorsed by government authorities, they would seem to indicate little about the author or the work other than the writer's desire to receive compensation for his or her labor. Indeed, the copyright pages of nearly all nineteenth-century texts appear emptier still: the protection they invoke has long since expired, and they serve only to mark the age of the volume being examined. The "possession" of the text is no longer in question: what was once the sole possession of the author or publisher can now be claimed by anyone with the desire and the resources to reproduce it.

Particularly with new technologies such as the Internet and CD-ROM, this transformation of private property into public property has been a boon for readers and scholars, and it appears to validate the claims set forth by opponents of copyright's temporal and geographic expansion. Most nineteenth-century texts can now be made available to a wide number of readers at less cost. Recent changes to copyright law, such as expanding the duration of copyright protection to the life of the author plus seventy years, have drawn criticism from scholars like Vaidhyanathan, who direct us once again to the "limited Times" clause in the Constitution. Indeed, the Supreme Court has recently heard a challenge to the constitutionality of this latest expansion of the copyright law.[1]

Such concern is not without merit in an age when multi-national corporations pour hundreds of thousands of dollars in campaign contributions into Washington D.C. in an attempt to influence legislation in order to maintain control of their property. This seriously limits the uses to which artists, writers and scholars can put these materials and potentially hampers creativity and debate. Such lobbying is nothing new; what is novel is the scale of resources accompanying these efforts. In response, critics of increased copyright protection have replicated the cries of monopoly power of the nineteenth century, but now these accusations are aimed as often at companies like the Walt Disney Corporation as at the publishing houses. It is not surprising, then, that publication and copyright are seen primarily as business matters and that critics have failed to examine how nineteenth-century authors could consider copyright in any other way. Authors have been seen not so much as in negotiation with the needs and desires of their audiences as, perhaps unwittingly or unwillingly, complicit with the rise of market capitalism in the nineteenth century.

Nowhere is this view more evident than in studies of the life and work of Emily Dickinson. While critics have taken to debating her true feelings regarding publication, one thing is clear: she never copyrighted her works. Most have described this as a principled stand, a purposeful rejection of the crass commercialism of the literary marketplace. Thus, Dickinson's poem 788—"Publication—is the Auction"—is read as a straightforward illustration of the poet's opinion and a fair comment on the process of publication. In the beginning of the poem, the speaker states,

> Publication—is the Auction
> Of the Mind of Man—
> Poverty—be justifying
> For so foul a thing
>
> Possibly—but We—would rather
> From our Garret go
> White—unto the White Creator—
> Than invest—Our Snow—(1–8)

The poet's niece, Martha Dickinson Bianchi, quoted the poem in 1935 when she wrote, "There can be no doubt of Aunt Emily's disinclination to see herself out in the world of print [. . .]. If she really wanted publicity, it was hers for the accepting, but she declared, publication is as 'foreign to my thought as firmament to fin'; and again, [quoting the first two lines above] admitting that poverty may justify it, but setting it outside her personal pale with finality" (27–8). Elizabeth Horan, who has written a detailed study of the battles over possession of rights to Dickinson's poetry, also quotes this well-known poem when she concludes, "With regard to the human spirit, the 'disgrace of price' reduced the lives of four, possibly five, women in disputes over the ownership of manuscripts. When it came to the market, Emily Dickinson was right" ("Todd, Bianchi" 88). In an understandable response to the bitter disputes over Dickinson's work, Horan accepts the poet's portrayal of publication and appears to blame "the disgrace of price"— the marketing of literature—for "reducing" the lives of the women involved. Horan suggests that the Todd and Dickinson women were somehow diminished by their efforts to control the poet's manuscripts, and, in her conclusion, Horan depicts the marketplace as a world dominated by squabbles over ownership, degrading to those who enter it.

Dickinson's poem does appear to contrast the "foulness" of publication with the speaker's desire to remain pure. The speaker "would rather / From our Garret go / White—unto the White Creator—." Purity requires that one resist entering the auction; to do so willingly is only acceptable if one has no other way of making a living. The diction here and elsewhere in the poem does not deny any kind of circulation, however. The speaker, who becomes the text both figuratively, in the metaphoric link between the text being auctioned and "the Mind of Man," and literally, in the marks on the page, expresses a wish to pass from the garret to the "White Creator." The text will change hands, yet the condition for such a transferal is a purity dependent upon being "White"—an unmarked, blank page. Avoiding the "auction" relies upon remaining obscure and uncirculated, "snow" that has not been "invested," either with meaning or in the marketplace.

This accords with the next three lines; Dickinson writes, "Thought belong to Him who gave it—/ Then—to Him Who bear / It's Corporeal illustration—[. . .]" (9–11). As Horan has noted of this line, the speaker splits the idea of a work from its material form ("Technically" 36). Yet the condition that seems to be set if one would maintain possession of "thought" is the total avoidance of putting that thought into any sort of "Corporeal illustration." The speaker/text must go "White"—blank—unto the "White Creator." Once "Thought" assumes material form, it is transferred from the original owner— "the one who gave it"—to the one who possesses the "Corporeal illustration." The diction makes it clear that this is not the same person.

Despite this apparently inevitable transaction, the speaker continues to resist the sale of an "embodied" thought by urging that one "Be the Merchant / Of the Heavenly Grace—/ But reduce no Human Spirit / To

Disgrace of Price—" (Dickinson 13–16). What has already become evident, however, is that once the "Human Spirit" has been expressed in written form, or "invested," it unavoidably becomes "disgraced." Once the "mind" is reproduced in writing, it becomes susceptible to market manipulation. Such manipulation does not need to come at the hand of cold corporate power. Martha Dickinson Bianchi quotes her aunt Lavinia Dickinson's declaration, "I will never give away to an outsider the ownership of my sister's brains" (qtd. in Horan "Technically" 38). Once Dickinson's "brains" are embodied in text, they are vulnerable. Because Dickinson left her thoughts in manuscript form, they are now subject to her sister Lavinia's ownership and sale. (She may not "give" them away, but she fervently pursued publishing them.) In an apparent acknowledgment of this inevitable transformation from idea as text to text as commodity, the speaker offers only impossible alternatives to "reducing" the human spirit to price: one cannot follow the injunction to "sell / The Royal Air—/ In the Parcel" (Dickinson 11–13) nor sell grace, but one can always hoard or sell the human spirit once it has been invested in text.

   This reading of Dickinson's poem is not intended as an argument that Dickinson herself either accepted or approved of publication. Ample evidence exists in her correspondence showing that she avoided publication. What is notable is how this poem, despite its apparent admission of inevitable defeat by publication inherent in its very creation, has been seen both as an expression of Dickinson's views and an accurate critique of the publishing industry. Our tendency is to view this poem and the practice of owning texts—"brains" or the "Human Spirit"—at least in part through the prism of the nineteenth-century debates over copyright law. This is particularly clear in the case of the works of Emily Dickinson: the careful hoarding of her manuscripts and the contentious battles for control of the rights of publication led to a situation where scholars and readers were excluded and forced to accept what was parceled out at the convenience of the manuscripts' owners.[2] While other nineteenth-century authors have long since entered the public domain, clearing the way for cheaper editions and Internet publication, Dickinson's works are still subject to legal oversight.[3]

   The situation has long been a source of frustration for scholars and readers. When Martha Dickinson Bianchi released another limited selection of her aunt's work, critic Morris U. Schappes noted in 1933, "The frequently offered suggestion that all available manuscripts be turned over to a group of capable scholars for scrupulous examination and editing has never been more pertinent than now. One almost wished for a state control of manuscripts such as exists in Russia, to provide scholars with the privilege of being scholars unhampered by property rights" (qtd. in Horan, "Todd, Bianchi" 85). This argument by now sounds familiar: it poses property rights against the advancement of knowledge, and property rights are meant to appear somewhat crass in the comparison. Interestingly, however, Schappes does not suggest that Dickinson's texts be made available in accordance with democratic principles; rather, he invokes communist Russia and the elimination of individual property rights in the manuscript. His qualified wish—Schappes apparently is not ready to go quite so far—recalls James Fenimore Cooper's most frequent critique of copyright opponents. Eliminating individual property rights is not the way to bring about greater democracy, Cooper always argued, but exactly the reverse. We can only imagine the chapters that might have been added to *The Littlepage Manuscripts* if a statement such as Schappes had been made about Cooper's works during his lifetime.

Bianchi writes of owning her aunt's manuscripts, "I like to feel my hand is on Emily's property" (qtd. in Horan 82). Bianchi's careful policing and possession of the manuscripts is certainly different from the poet's. While for a time Dickinson sewed her poems into small volumes, she also sent poems and portions of her poems in numerous letters, wrote them on loose slips of paper, and re-wrote them with different words for different audiences.[4] She did not practice the kind of tight control later exercised by her financially struggling niece. Horan suggests that Bianchi's interest in keeping her "hand" on the manuscripts was a matter of necessity, leading her only to care about those poems from which she could turn a profit: "Bianchi had no reason to trouble herself with texts that she could not readily copyright" (82). There is little reason to doubt Horan's assessment of Bianchi's motives. We can, however, contrast Bianchi's wish to control carefully the fate of the poems with her aunt's relationship to her work. The Dickinson family can be viewed harshly for the way they attempted to exercise control over the poet's work, and their motivations can be questioned. Greed, or at the very least financial necessity, cannot be ignored as a compelling factor in their close protection of their property and the piecemeal publication of Dickinson materials.

If we criticize them for being too guarded with the material, however, then it is only fair to consider Emily Dickinson's practices as a literary property owner. While her relatives may have made it difficult to gain access to these texts, the poet's own treatment of her manuscripts and her determination not to publish them nearly made access impossible. If we consider literary property ownership not simply as a practice that denies the public immediate and inexpensive access, but instead as a responsibility incumbent upon the author (as Clemens frequently portrayed it), then Dickinson's refusal to see to the protection and disposal of her work emerges not simply as a moral rejection of the "Auction of the Mind." Just as her poem paradoxically offers the blank page as the only text that can escape market circulation, her practice of simultaneously hoarding and mailing her manuscripts presents the possibility of oblivion as the sole alternative to publication. (This is particularly true when one recalls the common nineteenth-century practice of burning correspondence upon the death of the recipient.) According to the logic of copyright opponents, careful protection of literary property rights amounts to a kind of monopoly power that denies the public access to texts. Their arguments appear to be supported by the practice of Dickinson's heirs. At the same time, however, Emily Dickinson's treatment of her property reminds us that to disregard the careful management of literary property can just as easily rob the public of access.

Betsy Erkkila points out that one cannot read Dickinson's attitude about her literary property simply as a denial of a market economy: "Adhering to an essentially aristocratic and Carlylean notion of literature as the production of mind and genius for eternity, she set herself against not only the new commercialization and democratization but against the sentimental women writers of her time who had gained money and fame in the American marketplace" ("Emily" 20). For Dickinson, making her work available for sale was not wrong because it denied access to readers; rather, it made her work available to the "wrong" readers. In a careful study of the poems published during Dickinson's lifetime, Karen Dandurand has demonstrated that, in many cases, the audience who had access to the poetry was an "especially literary and sophisticated one" (256). Dandurand also provides evidence to suggest that Dickinson was conscious of her wider readership, even if she did not approve of the publication of her work (268). She resisted the entreaties to publish more of her work, Dandurand suggests, because she did not wish for the kind of intrusive publicity that was becoming a prevalent part of authorship. Erkkila links this refusal to engage a larger public with an aristocratic impulse. Widespread publication would have allowed for a leveling and an intermingling of class that, as Erkkila demonstrates, Dickinson had long criticized. As an alternative, the poet's hand-binding and private circulation of her manuscripts enacts a form of publication that attempts to deny both the economic and social effects of the marketplace ("Emily" 20).

In poem 709, Dickinson offers a critique of publication that appears to demand that one refrain from writing altogether and looks dismissively at those who must write because of poverty. Erkkila notes that the poem features "a highly charged political language in which the rhetoric of antislavery protest intersects with the rhetoric of protest against wage labor as a new form of human enslavement" (19). What is most disturbing about the rhetoric is not only the disapproving attitude the speaker shows to the poor who have no choice but to do "so foul a thing" as publish, but also that the image of the slave auction offers the slave no opportunity of liberation. Just as the writer apparently cannot avoid the marketplace unless he or she does not write at all (going "White" from her garret)—a self-negating alternative—the slave cannot choose to change the markings on his or her skin. As we have seen, it was not uncommon to employ the rhetoric of slavery in arguments regarding copyright law. In this regard, Dickinson's portrayal of publishing as an "auction of the mind" is not so different from Justice Grier's ruling in the Stowe *v.* Thomas case that, by publishing, Stowe had forfeited her rights to limit or control translations of her works. Both arguments undermine copyright protections by suggesting that publication is a willing, even a "foul," surrendering of property rights.

All nineteenth-century authors negotiated the demands of their readers, their artistic and political ideals, and the legal and business realities of writing and publishing. The discourse of literary property rights that emerged in the United States shaped and was shaped by the way authors pursued and portrayed their profession. While the reasons for Dickinson's apparent rejection of publication are open to debate and question, her refusal to copyright her work or publish it more widely did not exclude her from these negotiations. As Erkkila has argued, her refusal to publish and her eventual withdrawal from the public world did not free her from the questions of race, class, and gender of her time, just as withholding her poetry only delayed the struggles over its ownership until after her death.

The decision to copyright a work does not simply signify a desire to control one's property: as Dickinson's example suggests, the *refusal* to copyright a work can suggest an even *greater* desire to control possession. On the other hand, as Clemens so often argued, failure to copyright can signify a disregard for one's property, an abdication of authorial responsibility. Copyright cannot be read merely as an indication of an author's professional ambition, just as it cannot be read merely as a mechanism of transformation of author to owner. Copyright opponents often worked to present the law as unfairly elevating the property rights of an individual over the democratic ideals of equality and access to knowledge, yet the law could also function as the very mechanism to allow public access to works: Dickinson's uncopyrighted works remain among the only major nineteenth-century texts that are not part of the public domain, while the then-copyrighted works of her contemporaries are now freely available.

Authors such as Whitman, Cooper, Stowe, and Clemens, rejected or subverted the dichotomy suggested by the copyright debate even as they responded to the criticism leveled against them. As they sought to protect their literary property rights, each conceived of a unique view of copyright in accordance with his or her political and artistic beliefs. A greater understanding of nineteenth-century authorship demands that we acknowledge and examine the diversity of these views and consider copyright not as a peripheral legal or business matter but as a central concern for American readers and writers. As Whitman remarked, copyright is also "a question of honesty—of morals—of a literature, in fact." As authors, publishers, legislators, judges, lawyers, scholars, and readers continue to wrestle with issues of literary property rights, the question remains an open one.

Notes

NOTES TO THE INTRODUCTION

1. This is not to suggest that all recent critics agree with Chartier's claim that we have witnessed "the return of the author" (8). While Chartier argues, "In spite of striking differences, and indeed divergences, among them [approaches such as new historicism and bibliography], a common characteristic of all these approaches is that they reconnect the text with its author; the work with the desires or the positions of its producer" (9), some scholars working in copyright history, on the other hand, still embrace the notion of the author as primarily a legal construct or the product of European Romanticism. In their introduction to *The Construction of Authorship*, (published the same year as Chartier's essay in *Of Authors and Origins*— 1994), Martha Woodmansee and Peter Jaszi call on legal scholars to view the "author" with greater critical skepticism. In calling for an embrace of Derridean and Foucaultian analysis, they write "law has missed out on the contemporary 'critique of authorship'—the impulse, especially in literary studies, to put in question the naturalness and inevitability of Romantic ideas about creativity. Umberto Eco's 'open work' remains a closed book to the law, just as Roland Barthes' call in 'The Death of the Author' for a reversal of the conventional relation of author and reader has gone unheard by intellectual property lawyers" (8). If Chartier is correct in his assessment of the "return of the author"—and more recent studies such as Michael Newbury's suggest he was—then Woodmansee and Jaszi have begun calling on legal scholars to embrace post-structuralist critiques of authorship of the sixties and seventies just as literary scholars employing new historical and cultural approaches have once again begun recognizing the role of authorship.

NOTES TO CHAPTER ONE

1. For a detailed account of the kinds of problems faced by publishers in the early nineteenth century, see Kaser, David. *Messrs. Carey & Lea of Philadel-*

phia: A Study in the History of the Booktrade. (Philadelphia: U of Pennsylvania P, 1957). Often the profit margins for English novels published in America were decided by what amounted to footraces from the boats carrying copies of the texts to the competing publishing houses.

2. There are some critics who have studied these lesser-known texts, most often in surveys of Cooper's entire oeuvre, and dealt with them in greater detail. See, for example, Dekker, George. *James Fenimore Cooper: The American Scott.* (New York: Barnes & Noble, 1967) and McWilliams, Jr. John P. *Political Justice in a Republic: James Fenimore Cooper's America.* (Berkeley: U of California P, 1972).

3. Irving pleaded that he had been "confined to [his] room by an indisposition" and had been unable to act, but he suggested in the future that Cooper must send his work directly to a British publisher before printing it elsewhere (*Correspondence* 1: 89). He recommended John Miller, who subsequently sought out Cooper. Although there was no copyright for American authors *per se,* they could make arrangements with a British publisher, and, by publishing their works first in England, gain some measure of protection. Publishers would rarely pirate a text that one of their peers had already arranged to publish. As American piracy of British works flourished, American authors lost even this protection. Later in the century, American authors had to be "residing" in English territories when their books first were published, prompting many trips to Canada by authors such as Samuel Clemens.

4. A little more than a week after writing to his publishers, he also wrote to his friends in the Bread and Cheese Club, a group of writers, scholars, and professionals that Cooper organized and led during his years in New York. Once again, we see Cooper's sense of the issue as one of public, even more than legal, concern: "I feel sure that I may appeal to every individual among you to lend his aid in this desirable undertaking—As every thing depends on the force of Public Opinion, your names and characters cannot fail to produce a suitable effect in your respective spheres—" (*Letters* 1: 180). There is no evidence that the Bread and Cheese Club took any direct action in response to Cooper's appeal.

5. Dorothy Waples has suggested that a great deal of this criticism was politically motivated. See *The Whig Myth of James Fenimore Cooper.* Yale Studies in English. Vol. 88. (New Haven: Yale UP, 1938).

6. Although Cooper was greatly interested in assisting the aging Dunlap, it appears that his efforts largely failed. He did manage to gain Dunlap a fifty-pound down payment from Richard Bentley, but the book failed in England (*Letters* 2: 358n).

7. This argument, written by "An American," took up the cause of the petition and Clay's bill and was only part of a longer piece that offered several reasons for expanding copyright, including the fact that, according to Sackett,

authors were by nature no good with money (24)! Henry Clay had made a similar claim in his report, writing that authors "are frequently, from the nature of their pursuits, or the constitutions of their minds, incapable of applying that provident care to worldly affairs which other classes of society are in the habit of bestowing" (Putnam, *Question* 34). Authors had rights, it appears, but the protection of these rights here seems to be offered almost as an act of charity.

8. This legal case has been studied extensively and is written on in detail in nearly all legal texts dealing with the history of copyright. For a close textual reading of the case, see Meredith McGill's "The Matter of the Text: Commerce, Print Culture, and the Authority of the State in American Copyright Law." *American Literary History* 9 (1997): 21–59.

9. Walt Whitman, who agreed with Dickens regarding international copyright, still took Dickens to task in his article "Boz's Opinions of Us" for *The Evening Tattler* that same year (Whitman, *Journalism* 148). See Chapter Three.

10. For a thorough discussion of Charles Dickens and the question of international copyright law, see Moss, Sidney P. *Charles Dickens' Quarrel with America.* (Troy, NY: Whitson P, 1984).

11. See Cooper's emphatic letter to *The Evening Post* in July of 1843 in *Letters* 4: 393–397.

12. Nearly all of Cooper's biographers discuss his reaction to the Anti-Rent movement. See particularly Grossman, 197–201, Railton, 240–44, and Dekker's *James Fenimore Cooper,* 218–35.

13. While doing research at the American Antiquarian Society, I benefited greatly from discussions with Melissa A. Homestead, and I am grateful to her for directing me to this speech.

14. The success of this effort is debatable. Beard argues, "Cooper repeated unconsciously his strategic error in *A Letter to His Countrymen* and *Home as Found:* he identified himself and his personal associations too closely with his controversial materials" (*Letters* 5: 5). While it is true that Cooper's views are prominent in these texts, as critics writing at the time noted, it is clear that, for Cooper's part, he viewed differences in name and geography sufficient to establish the fictional nature of his characters. This is particularly evident in the libel trials over *Home as Found,* in which Cooper went to great lengths to demonstrate the differences between himself and his family and the Effinghams. See his letter to the *Philadelphia Public Ledger* in *Letters* 4: 72–87.

15. At other times, particularly in *Satanstoe,* the editor feels compelled to apologize for the narrator's "provincialism." See pages 94–5, for example.

16. Dekker and McWilliams note, "Neither *Satanstoe* nor *The Chainbearer,* two of Cooper's finest works, seems to have been accorded even one literary notice" (*Critical Heritage* 22).

17. While this spelling of Cooper's name did occasionally appear, particularly early on, it was not the preferred or proper spelling, as is made clear by the correctly spelled notice of Cooper's copyright.

18. An agreement between Cooper and Putnam for *Rural Hours* refers to Cooper as "the Agent for the author and Copyright owner of a certain work written by his daughter S. J. F. Cooper" (Agreement).

NOTES TO CHAPTER TWO

1. In fact, Barnes argues that with the notable exception of the Harpers, most prominent publishers were willing to put aside their competitive instincts and support international copyright: "by the mid-1840s the mania for cheapness had abated and trade courtesy began to be revived. Improved trade conditions brought greater stability. [. . .] As a result, from about 1845 until the depression of 1857 the American book trade experienced a remarkable prosperity and tranquility which augured well for an Anglo-American copyright agreement" (86). While it may be true that some large publishing houses generally put aside their more cutthroat practices, Stowe's experiences following the success of *Uncle Tom's Cabin* indicate that such respect was not always extended to authors.

2. As we will see, this was not the only time when slavery and authorship were juxtaposed.

3. Homestead discusses this aspect of Stowe's position as a married woman author in relation to the publication of *Uncle Tom's Cabin* in some detail, although she does not examine the difficulties this posed for Stowe as she attempted to secure copyrights overseas (119–29).

4. In an expression of gratitude, and perhaps an effort to encourage his behavior, Stowe wrote to thank Mr. Bentley for "transcend[ing] the mere legal & technical ideas of right" (qtd. in Coultrap-McQuin 89).

5. As Frank Luther Mott notes, *Graham's* was an important literary magazine throughout much of the 1840s, publishing Poe, Cooper, and Lowell among many others (546). By the early 1850s, the magazine was suffering from competition with *Harper's* and a rush to expand too quickly (552–3). In later years, Graham placed much of the blame for his magazine's failure on the unpopular reception of his Stowe editorials (553).

6. Melissa Homestead points out Justice Grier's steadfast support for the Fugitive Slave Law and suggests that his opinion in Stowe's case may have been motivated by his political sympathies.

7. The italicized phrases were included in the American Law Register's report on the case, but were not part of the initial federal court reporter's document. See *Stowe v. Thomas* 208.

8. This description of *Jefferys v. Boosey* is drawn from Barnes, 166–173.

9. Stowe's daughter, Eliza, who traveled with her mother to England, makes a melancholy note in her diary: "August 12. 13. 14 & 15 were spent in finishing Ma's book did not go out any where" (Diary).

10. Calvin Stowe wrote to Harriet in October, "Mr Low has not yet sent me the written statement as to his bargain for Dred, though I have twice written for it. The copy-right here stands in your name, so that is all safe" (Letter).

11. In a letter to Calvin, Stowe writes, "Since my last letter a great change has taken place in our plans, [. . .] so, if all goes well, we are due in Boston four weeks from this date. I long for home, for my husband and children, for my room, my yard and garden, for the beautiful trees of Andover. We will make a very happy home, and our children will help us" (qtd. in Fields 257). Forrest Wilson has suggested that this letter hints at some sort of domestic dispute (457).

12. Gaskell had occasion to meet Stowe while she traveled in England, beginning with her first trip in 1853. Gaskell seems to have been fond of her, telling a correspondent that she was "unspoiled & unspoilable," but remarking "she is not famous for keeping her engagements, as we know" (Gaskell 237).

13. When Stowe does turn her attention to the purchasing of goods, it is nearly always a means of indicting the morals or actions of a character. In *Pink and White Tyranny,* for example, the wife who cares only for the social scene and for the latest fashion is depicted as lavishly remodeling the home where her husband grew up; he, in turn, is forced to retreat to his sister's house, where he can lounge in comfort in familiar and comfortable surroundings.

14. It is worth noting that Mary Scudder's only flirtation with the moral danger represented by Aaron Burr comes after she takes one of these emotionally precious outfits and alters it to wear to a fashionable ball. These items are to be prized as family artifacts, not worn as ornaments.

NOTES TO CHAPTER THREE

1. Subsequently abbreviated *WW.*

2. An important exception is Terry Mulcaire's "Publishing Intimacy in *Leaves of Grass.*" *ELH* 60.2 (1993): 471–501. Mulcaire argues that Whitman's poetically imagined relationship with his reader depends upon the capitalistic conditions of mass production. While he does not examine Whitman's position on copyright extensively, Mulcaire does suggest that the poet embraces views held by both proponents and opponents of copyright by simultaneously imagining his books as products of his own body while at the same time figuring the body itself as emerging only through mass publication (482–3).

3. The fact that Whitman recorded two other references to the copyright bill the day it passed indicates the extent of his interest. At the end of a list of payments received for books, appropriately enough, Walt Whitman wrote this brief, non-descript entry: "Copyright bill pass'd" (*Daybooks* 2: 588). That same day, Whitman wrote his friend Dr. Richard Bucke and informed him, in a similarly understated fashion, "we have got the international copyright law pass'd here" (*Correspondence* 5: 173).

4. For Lowell's Senate testimony, see United States, Committee on Patents. *International Copyright.* 49th Cong., 1st sess. S. no. 161. Washington: GPO, 1886.

5. Gerard Genette has argued for closer attention to copyright pages and all of those "verbal or other productions" that "ensure the text's presence in the world" (1) in his recent work *Paratexts: Thresholds of Interpretation.* These "paratexts" can range from the author's name to the typeface of the book, or even to promotional interviews given by the author: Genette writes that "the paratext is what enables a text to become a book and to be offered as such to its readers and, more generally, to the public" (1).

6. See also Welsh, *From Copyright to Copperfield.* Welsh writes that "the evidence that Dickens intended to speak out on copyright is purely circumstantial: he arrived in America, and he spoke" (31).

7. This magazine, begun in Washington in 1837 and moved to New York in 1841, enjoyed a considerable literary standing through 1846, publishing Hawthorne, Bryant, Whittier, and occasionally Whitman himself. The strong nationalistic character of the magazine may account for this editorial's opposition to international copyright. See Mott, pages 677–84.

8. For more on this letter, see Buinicki, "'Boz's Opinions of Us': Whitman, Dickens, and the Forged Letter." *Walt Whitman Quarterly Review.* 21.1 (2003): 35–38.

9. Justin Kaplan touches on Whitman's defense of Dickens in the context of the debate over international copyright in *Walt Whitman: A Life,* pages 98–100.

10. See Gay Wilson Allen's *The Solitary Singer,* pages 60–66.

11. Grier suggests Whitman wrote this piece sometime between 1871 and 1873. In a remarkable feat of archival research, Martin Murray has discovered an article entitled "Washington as a Central Winter Residence" published in *The Washington Evening Star* on January 6, 1872. As Murray demonstrated in a presentation at the American Literary Association in May 2002, the article appears to be a published version of this Whitman manuscript. I am grateful to him for providing me with the text of the article.

12. In Whitman's published revision, he has eliminated his poetic catalogues and all references to the government receptions, as well as nearly all mention of administrative apparatus and authority. The reference to international copyright is also removed, thereby rendering the article almost

completely apolitical; "[. . .] the pleadings in the Supreme Court, and the debates in Congress" are presented as attractions primarily for students, who also come to enjoy the Botanic Gardens. Whitman's reference to international copyright in his draft version appears to be intended to incorporate authors into the democratic spectacle—"International copyright would be a benefit to Washington / Already many foreign authors visit here"—while in this published version, Washington is simply a tourist attraction designed particularly for American travelers. The poet writes, "The Americans are migratory and like change of scene. [. . .] Students are coming here from all parts of the country [. . .]." Whitman has narrowed his vision of Washington as a cosmopolitan destination, a narrowing that coincides with the deletion of his reference to international copyright.

13. In yet another apparent contradiction, Whitman decries the standards of present literary success: "[. . .] where is the man of letters, where is the book, with any nobler aim than to follow in the old track, repeat what has been said before—and, as its utmost triumph, sell well, and be erudite and elegant?" (999). This exclamation might indicate Whitman's own frustration at not finding a broader audience. While Whitman appears to be ridiculing the standard of "selling well" as a marker of success, it is not having a large sale that he is taking issue with here; rather, it is the standards that would allow a book of such pale imitation and propriety to have a large sale in the first place.

14. Ironically, *Franklin Evans* appeared immediately following Park Benjamin's pirated re-printing of Dickens' *American Notes* (Greenspan, *Walt Whitman* 46). Yet as Whitman himself made clear in his journalism, American authors were left with few publishing choices in the unregulated literary landscape.

15. Mulcaire argues that this vision of poetic contact is tied to the alienation of mass production: "Beginning with the Marxian insight that the commodity is in a real sense the projection of the living bodies of its producers, Whitman turns that insight on its head by proposing, in effect, that who touches any commodity touches a living projection of a human body; and the free exchangeability of commodities in the marketplace will take on for him the aspect of the free exchange of democratic 'camerados'" (472). What is important here is Mulcaire's observation that Whitman does not undermine capitalistic exchange so much as he re-imagines it.

16. Such a sentiment greatly resembles Elijah Paine's argument in the copyright infringement case of *Wheaton v. Peters* (1834) that Meredith L. McGill examines in "The Matter of the Text: Commerce, Print Culture, and the Authority of the State in American Copyright Law." While McGill rightly points out that such an argument, particularly in the case she describes, "overlooks the entire sphere of production" (31), the matter is complicated

in this situation by Whitman's close engagement with the production and distribution of *Leaves of Grass*.

17. This is a rather complex affair. As Edwin Haviland Miller points out, Whitman's version of events is "somewhat garbled" (196n). See *The Correspondence of Walt Whitman*, vol. 3, pages 196–98 for both Whitman's account and Miller's more complete recounting.

18. Whitman had made a good choice in identifying an advocate in this matter. In 1883, Gilder would become one of the founding members of the American Copyright League; clearly he was invested in issues of copyright and piracy. See James A. Rawley's "An Early History of the International Copyright Movement." *Library Quarterly* 6 (1941): 200–06.

19. Whitman's correspondence indicates that he is mistaken regarding the dates and amounts of these exchanges.

20. Whitman's total income in 1880 was $1,124.64, in 1881 $949.12, and in 1882 $2,120.30 (Miller xvi). These were fairly remarkable sums "in an era when one could buy a two-story house for $1,750.00" (xv).

21. Whitman would include a preface conveying this type of message in the 1887 British edition of *Specimen Days*, published there as *Specimen Days in America*. His preface, addressed "To the Reader in the British Isles," stresses that "in the volume, as below any page of mine, anywhere, ever remains, for seen or unseen basis-phrase, GOOD-WILL BETWEEN THE COMMON PEOPLE OF ALL NATIONS." In *Specimen Days in America*. London: Walter Scott, 1887.

22. The argument here once again echoes an argument employed by Elijah Paine in *Wheaton v. Peters* in 1834. See McGill, "Matter," pages 28–9.

23. In the 1856 edition, for example, the first and last names are separated by the break between the first two lines of the copyright notice (Myerson 24). In the 1860 edition, "BY WALT WHITMAN" occupies the entire second line and is printed in all capital letters (qtd. in Myerson 29). The 1870 edition notice includes "by" on the first line, leaving "WALT WHITMAN" to occupy the second line exclusively (qtd. in Myerson 50). These changes have the effect of featuring Whitman's name even within the institutionally mandated notice. To view all of the different copyright notices within a single volume, see Joel Myerson's invaluable *Walt Whitman: A Descriptive Bibliography*, pages 8–143.

24. This again raises questions concerning Whitman's dealings with Worthington. His reluctance to see older versions of *Leaves of Grass* competing with the most current expression seems offset by his willingness to consent to the circulation of his text once he becomes an informed participant in the exchange.

25. Whitman remarked to Traubel in 1888, "The other Spofford, A. R., [. . .] does not admit me. I mean by that that he has no use for me—that he suspects my work, sees no excuse for it. He throws nothing in my way, but he

does nothing to welcome me. I don't blame him—I am only putting down history for you to study—Whitman history. Spofford opposed when he might have benefited me" (1; 104). Whitman seems to have enlisted the librarian's help here in this final, unusual copyright page.

NOTES TO CHAPTER FOUR

1. He was also faced with the unique problem of being in danger of pirating his own work if he chose to use the letters he had written for the newspaper within his book. The discovery of this dilemma prompted a hasty trip to California to meet with the *Alta*'s editors. Fortunately, his case was helped considerably by his ill-fated lecture tour upon his return to the states: "The editors, made uncertain of the market for their book by the failure of Mark Twain's tour, relinquished their copyright in exchange for a simple acknowledgment in any eventual volume incorporating the letters" (Hoffman 137).

2. It is likely that Carey was motivated to re-issue his *Letters* by the apparently positive reception international copyright legislation was receiving in 1868. The Committee on the Library in the House of Representatives submitted a favorable report on bill H. R. No. 779, writing, "It would be an act of national justice and honor, in which we should find that justice is the wisest policy for nations and brings the richest reward" (United States 1). The committee had received a memorial in favor of international copyright signed by Francis Lieber, William Cullen Bryant, George Palmer Putnam, and others (Cameron 117–120).

3. Clemens had met the Shah while in London and written several travel letters describing him. He sent these to the New York *Herald* where they were published.

4. Clemens had used self-deprecation before in an apparent effort to defuse charges of selfishness. When he published a letter to the *Spectator* attacking Hotten for his piracies, he wrote, "My books are bad enough just as they are written; then what must they be after Mr John Camden Hotten has composed half-a-dozen chapters and added the same to them?" (qtd. in Welland 21).

5. In fact, Clemens had counted on his letters being reprinted; because he had anticipated publishing the proposed pamphlet from the moment he began writing, Clemens told Bliss that he had not copyrighted his letters on the Shah when he sent them back to the states: "Have begun to write about the Shah to N.Y. Herald—don't want them copyrighted. You seize them as they appear, & turn them into a 25 cent pamphlet (my royalty 10 per cent) & spread them over the land your own way, but be quick! Don't let it get cold before you are out" (*Letters* 5: 384). Clemens was not afraid to use the piratical tendencies of American newspaper editors to his own advantage.

6. He was clearly more than a "tacit accessory." His purposeful decision *not* to copyright his letters demonstrates his agency and puts into question his "objection to republication."

7. Hoffman notes only "Sam did not want to lead the fight for the law because he was its most obvious beneficiary" (238). All of the authors whose signatures he sought would have been in the same position. Doyno makes passing reference to these letters, noting, "Twain and Howells were planning a campaign to improve the situation for authors" (21). This is true, but it does not address Clemens' odd tentativeness.

8. If one recalls Clemens' anger at the *Alta* for copyrighting the letters he intended to use in *Innocents Abroad,* it becomes apparent that $10,000 was Clemens' default sum for losses due to copyright issues.

9. It is important to recall that Clemens was selling his book through subscription publication. The sale of cheaper Canadian editions would thus not only compete with his books in terms of price, but it would cost him subscribers not willing to wait for the arrival of their subscription copy.

10. Others did not share Clemens' optimism that he had "solved the problem of International Copyright" with his trademark victory (*Letters to his Publishers* 112). When he wrote his publisher at the American Publishing Company, Bliss responded, "I was in hopes you had unearthed some point of law that would lift Am Authors and Publishers out of the Copyright slough, but by your card I see the thing flatted out" (113n).

11. Clemens followed this logic after he became a publisher, as well, telling his partner Charles Webster in 1887, "And I would make it the rule of the house to give *any* respectable author permission to use extracts amounting in bulk to even a whole *tenth* of any book of ours—he to name page and matter as this lady has done. I quite understand that 1/10 of the Memoirs would be all of 100 pages. *And a very generous advertisement for us, gratis—* well worth having. It isn't a newspaper's *review* of a book that makes the book sell; it is the *extracts* copied from the book that does it." (*Letters to His Publishers* 225). Clemens does make republication contingent upon both an author's request and the publisher's permission, a condition mandating the control he had always advocated; however, as both a writer and a publisher he held firmly to the belief that a book's sale relief in large part upon the widespread circulation of substantial portions of that book.

12. It is worth noting, of course, that now that Clemens is trying to downplay his copyright losses, the familiar figure of $10,000 is replaced by $5,000.

13. Though only commenting on it in passing, Christopher P. Wilson notes of Clemens' testimony, "At the time, Twain's candor seemed to do little more than ruffle the vanity of the crusade; in retrospect, his skeptical inference carries more weight" (65). Wilson believes that Clemens' comments foreshadow the "*coalition* of interests which included writers, publishers, printers, and protectionists" that eventually helped pass an international

copyright bill (65). While this may be so, Wilson downplays the fact that, in his testimony, Clemens *cedes* authorial primacy to these other interests and undermines the arguments of his colleagues. The transcripts suggest that the effect of Clemens' remarks was to strengthen the arguments of copyright opponents during the hearings.

NOTES TO THE CONCLUSION

1. The case, *Eldred v. Ashcroft*, has received widespread, if not prominent, media coverage. A recent article on the case published in *The Chronicle of Higher Education* indicates the interest it holds for scholars. While the piece outlines the main arguments, it devotes most of its time to a flattering profile of the plaintiff, an independent Internet publisher. One legal scholar is cited in the article as noting, "Mr. Eldred is a striking example of how one person's efforts to advance scholarship and the public domain have been stifled by Congress's kowtowing to entertainment interests" (Foster A35). As for Eldred himself, "Literature, he says, should not be 'locked up in a library and accessible [only] to high priests of academia . . . People have as much power as a printing press' in their own computers" (A35). While the players and the technologies have changed, the rhetoric and the oppositional logic—the people versus the elite—seem quite familiar.

2. One of the earliest attempts to explain the story of the possession and publication of Dickinson's manuscripts is Millicent Todd Bingham's *Ancestors' Brocades*. In it, Bingham tells the story of her mother Martha Todd's editing, with Thomas Wentworth Higginson, of the first edition of Dickinson's poems. Lavinia Dickinson, the poet's sister, originally sought their assistance in preparing the manuscripts but came to resent their involvement. Bingham writes, "She was jealous for Emily, but more jealous of her own rights as Emily's representative" (286). This resentment contributed to a growing enmity between Todd, who had possession of a number of manuscripts, and the Dickinson family. In her studies of the dispute, Elizabeth Horan details how this dispute resulted in a state of affairs in which "no individual or corporation has ever been able to assert exclusive rights" ("Technically" 34). See also "To Market: The Dickinson Copyright Wars" *The Emily Dickinson Journal* 5.1 (1996): 88–120.

3. Horan argues that, because of the tangled legal history of ownership of Dickinson's manuscripts, "any attempts at monopoly within Dickinson publication" would, in her opinion, end in "probable failure" ("Technically" 34): "The legal uncertainties involved in the copyright status of Dickinson texts have been and can continue to be a boon for prospective publication" (34). Horan's study seems designed to offer support for "the prospect of making Dickinson available online" (34). The fact that any such publication would have to rely on "legal uncertainties" demonstrates the unique

status of Dickinson's works compared to those of other nineteenth-century authors.

4. Betsy Erkkila notes that the sewing of her poems into small groupings may suggest either preparation for publication or "a private form of publication [. . .] her own form of productive industry" ("Homoeroticism and Audience" 173).

Works Cited

Adamson, Thomas. *A Reply to "Considerations and Arguments, Proving the Inexpediency of an International Copyright Law, by John Campbell."* New York: Bartlett & Welford, 1844.

Allen, Gay Wilson. *The Solitary Singer.* New York: Grove Press, 1955.

Archer, Stevenson. *International Copyright. Speech of Hon. Stevenson Archer, of Maryland, Delivered in the House of Representatives, March 23, 1872.* Washington: F. & J. Rives & Geo. A. Bailey, 1872.

Austin, James C. *Fields of the* Atlantic Monthly. San Marino: Huntington Library, 1953.

Barnes, James J. *Authors, Publishers and Politicians: The Quest for an Anglo-American Copyright Agreement, 1815–1854.* Columbus: Ohio State UP, 1974.

Bianchi, Martha Dickinson. *Emily Dickinson Face to Face.* Boston: Houghton Mifflin Co., 1932.

Bingham, Millicent Todd. *Ancestor's Brocades: The Literary Debut of Emily Dickinson.* New York: Harper and Brothers, 1945.

Bourdieu, Pierre. *Language and Symbolic Power.* Ed. John B. Thompson. Trans. Gino Raymond and Matthew Adamson. Cambridge: Harvard UP, 1991.

Boyd, Richard. "Models of Power in Harriet Beecher Stowe's *Dred.*" *Studies in American Fiction* 19.1 (1991): 15–30.

Brown, Gillian. "The Problem of Sentimental Fiction." *Approaches to Teaching Stowe's* Uncle Tom's Cabin. Ed. Elizabeth and Susan Belasco Ammons. Approaches to Teaching World Literature. New York: MLA, 2000. 111–19.

Bryant, William Cullen. "The International Copyright Plans." *The Evening Post* 6 Feb. 1872: n.p.

———. Editorial. *The Evening Post* 13 Feb. 1872: n.p.

Budd, Louis J. *Mark Twain: The Contemporary Reviews.* American Critical Archives 11. Cambridge, UK: Cambridge UP, 1999.

Cameron, Kenneth Walter. "Melville, Cooper, Irving and Bryant on International Matters." *Emerson Society Quarterly* 51 (1968): 108–36.

Campbell, John. *Considerations and Arguments Proving the Inexpediency of an International Copyright Law.* New York: William E. Dean, 1844.

Carey, H. C. *Letters on International Copyright.* 2nd ed. New York: Hurd and Houghton, 1868.

Carey, Henry and Isaac Lea. Letter to James Fenimore Cooper. 23 April 1827. Papers; Cooper Manuscripts, Mss. Boxes C; Box 2, folder 13. AAS, Worcester, MA.

Chace, Jonathan. *International Copyright.* US 49th Cong., 1st sess. S. Rept. 1188. Washington: GPO, 1886.

Chartier, Roger. "Figures of the Author." *Of Authors and Origins: Essays on Copyright Law.* Ed. Brad Sherman and Alain Strowel. Oxford: Oxford UP, 1994. 7–22.

Charvat, William. "Cooper as Professional Author." *James Fenimore Cooper: A Re-Appraisal.* Ed. Mary E. Cunningham. Cooperstown, NY: NY State Historical Association, 1954. 128–43.

——. *Literary Publishing in America: 1790–1850.* Philadelphia: U of Pennsylvania P, 1959.

——. *The Profession of Authorship in America, 1800–1870.* n.p.:Ohio State UP, 1968.

Clark, Aubert J. "The Movement for International Copyright in Nineteenth-Century America." Dissertation. Catholic University of America, 1960.

Clemens, Samuel L. *The Adventures of Huckleberry Finn.* 1884. New York: Penguin Books, 1985.

——. "American Authors and British Pirates: A Private Letter and a Public Postscript." *New Princeton Review* 5.1. (1888): 47–54.

——. *Mark Twain's Autobiography.* Stormfield ed. Vol. 1. New York: Harper & Brothers, 1924.

——. *Mark Twain's Letters.* The Mark Twain Papers. Ed. Lin Salamo and Harriet Elinor Smith. Vol. 5. Berkeley: U of California P, 1997.

——. *Mark Twain's Letters to His Publishers.* Ed. Hamlin Hill. The Mark Twain Papers. Ed. Donald Coney Walter Blair, Henry Nash Smith. Berkeley: U of California P, 1967.

——. *Mark Twain's Notebooks and Journals Vol. 3.* Ed. Frederick Anderson. The Mark Twain Papers. Ed. Claude M. Simpson Walter Blair, Henry Nash Smith. Berkeley: U of California P, 1979.

——. *Mark Twain Speaking.* Ed. Paul Fatout. Iowa City: U of Iowa P, 1976.

——. *The Prince and the Pauper.* 1881. *The Complete Works of Mark Twain.* Vol. 21. New York: Harper and Bros., 1909.

——. *Roughing It.* First ed. Hartford: American Publishing Co., 1872.

——. *Roughing It.* 1872. Ed. Harriet Elinor Smith and Edgar Marquess Branch. *The Works of Mark Twain.* Ed. Robert Hirst. Vol. 2. Berkeley: U of California P, 1993.

——. *Sketches New and Old.* 1875. *The Complete Works of Mark Twain.* Vol. 19. New York: Harper and Bros., 1917.

Cooper, James Fenimore. Agreement with Putnam. Dec. 1850. Papers; Cooper Manuscripts, Mss. Boxes C; Box 5, folder 22. AAS, Worcester, MA.

———. *The American Democrat*. 1838. New York: Liberty Fund, Inc., 1981.

———. *The Chainbearer*. The Works of James Fenimore Cooper. Vol. 6. New York: Greenwood P, 1969.

———. *The Chainbearer; or the Littlepage Manuscripts*. First ed. Vol. 1. 2 vols. New York: Burgess, Stringer & Company, 1845.

———. Contract. 22 Dec. 1849. Papers; Cooper Manuscripts, Mss. Boxes C; Box 5, Folder 22. AAS, Worcester, MA.

———. *The Pioneers*. 1823. New York: Penguin, 1988.

———. *The Correspondence of James Fenimore-Cooper*. Ed. James Fenimore Cooper. 2 vols. New Haven: Yale UP, 1922.

———. *Home as Found*. 1838. Works of James Fenimore Cooper. Vol. 6. 10 vols. New York: Greenwood P, 1969.

———. *A Letter to His Countrymen*. New York: John Wiley, 1834.

———. *The Letters and Journals of James Fenimore Cooper*. Ed. James Franklin Beard. 6 vols. Cambridge: Harvard UP, 1960.

———. *Notions of the Americans: Picked up by a Traveling Bachelor*. 1828. The Writings of James Fenimore Cooper. Ed. James Franklin Beard. New York: SUNY P, 1991.

———. *The Redskins*. 1893. The Works of James Fenimore Cooper. Vol. 6. New York: Greenwood P, 1969.

———. *Satanstoe, or the Littlepage Manuscripts a Tale of the Colony*. 1845. The Writings of James Fenimore Cooper. Ed. James P. Elliott James Franklin Beard, and Lance Schachterle. New York: SUNY P, 1990.

———. *Satanstoe, or the Littlepage Manuscripts. A Tale of the Colony*. First ed. Vol. 1. 2 vols. New York: Burgess, Stringer and Company, 1845.

Coultrap-McQuin, Susan. *Doing Literary Business: American Women Writers in the Nineteenth-Century*. Gender and American Culture. Ed. Linda K. and Nell Irvin Painter Kerber. Chapel Hill: U of North Carolina P, 1990.

Crozier, Alice C. *The Novels of Harriet Beecher Stowe*. New York: Oxford UP, 1969.

Dandurand, Karen. "Dickinson and the Public." *Dickinson and Audience*. Ed. Martin Orzeck and Robert Weisbuch. Ann Arbor: U of Michigan P, 1996.

Dekker, George. *James Fenimore Cooper: The American Scott*. New York: Barnes & Noble, 1967.

Dekker, George and John P. McWilliams, ed. *Fenimore Cooper: The Critical Heritage*. London: Routledge and Kegan Paul, 1973.

Dickinson, Emily. *The Poems of Emily Dickinson: Reading Edition*. Ed. R.W. Franklin. Cambridge: Harvard UP, 1999.

Doyno, Victor A. *Writing* Huck Finn: *Mark Twain's Creative Process*. Philadelphia: U of Pennsylvania P, 1991.

Eaton, Andrew J. "The American Movement for International Copyright." *The Library Quarterly* 15 (1945): 95–122.

Elderkin, John. "International Copyright. A New Form Suggested." Letter to the Editor. *The Evening Post* 10 Feb. 1872, Third ed.: n.p.

"English Copyright for American Authors." *The Nation* 46.1180 (1888):110–11.

Erkkila, Betsy. "Emily Dickinson and Class." *American Literary History* 4.1 (1992): 1–27.

——. "Homoeroticism and Audience: Emily Dickinson's Female 'Master.'" *Dickinson and Audience*. Ed. Martin Orzeck and Robert Weisbuch. Ann Arbor: U of Michigan P, 1996. 161–80.

Fields, Annie, ed. *Life and Letters of Harriet Beecher Stowe*. Cambridge: Riverside Press, 1897.

Fink, Steven. "Margaret Fuller: The Evolution of a Woman of Letters." *Reciprocal Influences: Literary Production, Distribution, and Consumption in America*. Ed. Steven Fink and Susan S. Williams. Columbus: Ohio State UP, 1999: 55–74.

Foster, Andrea L. "Copyright Fight." *Chronicle of Higher Education* 25 Oct. 2002: A35.

Foucault, Michel. *The Archaeology of Knowledge*. Trans. A. M. Sheridan Smith. New York: Pantheon, 1972.

——. "What is an Author?" Trans. Josue V. Harari. *The Foucault Reader*. Ed. Paul Rabinow. New York: Pantheon, 1984. 101–21.

Gaskell, Elizabeth Cleghorn (Stevenson). *The Letters of Mrs. Gaskell*. Ed. J.A.V Chapple and Arthur Pollard. Manchester: Manchester UP, 1966.

Genette, Gerard. *Paratexts: Thresholds of Interpretation*. Trans. Jane E. Lewin. New York: Cambridge UP, 1997.

Graham, George. "Black Letters; or Uncle Tom-Foolery in Literature." *Graham's Magazine* Feb. 1853: 209–215.

——. "Editor's Table." *Graham's Magazine* Mar. 1853: 365.

Greenspan, Ezra. "Pioneering American Authorship: James Fenimore Cooper in the 1820s." *The Professions of Authorship: Essays in Honor of Matthew J. Bruccoli*. Ed. Richard Layman and Joel Myerson. Columbia, SC: U of South Carolina P, 1996. 106–20.

——. *Walt Whitman and the American Reader*. New York: Cambridge UP, 1990.

Gribben, Alan. "Autobiography as Property: Mark Twain and His Legend." *The Mythologizing of Mark Twain*. Ed. Sara deSaussure Davis and Philip D. Beidler. University, Alabama: U of Alabama P, 1984. 39–55.

Grossman, James. *James Fenimore Cooper*. The American Men of Letters Series. Ed. Joseph Wood Krutch, Margaret Marshall, Lionel Trilling, Mark Van Doren. London: Methuen & Co., 1950.

Hedrick, Joan D. *Harriet Beecher Stowe: A Life*. New York: Oxford UP, 1994.

Hoffman, Andrew. *Inventing Mark Twain: The Lives of Samuel Langhorne Clemens*. New York: William Morrow and Co., Inc., 1997.

Homestead, Melissa J. "Imperfect Title: Nineteenth-Century American Women Authors and Literary Property." Dissertation. University of Pennsylvania, 1998.

Horan, Elizabeth. "Mabel Loomis Todd, Martha Dickinson Bianchi, and the Spoils of the Dickinson Legacy." *A Living of Words*. Ed. Susan Albertine. Knoxville: U of Tennessee P, 1995. 65–93.

——. "Technically Outside the Law: Who Permits, Who Profits, and Why." *The Emily Dickinson Journal* 10.1 (2001): 34–54.

——. "To Market: The Dickinson Copyright Wars." *The Emily Dickinson Journal* 5.1 (1996): 88–120.

House, Kay Seymour. Historical Introduction. *Satanstoe*. By James Fenimore Cooper. *The Writings of James Fenimore Cooper*. Ed. James Franklin Beard. Albany: SUNY, 1990.

Hovet, Theodore R. *The Master Narrative: Harriet Beecher Stowe's Subversive Story of Master and Slave in* Uncle Tom's Cabin *and* Dred. Lanham, MD: UP of America, 1989.

"The International Copyright Question." *The United States Magazine and Democratic Review* 12 (1843): 115–122.

J.K.A. "Literary Property." *The American Jurist, and Law Magazine* X.XIX (1833): 62–80.

Kaplan, Justin. *Walt Whitman: A Life*. New York: Simon, 1980.

Kaser, David. *Messrs. Carey & Lea of Philadelphia: A Study in the History of the Booktrade*. Philadelphia: U of Pennsylvania P, 1957.

Leaffer, Marshall L. *Understanding Copyright Law*. Legal Text Series. 3rd ed. New York: Matthew Bender, 1999.

"Literary Property." *The American Jurist, and Law Magazine* 2.4 (1829): 248–67.

Long, Robert Emmet. *James Fenimore Cooper*. New York: Continuum, 1990.

Lowry, Richard S. *"Littery Man": Mark Twain and Modern Authorship*. Commonwealth Center Studies in American Culture. New York: Oxford UP, 1996.

Malone, Dumas, ed. *Dictionary of American Biography*. Vol. 5. 10 vols. New York: Scribners, 1958–1964.

Mathews, Cornelius. *The Better Interests of the Country in Connexion with International Copyright. [a Lecture Delivered at the Lecture-Room of the Society Library, Feb. 2, 1843]*. New York and London: Wiley and Putnam, 1843.

Matthews, Brander. "American Authors and British Pirates." *New Princeton Review* 4.5 (1887): 201–212.

——. "American Authors and British Pirates: An Open Letter to Close a Correspondence." *New Princeton Review* 5.1 (1888): 54–65.

——. *Cheap Books and Good Books*. First ed. New-York: The American Copyright League, 1888.

——. *These Many Years, Recollections of a New Yorker*. New York: Charles Scribner's Sons, 1917.

McGill, Meredith L. "The Duplicity of the Pen." *Language Machines: Technologies of Literary and Cultural Production*. Ed. Jeffrey Masten, Peter Stallybrass, and Nancy J. Vickers. New York: Routledge, 1997: 39–71.

——. "The Matter of the Text: Commerce, Print Culture, and the Authority of the State in American Copyright Law." *American Literary History* 9 (1997): 21–59.

McWilliams, Jr. John P. *Political Justice in a Republic: James Fenimore Cooper's America.* Berkeley: U of California P, 1972.

A Memorial of American Authors. Z715 M533 Mnd n.p., n.d. AAS, Worcester.

Merish, Lori. "Sentimental Consumption: Harriet Beecher Stowe and the Aesthetics of Middle-Class Ownership." *American Literary History* 8.1 (1996): 1–33.

——. *Sentimental Materialism: Gender, Commodity Culture, and Nineteenth-Century American Literature.* New Americanists. Ed. Donald E. Pease. Durham: Duke UP, 2000.

Miller, Edwin Haviland. Introduction. *Walt Whitman: The Correspondence.* By Walt Whitman. Ed. Miller. Vol. 6. New York: New York UP, 1977. xi–xxxvi.

Morrill, Lot Myrick. *International Copyright.* US 42nd Cong., 3rd sess. S. Rept. 409. Washington: GPO, 1873.

Moss, Sidney P. *Charles Dickens' Quarrel with America.* New York: Whitson Pub., 1984.

Mott, Frank Luther. *A History of American Magazines: 1741–1850.* Vol. 1. 5 vols. Cambridge, MA: Harvard UP, 1938.

Mulcaire, Terry. "Publishing Intimacy in *Leaves of Grass.*" *ELH* 60.2 (1993): 471–501.

Murray, Martin. "Walt Whitman's Washington Reading List." Walt Whitman Session. ALA Conference. Hyatt Regency, Long Beach. 1 June 2002.

Myerson, Joel. *Walt Whitman: A Descriptive Bibliography.* (Pittsburgh Series in Bibliography.) Pittsburgh and London: University of Pittsburgh Press, 1993.

Newbury, Michael. *Figuring Authorship in Antebellum America.* Stanford: Stanford UP, 1997.

Paley, Morton D. "John Camden Hotten and the First British Editions of Walt Whitman—'A Nice Milky Cocoa-Nut.'" *Publishing History* 6 (1979): 5–35.

Parton, James. "International Copyright." *Topics of the Time.* Boston: James R. Osgood And Company, 1871. 95–131.

Patterson, Lyman. *Copyright in Historical Perspective.* Nashville: Vanderbilt UP, 1968.

Perkins, Mary (Beecher), Mrs. Thomas Clap. Letter to Perkins, Thomas Clap. 23–25 August 1856. Day, Katharine S., Coll. Stowe Center, Hartford, CT.

Putnam, George Haven. *George Palmer Putnam: A Memoir.* New York and London: G. P. Putnam's Sons, 1912.

——. *International Copyright Considered in Some of Its Relations to Ethics and Political Economy; an Address Delivered January 29th, 1879, before the New York Free-Trade Club.* Economic Monographs. No. Xv. New York: G. P. Putnam's Sons, 1879.

——. *The Question of Copyright.* 1891. 2nd ed. New York: G.P. Putnam's Sons, 1896.

Putnam, George Palmer. *American Facts.* London: Wiley and Putnam, 1845.

——. Letter to James Fenimore Cooper. 27 March 1850. Papers; Cooper Manuscripts, Mss. Boxes C; BOX 3, Folder 21. AAS, Worcester, MA.

Railton, Stephen. *Fenimore Cooper: A Study of His Life and Imagination.* Princeton: Princeton UP, 1978.

Rawley, James A. "An Early History of the International Copyright Movement." *Library Quarterly* 11 (1941): 200–06.

Register of Debates in Congress. Vol. 7. Washington: Gales and Seaton, 1831.

Rice, Grantland S. *The Transformation of Authorship in America.* Chicago: U of Chicago P, 1997.

Rose, Mark. "The Author as Proprietor: Donaldson V. Becket and the Genealogy of Modern Authorship." *Of Authors and Origins: Essays on Copyright Law.* Ed. Brad Sherman and Alain Strowel. Oxford: Oxford UP, 1994. 23–56.

Sackett, Grenville A. *A Plea for Authors, and the Rights of Literary Property. By an American.* New York: Adlard and Saunders, 1838.

Smith, Henry Nash and William M. Gibson, ed. *Mark Twain—Howells Letters: The Correspondence of Samuel L. Clemens and William D. Howells, 1872–1910.* Vol. 1. 2 vols. Cambridge, MA: Belknap P of Harvard UP, 1960.

Spiller, Robert E. *Fenimore Cooper: Critic of His Times.* New York: Minton, Balch, and Co., 1931.

Stowe, Calvin E. Letter to Harriet B. Stowe. 2 February 1857. Acquisitions. Stowe Center, Hartford, CT.

——. Letter to Harriet B. Stowe. 23 February 1857. Acquisitions. Stowe Center, Hartford, CT.

——. Letter to Harriet B. Stowe. 23 February-March [?] 1857. Acquisitions. Stowe Center, Hartford, CT.

——. Letter to Harriet B. Stowe. 2 March 1857. Acquisitions. Stowe Center, Hartford, CT.

——. Letter to Harriet Beecher Stowe. 13 October 1856. Acquisitions. Stowe Center, Hartford, CT.

——. Letter to Harriet Beecher Stowe. 17 June 1853. Acquisitions. Stowe Center, Hartford, CT.

——. "Statement of Facts." Manuscript. Acquisitions. Stowe Center, Hartford, CT.

Stowe, Charles Edward. *Life of Harriet Beecher Stowe, Compiled from Her Letters and Journals.* Boston: Houghton, Mifflin, 1890.

Stowe, Eliza Taylor. Diary: Andover, Ma, and Paris, France. Diaries. Stowe Center, Hartford, CT.

Stowe, Harriet Beecher. *Dred.* 1856. Ed. Judie Newman. Halifax, UK: Ryburn Pub., 1992.

——. Letter to Gaskell, Elizabeth Cleghorn (Stevenson). 10 July 1860. Acquisitions, Stowe Center, Hartford, CT.

——. Letter to James T. Fields. 25 January 1862. Day, Katharine S. Coll. Stowe Center, Hartford, CT.

——. Letter to Mr. Phillips (of Phillips & Sampson). 1856. Day, Katharine S. Coll. Stowe Center, Hartford, CT.

——. Letter to Mr. Philips [Sic]. 2 January 1859. Acquisitions. Stowe Center, Hartford, CT.

——. Letter to Messrs Smith & Elder. 25 January 1862. Acquisitions. Stowe Center, Hartford, CT.

——. *The Minister's Wooing.* 1859. Ed. Susan K Harris. New York: Penguin, 1999.

——. *Oldtown Folks.* 1869. American Women Writers. Ed. Joanne Dobson, Judith Fetterley, and Elaine Showalter. New Brunswick: Rutgers UP, 1987.

——. *Pink and White Tyranny.* 1871. Plume American Women Writers. New York: NAL Penguin, 1988.

Stowe v. Thomas. 23 Fed. Cases 201–208. PA Circuit Ct., 1853.

Sumner, Charles. Letter to William Prescott. 10 July 1843. Papers, 1834–1874; Miscellaneous Manuscript Boxes "S"; Folder 1. AAS, Worcester, MA.

"The Uncle Tom Epidemic." *The Literary World* 4 Dec. 1852: 355–8.

Thomas, M. Wynn. *The Lunar Light of Whitman's Poetry.* Cambridge, MA: Harvard UP, 1987.

Traubel, Horace. *With Walt Whitman in Camden.* Ed. Horace Traubel et al. 9 vols. Various publishers, 1906–96.

"Uncle Tomitudes." *Putnam's Monthly.* Jan. 1853: 97–102.

United States. *An Act to amend the several acts respecting copyrights.* US 21st Cong., 2nd sess. Ch. 16. Washington: GPO, 1831.

——.——. Committee on the Library. *Report. [To accompany bill H. R. No. 779].* 40th Cong., 2d sess. Report No. 16. Washington: GPO, 1868.

——.——. Committee on Patents. *International Copyright.* 49th Cong., 1st sess. S. no. 161. Washington: GPO, 1886.

——.——. Committee on Patents and the Patent Office. *Report [To accompany Senate Bill No.32.].* 225th Cong. 2d sess. Washington: GPO, 1838.

——.——. Copyright Office. *Copyright in Congress: 1789–1904.* Copyright Office Bulletin No. 8. Washington: GPO, 1905.

——.——. House Committee on the Judiciary. *Testimony Before the House Committee on the Judiciary on International Copyright.* Washington: GPO, 1890.

Vaidhyanathan, Siva. *Copyrights and Copywrongs: The Rise of Intellectual Property and How It Threatens Creativity.* New York: NYU P, 2001.

Waples, Dorothy. *The Whig Myth of James Fenimore Cooper.* Yale Studies in English. Vol. 88. New Haven: Yale UP, 1938.

Welland, Dennis. *Mark Twain in England.* Atlantic Highlands, N.J.: Humanities P, 1978.

Welsh, Alexander. *From Copyright to Copperfield.* Cambridge, MA: Harvard UP, 1987.

Whitman, Walt. *The Correspondence.* Ed. Edwin Haviland Miller. 6 vols. New York: New York UP, 1961–77.

——. *Daybooks and Notebooks.* Ed. William White. Vol. 2. New York: New York UP, 1978.

——. *The Journalism.* Ed. Herbert Bergman. Vol. 1. New York: Peter Lang Pub., 1998.

——. *Leaves of Grass.* Philadelphia, 1891. Special Collections Department of the Main Library, University of Iowa.

——. *Notebooks and Unpublished Manuscripts.* Ed. Edward F. Grier. Vol. 2. New York: New York UP, 1984.

——. *Walt Whitman: Poetry and Prose.* Ed. Justin Kaplan. New York: Library of America, 1996.

——. *Specimen Days in America.* London, 1887. Special Collections Department of the Main Library, University of Iowa.

——. "Washington as a Central Winter Residence." *The Washington Evening Star* 6 Jan. 1872. n.p.

Whitney, Lisa. "In the Shadow of Uncle Tom's Cabin: Stowe's Vision of Slavery from the Great Dismal Swamp." *The New England Quarterly* 66.4 (1993): 552–69.

Wilson, Christopher P. *The Labor of Words: Literary Professionalism in the Progressive Era.* Athens: U of Georgia P, 1985.

Wilson, Forrest. *Crusader in Crinoline.* Philadelphia: J. B. Lippincott, 1941.

Winship, Michael. "The Transatlantic Book Trade and Anglo-American Literary Culture in the Nineteenth Century." *Reciprocal Influences: Literary Production, Distribution, and Consumption in America.* Ed. Steven Fink and Susan S. Williams. Columbus: Ohio State UP, 1999: 98–122.

Woodmansee, Martha and Peter Jaszi, ed. *The Construction of Authorship: Textual Appropriation in Law and Literature.* Durham: Duke UP, 1994.

Index